Anonymous

Appletons' Illustrated Hand-book of American Winter Resorts for Tourists and Invalids

Anonymous

Appletons' Illustrated Hand-book of American Winter Resorts for Tourists and Invalids

ISBN/EAN: 9783337258368

Printed in Europe, USA, Canada, Australia, Japan

Cover: Foto ©Andreas Hilbeck / pixelio.de

More available books at **www.hansebooks.com**

APPLETONS'

ILLUSTRATED HAND-BOOK

OF

AMERICAN

WINTER RESORTS;

FOR TOURISTS AND INVALIDS.

WITH MAP, ILLUSTRATIONS, AND TABLE OF RAILWAY FARES.

REVISED FOR SEASON OF 1886–'87.

NEW YORK:
D. APPLETON AND COMPANY,
1, 3, AND 5 BOND STREET.
1887.

Uniform with this volume:
"Hand-Book of Summer Resorts." Illustrated.

CONTENTS.

	PAGE
MAP OF THROUGH ROUTES SOUTH..Face p.	3
MAP OF FLORIDA...	3
FLORIDA..	3
General Description..	4
Jacksonville..	6
St. Augustine..	8
Pablo Beach. Fernandina and Cedar Keys..	14
Internal Travel Lines...	15
The St. John's River...	16
Indian River..	21
The Tallahassee Country..	22
Western Florida...	24
Up the Ocklawaha...	25
The Gulf Coast...	26
Key West..	27
Southern Florida...	28
Hints for Sportsmen...	29
GEORGIA RESORTS...	30
Savannah...	32
Augusta...	36
Thomasville..	38
Mineral Springs..	38
Mountain Region and Scenery...	39
SOUTH CAROLINA RESORTS...	41
Charleston...	42
Summerville...	49
Aiken...	49
Mineral Springs...	53
The Mountain Region..	54
NORTH CAROLINA RESORTS...	55
The Mountain Region..	57
Asheville..	59
The Warm Springs...	62
MINNESOTA RESORTS...	65
St. Paul...	67
Minneapolis and St. Anthony..	68
Winona...	69
Red Wing and Frontenac...	69
Faribault...	70
ARKANSAS HOT SPRINGS...	71

CONTENTS.

	PAGE
COLORADO RESORTS	72
Denver	75
Colorado Springs and Vicinity	75
Pueblo and the Boiling Springs	77
Idaho Springs and Georgetown	77
North Park, Middle Park, and Hot Springs	78
South Park and San Luis Park	79
CALIFORNIA RESORTS	80
San Francisco	83
Santa Barbara	84
San Diego and Los Angeles	85
San Bernardino	86
Paso Robles Hot Springs	87
Sacramento	87
Stockton and Visalia	88
San José and the Santa Clara Valley	89
San Rafael and Monterey	90
Napa City and Calistoga	90
The Geyser Springs	91
ALONG THE LOWER MISSISSIPPI	92
New Orleans	97
THE WEST INDIES	104
Cuba	104
Isle of Pines	109
The Bahamas—Nassau	109
Jamaica	110
Hayti and Santo Domingo	112
Porto Rico	115
St. Thomas	116
Santa Cruz or St. Croix	117
St. Vincent	117
Barbadoes	117
Curaçoa	118
"Down the Islands"	118
THE BERMUDAS	121
THE SANDWICH ISLANDS	127
Honolulu	128
Maui and Lahaina	130
Hilo and the Volcanoes	131
Kauai	132
MEXICO	134
Vera Cruz	136
Puebla	137
The City of Mexico	138
Central Mexico	140

CONTENTS.

NORTHERN MEXICO	141
Chihuahua	141
The Volcanoes	141
The Mines	142
OTHER RESORTS	143
Atlantic City	143
Eastman, Ga.	143
Old Point Comfort, Va.	144
Las Vegas Hot Springs, N. M.	144
Lakewood, N. J.	146
Newport News, Va.	146
Bailey Springs, Ala.	146
Camden, S. C.	147
Columbia, S. C.	147
Mobile, Ala.	148
TABLE OF RAILWAY FARES	149

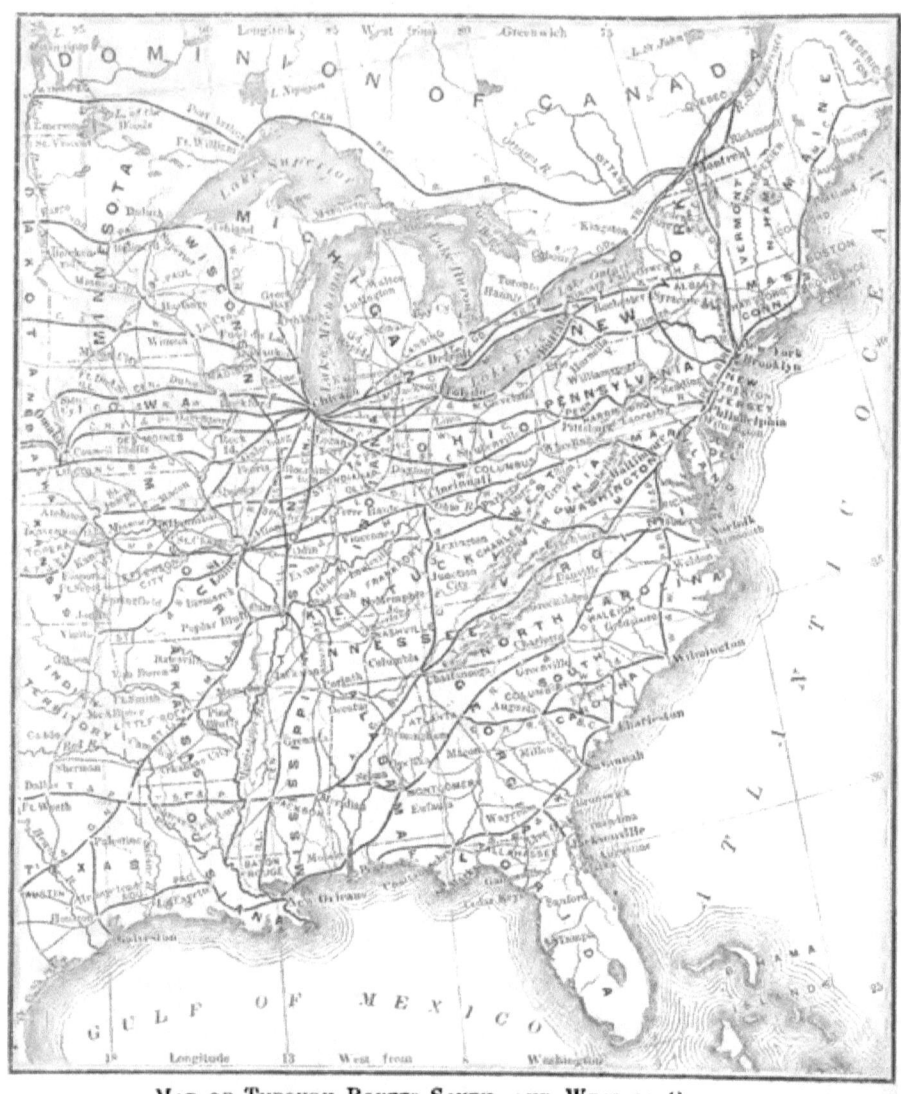

MAP OF THROUGH ROUTES SOUTH, AND WEST TO OMAHA.

HAND-BOOK OF AMERICAN WINTER RESORTS.

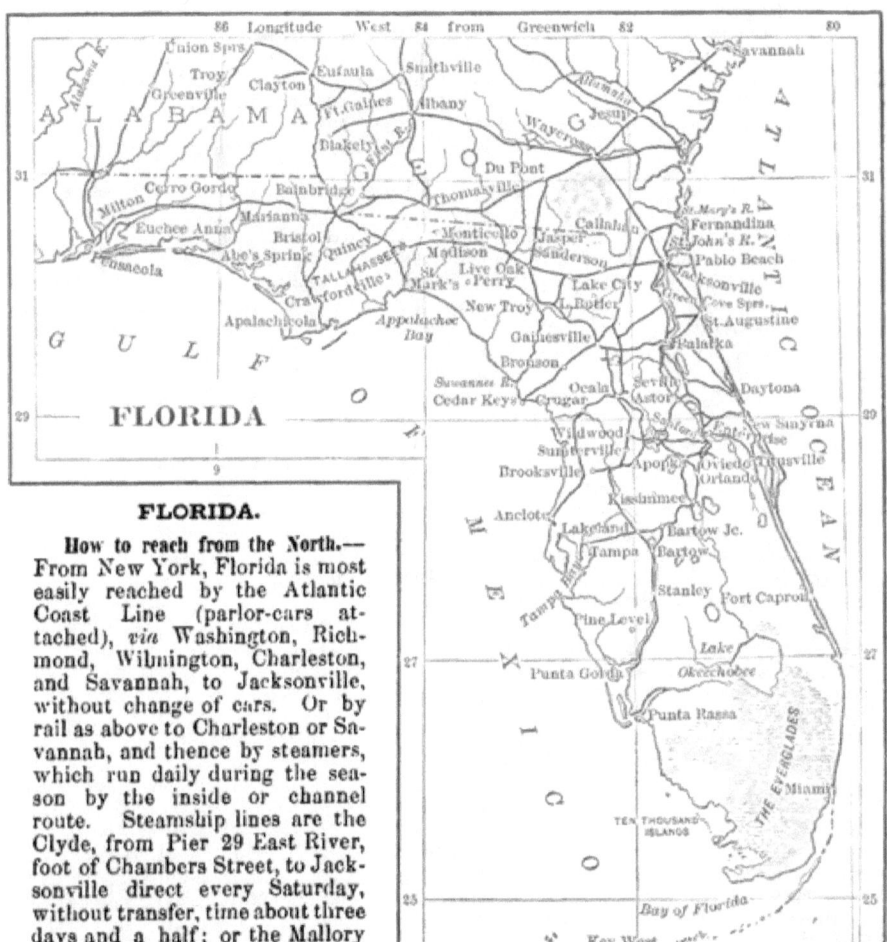

FLORIDA.

How to reach from the North.—From New York, Florida is most easily reached by the Atlantic Coast Line (parlor-cars attached), *via* Washington, Richmond, Wilmington, Charleston, and Savannah, to Jacksonville, without change of cars. Or by rail as above to Charleston or Savannah, and thence by steamers, which run daily during the season by the inside or channel route. Steamship lines are the Clyde, from Pier 29 East River, foot of Chambers Street, to Jacksonville direct every Saturday, without transfer, time about three days and a half; or the Mallory line, from Pier 21 East River, foot of Fulton Street, to Fernandina every Tuesday and Friday, and thence to Jacksonville (32 miles) by steamer or rail. Fare on either route, $24. Steamers also sail three times a week from **Pier 29 East** River to Charleston, and three times a week from

Pier 35 North River to Savannah (time, about 60 hours; fare, $20), whence the journey can be continued by rail, or by steamer through the Sea Islands or channel route. For fares by rail, see Table of Railway Fares, p. 149.

How to reach from the West.—Two daily express trains, with parlor-cars attached, run direct, without change, from Cincinnati, *via* Chattanooga, Atlanta, and Jesup, to Jacksonville. Or, from Chattanooga or Atlanta, rail can be taken to Charleston or Savannah, whence the journey to Florida may be made by rail on the Atlantic Coast Line route, or by steamers by the channel route. From Nashville two daily express trains, with parlor-cars attached, run direct through Montgomery and Thomasville to Jacksonville.

From New Orleans and the South, Florida can be reached by the C. L. & N. O. R. R. to Flomaton, thence by Pensacola R. R. to Pensacola, where connection is made with the Pensacola & Atlantic R. R. to all parts of Florida.

General Description.—Florida is the southernmost State of the Union, and is situated between lat. 24° 30′ and 31° N., and lon. 80° and 87° 45′ W. Exclusive of islands, it consists of a long, narrow strip of territory, extending in the form of a peninsula south from Georgia and Alabama, through five degrees of latitude, and containing 58,680 square miles. Its entire area eastward lies upon the Atlantic, and the Gulf of Mexico washes almost the whole of the western side. The coast-line is of much greater extent than that of any other State, having a length of 472 miles on the Atlantic, and 674 miles on the Gulf; but this immense stretch of sea-front is almost inaccessible on account of shallow soundings, and has few good harbors. South from the mainland a chain of small, rocky islands, called "Keys," extends southwest, ending in a cluster of rocks and sand-banks, called the Tortugas. South of the bank upon which these keys arise, and separated from them by a navigable channel, is a long, narrow coral-reef, known as the Florida Reef, which here constitutes the left bank of the Gulf Stream. The most important of the keys is Key West. The surface of Florida is for the most part level, yet undulating, being nowhere more than 250 or 300 feet above the sea. About 5,000 square miles in the southern part of the peninsula is a swamp, called the Everglades, which, during the rainy season, between June and October, is impassable. North of this tract to Georgia the surface is generally a dead level, but in some parts it is undulating and occasionally hilly. West of the neck of the peninsula the ground is more uneven and rugged, though the elevations are still slight and of very limited extent. The lands are almost *sui generis*, very curiously distributed, and may be designated as high hummock, low hummock, swamps, savannas, and the different qualities of pine-land. High hummock is usually timbered with live and other oaks, with magnolia, laurel, etc., and is considered the best description of land for general purposes. Low hummock, timbered with live and water oak, is subject to overflows, but when drained is preferred for sugar. Savannas, on the margins of streams and in detached bodies, are usually very rich and alluvious, yielding abundantly in dry seasons, but needing, at other times, ditching and diking. Marsh savannas, on the borders of tide-streams, are very valuable, when reclaimed, for rice or sugar-cane. The lake called the Everglades is filled with islands covered with a dense jungle of vines and evergreens, pines, and palmettos. It lies south of Okechobee, and is 160 miles long and 60 broad. Its depth varies from one to fifty feet. A rank tall grass springs from the vegetable deposits at the bottom, and, rising above the surface of the water, gives the lake the deceitful air of a beautiful verdant lawn. Throughout the State the warmth and humidity of the climate compensate, in a great measure, for the inferior character of the soil, and give it a vegetation of great variety and luxuriance. The productions are chiefly those which require a tropical sun: cotton, coffee, cocoa, sugar-cane, tobacco, rice, etc. Oranges, lemons, limes, pineapples, bananas, olives, and grapes, flourish luxuriantly; and garden vegetables are produced in the greatest abundance. The driest seasons are relieved by heavy dews, and the sun that would bake the earth in other parts and wither vegetation is so tempered by the prevailing moisture as to cover the surface with perennial verdure.

The rivers of Florida are numerous, and many of them afford excellent facilities for internal navigation. The most important are the St. John's, Indian River, Caloosahatchee and Withlacoochee, the Suwanee, the Appalachicola, and the St. Mary's. A multitude of lakes dot the surface of the country, some of which are navigable for large steamers. Lake Okechobee, north of the Everglades, is about 40 miles long and 30 wide. Many of these waters are extremely picturesque in their unique beauty of wild and rank tropical vegetation, presenting everywhere to

Light-house on Florida Keys.

the eye of the stranger very novel attractions, in the profusion and variety of the trees and shrubs and vines which line all their shores and bayous.

The Climate.—The climate of Florida is one of the finest in the world: though ten degrees nearer the equator than Southern Italy, the temperature is no warmer, and the air far more equable and dry. The reason for this has never been clearly established; but it is well known that, while the Gulf Stream carries off immense quantities of the surplus heat of the region, branches of the returning arctic current also lave its shores and assist in maintaining the surprising equilibrium of its temperature. Be the cause what it may, however, there can be no doubt of the fact, which has been established by a long series of the most careful observations. In the south the temperature scarcely changes the year round, and summer is only distinguished by the copiousness of its showers. The average mean temperature of the State is 73° F., and the difference between summer and winter does not generally exceed 20°, while at Key West it is not more than 11°. The thermometer seldom rises above 90° in summer, and rarely falls below 30° in winter; on the average the winters are thirty or forty degrees warmer than in New York, while the summer months of the latter are ten or fifteen degrees hotter than in Florida. Frost is unknown in Southern Florida, and is comparatively light even in the northern part of the State. It occurs most frequently between November and March, being most frequent in December and January, and rarely showing itself in October and April as far north as Jacksonville. As a general thing no frost occurs throughout the year below lat. 28° N. Summer being the rainy season in Florida, the winters are usually clear and dry. By observations taken for a period of twenty-two years at Jacksonville, it was found that January averaged 20 clear days; February, 19; March, 20; April, 25; May, 22; June, 17; July, 18; August, 19; September, 17; October, 19; November, 20; and December, 20. It must not be inferred, however, that rain fell on all the days which could not be registered as clear; it may be said in general terms that from October to May there are not more than four or five rainy days in a month. In addition to the mildness of the climate, it is believed that the immense pine-forests which cover a large part of the State contribute greatly to its healthfulness. The delicious terebinthine odors exhaled by these forests not only purify the atmosphere, but impart to it a healing, soothing, and peculiarly invigorating quality.

Healthfulness, etc.—Owing to the evenness and salubrity of its climate, as above indicated, Florida has long been a popular resort for invalids, and especially those afflicted with pulmonary complaints. Of the total deaths from all causes in Florida in 1870, as reported by the Federal census, only 131 were from consumption. There were 17.3 deaths from other causes to one from consumption. The advantages of the climate in this respect are further shown by a comparison of the statistics relating to consumption as reported by the census of 1870, from which it appears that the ratio of deaths from consumption to those from all causes was less in Florida than in any other State except Nevada; and this advantage becomes still greater when it is considered that, Florida being a popular resort for consumptives, a large proportion of those who die there from that cause came with the disease from other States. Including only the resident population, the deaths from consumption in Florida average 1 in 1,457, while in Massachusetts the average is as high as 1 in 254. "The mortality among visitors suffering from consumption is not very large," says Dr. Howe, in his "Winter Homes for Invalids," "but would be less if physicians, with little knowledge and less conscience, would abstain from sending their patients there in the last stages of the disease, when every earthly hope of their recovery had gone. Many unfortunates are sent every year to Florida with life ebbing out rapidly, and by men who can not possibly have an intelligent hope of their recovery. Needing nothing but the soothing attentions of the home circle, of sympathizing friends to comfort them as they pass down the dark valley, they are torn away, sent on a wearisome journey to a strange land, among strangers to die. This course is so cruel and absurd that it would almost seem needless to reiterate the advice previously given, that only those in the incipient stages of consumption should venture from a good home for the uncertainties of recovery in a distant country."

A common impression about Florida is that, while its climate is beneficial to consumptives, it is peculiarly productive of malarial diseases, and that the mortality from these diseases is excessive. How utterly mistaken this impression is, is shown by the following extract from a report of U. S. Surgeon-General Lawson: "The statistics in this bureau demonstrate the fact that the diseases which result from malaria are of a much milder type in the peninsula of Florida than in any other State in the Union. . . . In the Middle Division of the United States the proportion is one death to thirty-six cases of remittent fever; in the Northern Division, one to fifty-two; in the Southern Division, one to fifty-four; in Texas, one to seventy-eight; in California, one to one hundred and twenty-two; in New Mexico, one to one hundred and forty-eight; while in Florida it is but *one to two hundred and eighty-seven*." It may be added that malarial fevers are rarely originated except in the "hummocks," where the clayey soil holds the water, and the drainage is consequently imperfect.

Jacksonville.

How to Reach.—Jacksonville is reached from the North by any of the routes given at the commencement of this chapter. It is at the terminus of the Savannah, Florida & Western R. R., which forms an all-rail line between Jacksonville and

Savannah, over which through-trains run twice a day. The two main trunk-lines, known as the Florida Railway and Navigation Company's R. R., and Jacksonville, Tampa & Key West R. R., connect at Jacksonville for Tallahassee, Monticello, Chattahoochee, Gainesville, Leesburg, Tampa, St. Augustine, Palatka, Sanford, Orlando, and all points south, west, and east. At Callahan (20 miles from Jacksonville) the S., F. & W. R. R. is crossed by the Florida Railway and Navigation Company's road, which connects Fernandina on the Atlantic with Cedar Keys on the Gulf coast. A line of commodious steamers, large and well equipped, running tri-weekly, plies between Savannah and Charleston to Fernandina, connecting with trains to Jacksonville. Daily lines of steamers run up the St. John's River to Sanford and Enterprise (205 miles), and small steamboats run from Jacksonville up the Ocklawaha. The St. Augustine branch of the Jacksonville, Tampa & Key West R. R. puts Jacksonville in direct communication with St. Augustine by a ride of a little over an hour. This is the most direct route. It may also be reached by daily river-steamers, which connect with the St. John's Railway at Tocoi, and terminating after a fourteen-mile ride in the western portion of St. Augustine.

Hotels and Boarding-Houses.—The principal hotels are the *St. James*, the *Windsor*, the *Carlton*, the *Everett*, the *Duval*, the *Tremont*, the *Togni*, the *Grand View*, the *Bay State House*, conducted by Northern men with Northern cooks, the *Grand Union*, and the *St. John's*. There are said to be upward of a hundred boarding-houses. Of these, the *Mattair House*, the *Revere House*, the *Bigelow*, *Oakland Grove*, the *Pennsylvania*, the *Victoria*, the *Elmwood*, and the houses kept by Mrs. Day, Mrs. Tibbitts, Mrs. Earle, and Mrs. Henderson are the best. The prices at the first six hotels mentioned range from $3 to $5 per day; at the others, from $1 to $2.50 per day. At first-class boarding-houses the charges are from $8 to $20 per week. Good furnished rooms, including lights, fuel, and attendance, may be had in private houses for from $3 to $6 per week, and board without room is about $11 per week at the hotels, and less at the boarding-houses. Unfurnished cottages can be hired for from $20 to $30 per month.

Jacksonville, the largest city in Florida, is situated on the right bank of the St. John's River, about 25 miles from its mouth. It was named after General Andrew Jackson, was laid out as a town in 1822, had a population of 1,045 in 1850, and of 6,912 in 1870. In 1886 its resident population was about 22,000, which is largely increased during the winter by transient visitors. The city is regularly laid out, with streets crossing each other at right angles and shaded with trees. The principal thoroughfare is Bay Street, and on this are situated the leading business houses. On the northwest side of the city is a picturesque bluff, covered with fine residences and commanding a beautiful view of the river. There are several suburban villages (East Jacksonville, Springfield, La Villa, Brooklyn, River Side, Oakland, Arlington, South Jacksonville, and Alexandria), and those on the other side of the river are connected with the city by ferry. Besides several good schools, Jacksonville contains Catholic, Episcopal, Presbyterian, Methodist, and Baptist churches; a circulating library, a commodious *Opera-House*; three daily newspapers; banks, public halls, and telegraphic connections with all parts, and four street railways. The commerce of the city is extensive, the chief business being the cutting and shipment of lumber. There are several large saw-mills. Cotton, sugar, fruit, fish, and early vegetables are also shipped to Northern and foreign ports. Jacksonville is much resorted to by invalids on account of its mild and salubrious climate, the details concerning which are given on a preceding page under "Climate." A system of water-works, drawing excellent water from artesian wells, and also a system of sewerage, have been constructed; and the unwholesome marshy ground west of the city has been thoroughly drained and laid out in gardens. Many prefer remaining here to going farther into the interior, on account of the superior accommodations which it offers and its social advantages. Among the amusements are excursions on the river and drives on the excellent shell-roads which lead out of the city. A favorite drive is to *Moncrief's Springs* (4 miles), a mineral spring whose waters are said to cure malarial diseases. There are bath-houses here, a restaurant, a bowling-alley, a dancing-pavilion, and a race-course.

St. Augustine.

How to reach.—St. Augustine is reached from Jacksonville most directly by the Jacksonville, St. Augustine and Halifax River Railroad. The cars start from the depot in South Jacksonville, a point which is reached by a ferry-boat, which leaves the wharf every fifteen minutes. It may also be reached by a steamboat up the river to Tocoi, 49 miles, and from there by the St. John's Railway, 18 miles farther; or, by train up the west bank of the river to West Tocoi, at which point a ferry connects with the same railway.

Hotels and Boarding-Houses.—The principal hotels are the new extensive *St. Marco*, outside the gate of St. George: this immense building contains all the modern improvements, and commands a full view of the river; the *St. Augustine*, fronting on the Plaza and Charlotte St.; the *Magnolia*, St. George St. near the Plaza; the *Marion*, Charlotte St. north of the Plaza; the *Ocean View*, on Bay St., and others. There are also numerous boarding-houses at which board and rooms may be had for from $8 to $15 a week; among them may be mentioned those of T. F. House, E. J. de Medicis, Mrs. J. V. Hernandez, William Mickler, Mrs. Patterson, and Mrs. Collins.

Location, Climate, and History.—St. Augustine is situated on the Atlantic coast of Florida, about 40 miles south of the mouth of the St. John's River, and 33 southeast of Jacksonville. It occupies a narrow peninsula formed by the Matanzas River on the east, and the St. Sebastian on the south and west, the site being a flat, sandy level, encompassed for miles around by a tangled undergrowth of low palmettos and bushes of various descriptions. Directly in front lies Anastasia Island, forming a natural breakwater, and almost entirely cutting off the sea-view. On the north end of the island is a lighthouse with a revolving light, situated in lat. 29° 53' N., and long. 81° 16' W.

The *climate* of St. Augustine is singularly equable both winter and summer, the mean annual temperature being 70°. The mean temperature for winter is 58.08°; for spring, 68.54°; for summer, 80.27°; and for autumn, 71.73°. Frosts seldom occur even in mid-winter, and the sea-breezes temper the heats of summer so that they are quite endurable. Many consumptives frequent St. Augustine, and with marked benefit; but the air is regarded as rather "strong" for those who have passed the earlier stages of the disease, and no one should remain there in January and February who cannot stand an occasional cold northeaster. Asthma is also thought to be relieved by residence at St. Augustine, and the place is exceptionally free from malarial diseases.

St. Augustine is the oldest European settlement in the United States, and its history carries us back almost to the middle ages. It was founded by the Spaniards in 1565, more than half a century before the landing of the Pilgrims at Plymouth, and was from the start a place of note, and the scene of interesting historical events. Its founder, Don Pedro Menendez, was one of the most eminent men of Spain, and a famous commander during the reign of Philip II., by whom he was sent to Florida at the head of an expedition comprising 34 vessels and 2,600 persons, to colonize the country and suppress a Huguenot settlement made in 1564 near the mouth of the St. John's. He landed at St. Augustine on August 28, 1565, established his colony, and then marched to exterminate the Huguenots, which he effected with great vigor and cruelty, putting to death all his prisoners, "not because they are Frenchmen, but because they are heretics and enemies of God." Two years later, this massacre was avenged by a French adventurer, Dominique de Gourgues, who, with a small force of volunteers, attacked and captured the Spanish forts on the St. John's, and hanged his prisoners, "not because they are Spaniards, but because they are traitors, robbers, and murderers." De Gourgues, however, made no attempt to retain his conquest, but, after his deed of retribution was accomplished, sailed back to France. Menendez was absent in Spain during this attack by De Gourgues, and did not return until the affair was over. He continued for some years longer to rule the colony, but finally returned to Spain, where his reputation for ability was so high that he was made captain-general of the navy, soon after which he died, at the age of fifty-five. His career in Florida, though stained with cruelty, was distinguished for energy and perseverance, and to him, undoubtedly, is due the credit of establishing the first permanent settlement in the United States.

In 1586 Sir Francis Drake, the famous English explorer, returning from an expedition against the Spanish West Indies, appeared off St. Augustine, and so terrified the Spaniards that they abandoned the fort and the town to him without any attempt at resistance, and fled to the shelter of the forts on the St. John's. Drake took possession, and pillaged and burned the town, carrying away considerable booty. The principal public buildings of the place at that time were a court-house, a church, and a monastery. After the departure of Drake, the Spaniards returned and rebuilt the town, which, however, grew so slowly that in 1647 there were within its walls only 300 families, or 1,500 inhabitants, including 50 monks of the order of St. Francis. In 1665 a party of English buccaneers, commanded by Captain John Davis, made a descent upon St. Augustine with seven small vessels, and pillaged the town. The garrison, though consisting of 200 men, do not appear to have resisted the attack, which, it is probable, was made from the south by boats. In 1702, Spain and England being at war, an expedition against St. Augustine was organized in South Carolina, by Governor Moore, of that colony. It consisted of 600 whites, and as many Indian allies, and its plan of operations comprised a march by land of one portion of the force, and an attack by sea of the other. The land force was commanded by Colonel Daniel, the naval force by Governor Moore himself. The forces under Colonel Daniel reached St. Augustine before the naval part of the expedition appeared, and easily captured the town; the governor, Don Joseph Cuniga, and the inhabitants, taking refuge in the castle, which was well supplied with provisions, and contained a considerable garrison. Governor Moore, with the fleet, soon after arrived, and invested the fortifications, but, not having siege-guns of sufficient calibre, could make no impression on the walls of the fort. Colonel Daniel was sent to Jamaica to procure heavier guns. While he was absent two Spanish vessels appeared off the harbor. Governor Moore, fearing that he was about to be attacked by a superior force and his retreat cut off, hastily raised the siege, destroying such of his munitions as he could not remove, and barbarously burning the town. He retreated by land, abandoning his vessels for fear of the Spanish squadron. Shortly afterward, Colonel Daniel returned from Jamaica with mortars and heavy guns, but found Moore gone, and was himself nearly captured. The expedition returned to Carolina in disgrace, but without the loss of a man. It cost the colony of South Carolina £6,000, and led to the issue of the first paper-money ever circulated in America. In 1727 Colonel Palmer, an energetic officer, made a raid into Florida with about 300 Carolina militia, and carried destruction by fire and sword to the very gates of St. Augustine, which, however, he dared not attack, though he sacked a Yemassee village about a mile north of the city. In 1740, war again existing between Spain and England, an expedition against St. Augustine was organized by the famous General Oglethorpe, then Governor of Georgia. He obtained assistance from South Carolina, and from England a naval force of six ships. About the 1st of June his forces reached St. Augustine, which was defended by a not very numerous garrison commanded by Don Manuel de Monteano, the Governor of Florida, a man of energy and resolution. After a siege of five or six weeks, carried on chiefly by bombardment from Anastasia Island, Oglethorpe became satisfied that he could not take the place, especially as his fleet had withdrawn in apprehension of bad weather, and he accordingly embarked his troops and sailed away on July 9th. Two years later, the Spanish Governor of Florida, the energetic Monteano, having received reenforcements from Cuba, sailed from St. Augustine with 36 vessels and 3,000 men to attack the English settlements in Georgia. He met with some success at first, but was finally baffled, partly by the force and partly by the *finesse* of Oglethorpe, and returned to Florida. In the following year (1743) Oglethorpe made a raid into the Spanish dominions to the gates of St. Augustine, advancing with such celerity and secrecy that the Indians attached to his force captured and scalped forty of the Spanish troops under the very walls of Fort St. Marks, the chief defense of the city. The British kept possession of Florida about 20 years, and then, in 1783, receded it to Spain in exchange for the Bahama Islands. St. Augustine, at that time, contained 3,000 inhabitants. In 1819 it was transferred to the United States. During the civil war it changed masters three times. The resident population at the present

A Street in St. Augustine.

time is about 2,200; but this is increased by from 7,000 to 10,000 visitors during the winter, and St. Augustine is then one of the gayest places in the South.

Streets, Drives, etc.—"The aspect of St. Augustine," says Mrs. Beecher Stowe, "is quaint and strange, in harmony with its romantic history. It has no pretensions to architectural richness or beauty; and yet it is impressive from its unlikeness to anything else in America. It is as if some little, old, dead-alive Spanish town, with its fort and gateway and Moorish bell-towers, had broken loose, floated over here, and got stranded on a sand-bank. Here you see the shovel-hats and black gowns of priests; the convent with gliding figures of nuns; and in the narrow, crooked streets meet dark-browed people, with great Spanish eyes and coal-black hair. The current of life here has the indolent, dreamy stillness that characterizes life in Old Spain. In Spain, when you ask a man to do anything, instead of answering as we do, 'In a minute,' the invariable reply is, 'In an hour'; and the growth and progress of St. Augustine have been according." This was true, no doubt, when it was written, but a change has taken place in every respect. There are four principal streets which extend nearly the whole length of the city—Tolomato, St. George (the Fifth Avenue of the place), Charlotte, and Bay. The latter commands a fine view of the harbor, Anastasia Island, and the ocean. All the streets are extremely narrow, the thoroughfares being only 12 or 15 feet wide, while the cross-streets are narrower still. An advantage of these narrow streets in this warm climate is that they give shade, and increase the draught of air through them as through a flue. The principal streets were formerly paved with shell-concrete, portions of which are still to be seen above the shifting sand; and this flooring was so carefully swept that the dark-eyed maidens of Old Castile, who then led society here, could pass and repass without soiling their satin slippers. No rumbling wheels were permitted to crush the firm road-bed, or to whirl the dust into the airy verandas. All the old Spanish residences are built of coquina-stone, which is first stuccoed and then white-washed. Many of them have hanging balconies along their second stories, which in the narrow streets seem almost to touch, and from which their respective occupants can chat confidentially and even shake hands. It must not be supposed, however, that St. Augustine is built wholly of coquina and in the Spanish style; there are many fine residences there in the American style, and in a few years St. Augustine will rival Newport in the number of its villas. A profusion of oranges, lemons, bananas, figs, date-palms, and all manner of tropical flowers and shrubs, ornament

St. Augustine Cathedral.

their grounds. "A charming drive is out St. George Street, through the City Gate to the beach of the San Sebastian.

Places of Resort.—The most interesting feature of the town is the old Fort of San Marco (now *Fort Marion*), which is built of coquina, a unique conglomerate of fine shells and sand found in large quantities on Anastasia Island, at the entrance of the harbor, and quarried with great ease, though it becomes hard by exposure to the air. It is quarried in large blocks, and forms a wall well calculated to resist cannon-shot, because it does not splinter when struck. The fort stands on the sea-front at the northeast end of the town. It was a hundred years in building, and was completed in 1756, as is attested by the following inscription, which may still be seen over the gateway, together with the arms of Spain, handsomely carved in stone: " Don Fernando being King of Spain, and the Field-Marshal Don Alonzo Fernando Herida being governor and captain-general of this place, St. Augustine of Florida and its provinces, this fort was finished in the year 1756. The works were directed by the Captain-Engineer Don Pedro de Brazos y Gareny." While owned by the British, this was said to be the prettiest fort in the king's dominions. Its castellated battlements; its formidable bastions, with their frowning guns; its lofty and imposing sally-port, surrounded by the royal Spanish arms; its portcullis, moat, and drawbridge; its circular and ornate sentry-boxes at each principal parapet-angle; its commanding lookout tower; and its stained and moss-grown massive walls—impress the external observer as a relic of the distant past; while a ramble through its heavy casemates—its crumbling Romish chapel, with elaborate portico and inner altar and holy-water niches; its dark passages, gloomy vaults, and more recently-discovered dungeons—bring you to ready credence of its many traditions of inquisitorial tortures; of decaying skeletons, found in the latest-opened chambers, chained to the rusty ring-bolts; and of alleged subterranean passages to the neighboring convent. Next to the fort the great attraction is the Sea-Wall, which, beginning at the water-battery of the fort, extends southward for nearly a mile, protecting the entire ocean-front of the city. It is built of coquina, with a granite coping four feet wide, and furnishes a delightful promenade of a moonlight evening. In full view of this is the old lighthouse on Anastasia Island, built more than a century ago, and a new one surmounted with a revolving lantern. Near the south end of the wall are the *United States Barracks*, which are among the finest and most complete in the country. The building was formerly a Franciscan monastery, but has undergone extensive modifications and repairs. The old Spanish wall, which extended across the peninsula from shore to shore and protected the city on the north, has crumbled down or been removed, but the City Gate, which originally formed a part of it, still stands at the head of St. George Street. It is a picturesque and imposing structure, with its ornamented lofty towers and loop-holes and sentry-boxes in a fair state of preservation.

In the centre of the town is the *Plaza de la Constitucion*, a fine public square, surrounded by a fence and furnished with seats which are seldom unoccupied during the winter season. Nearly in the centre of the square stands a monument, about 20 feet high, erected in 1812 in commemoration of the Spanish Liberal Constitution. Fronting on the Plaza are several imposing buildings, the most striking of which is the old Catholic Cathedral, erected in 1793 at a cost of $17,000. Its quaint Moorish belfry, with four bells set in separate niches, together with the clock, form a perfect cross. One of the bells bears the date of 1682. A neat Episcopal church also fronts on the Plaza, and there are Methodist, Baptist, and Presbyterian churches in the city. The old *Convent of St. Mary's*, located on St. George Street, just west of the Cathedral, has lately been demolished to make room for a new building. In its rear is the Bishop's Palace. The new *Convent of the Sisters of St. Joseph* is a tasteful coquina building on St. George Street, south of the Plaza; the old convent of this sisterhood was on Charlotte Street north of the Barracks. The nuns are mainly occupied in teaching young girls, but they also manufacture lace of a very fine quality, and excellent palmetto hats. After the Cathedral, the most imposing edifice on the Plaza is the *Governor's Palace*, formerly the residence of the Spanish Governors, but now used as Post-Office, City Clerk's Office, and Public Library. It is situated at the corner of St. George and King Streets. An older house than this, formerly occupied by the Attorney-General, was pulled down a few years ago. Its runs are still a curiosity, and are called (though incorrectly) the Governor's house.

The Convent-Gate.

The old **Huguenot Burying-Ground,** on King Street near the City Gate, is a spot of much interest; and so is the *Military Burying-Ground* (just south of the Barracks), where rest the remains of those who fell near here during the prolonged Seminole War. Under three pyramids of coquina, stuccoed and whitened, are the ashes of Major Dade and 117 men of his command, who were massacred by Oceola and his band. The *Soldiers' Monument,* erected in 1871, in honor of the Confederate dead, is located on St. George Street, just south of Bridge Street. On St. George Street, near the City Gate, is a famous *Rose-tree* of many years' growth; the trunk is as large as a man's arm, and the tree bears from 500 to 1,000 roses in a season. During the last few years many handsome residences have been erected, by Mr. Lorillard, Mr. Smith, Mr. Ammidown, and others.

The harbor affords excellent opportunities for boating, and numerous points of interest attract excursion-parties. Among the most popular of these are those to the *North Beach,* one of the finest on the coast, affording an admirable view of the ocean; to the *South Beach;* to the sand-hills, where General Oglethorpe planted his guns and laid siege to Fort Marion; to *Fish's Island;* and to the lighthouses and coquina-quarries on Anastasia Island. A pleasant trip is to *Matanzas,* where are the ruins of a fortress more ancient than any structure in the city itself; and *Matanzas Inlet* affords excellent camping-places for hunting and fishing parties. About 2½ miles off Matanzas an immense *Sulphur Spring* boils up out of the ocean where the water is 132 feet deep, and is well worth a visit. Salt-water bathing may be practised at St. Augustine in suitable bathing-houses, but the sharks render open sea-bathing dangerous.

Pablo Beach.

The most popular local resort near Jacksonville, next to St. Augustine, bears a name almost new to the general public. It is Pablo Beach. This is a beautiful location on the Atlantic beach, a few miles south of the mouth of the St. John's. It is connected with Jacksonville by a short but thoroughly equipped railroad, known as the Jacksonville & Atlantic R. R. Both this railroad and Pablo Beach are the result of Jacksonville enterprise. A ride of thirty minutes lands the tourist or pleasure-seeker upon a beach incomparable in hardness, smoothness, and extent. On this beats the Atlantic, and the finest of marine views opens before him. The entire enterprise dates its inception only fourteen months back, while the road has been in active operation less than six months. In this short time a hotel, *Murray Hall*, perhaps the most graceful in architecture and most picturesque and tasteful in design of any in the entire State, and capable of accommodating 400 guests, has been erected here. It has been filled to overflowing the entire summer. The growth of Pablo Beach has been phenomenal. It is within the past six months that the first cottage was erected, and in that time 70 buildings have been completed and occupied by private citizens. The railroad company have put up extensive buildings, bath-houses, pavilions for dancing, skating, etc., handsome pagodas, and other attractive improvements. Aside from the disbursements of the railroad company, $300,000 have been expended in the development of the place. It seems to have filled a need of Jacksonville. It has certainly attained an unparalleled popularity with the people and sojourners of that city. By actual count, 55,000 persons enjoyed the delights of the seaside at this point from July 1 to September 15, 1886. The attractions and amusements are hunting, fishing, boating, bathing in an unequalled surf, and riding, driving, and bicycle-riding on the magnificent beach. This beach stretches away in an unbroken line to St. Augustine on the south, and to Mayport at the mouth of the St. John's on the north.

Fernandina and Cedar Keys.

Fernandina is an interesting old seaport town, situated on the west shore of Amelia Island, at the mouth of Amelia River, 50 miles north of Jacksonville. It is reached by rail from Jacksonville, and from Charleston by railroad and steamer; by steamer direct from New York; and by the inside line of steamers from Savannah. Fernandina was founded by the Spaniards in 1632, and has a population of about 3,000, largely increased during the winter season. Its harbor is the finest on the coast south of Chesapeake Bay, being landlocked and of such capacity that, during the War of 1812, when the town was Spanish and neutral, more than 300 square-rigged vessels rode at anchor in it at one time. Vessels drawing 19 or 20 feet of water can cross the bar at high tide, and the largest ships can unload at the wharves. It is the initial point of the Florida Railway and Navigation Company's system, whence lines run to Cedar Keys and through Jacksonville to Chattahoochee. The *climate* of Fernandina is very similar to that of St. Augustine; mild and equable in winter, and in summer tempered by the cool sea-breezes. It is entirely free from malaria, and is altogether one of the healthiest places in Florida, though like St. Augustine, and for the same reasons, its air is considered too strong for consumptives in advanced stages of the disease. The town, which is the seat of the Episcopal bishopric of Florida, contains seven churches, a flourishing young ladies' seminary, and a weekly newspaper. Fernandina possesses other attractions for visitors besides its delightful climate. There is, for instance, a fine shell-road, 2 miles long, leading to the ocean-beach, which affords a remarkably hard and level drive of nearly 20 miles, and on which is a fine hotel. A favorite excursion is to *Dungeness*, the home of the Revolutionary hero, General Nathanael Greene. This estate, of about 10,000 acres of choice land, was the gift of the people of Georgia to the general, in recognition of his services as commander of the Southern provincial army. The grounds are beautifully laid out, and are embellished with flower-gardens, and handsome groves, and avenues of olive-trees, and live-oaks draped with long festoons of the graceful Spanish moss. On the beach, about half a mile from the Dungeness mansion, is the grave of another Revolutionary hero, General Henry Lee, marked by a headstone erected by his son, General Robert E. Lee. Cumberland Island, on which Dungeness is situated, was purchased in 1884 by Mr. Thomas M. Carnegie, who rebuilt the old mansion. The hotels at Fernandina are the *Egmont Hotel*, one of the finest in the South, the *Mansion House*, the *Riddell House*, the *Florida House*, and the *Tourists' Hotel*. Rates from $2.50 to $3.50 a day. Board may be had in private families at from $6 to $12 a week.

Internal Travel Lines.

A.—FLORIDA RAILWAY & NAVIGATION COMPANY.

Central Division.—Beginning at Fernandina, the Florida Railway & Navigation Company extends directly across the State to Cedar Keys, on the Gulf coast (154 miles), crossing at *Callahan* the Savannah, Florida & Western R. R. (Waycross Branch). *Baldwin*, at the crossing of the Western Division of the Florida Railway & Navigation Company from Jacksonville to Chattahoochee, is 47 miles from Fernandina, 20 from Jacksonville, and 107 from Cedar Keys, and the telegraph-line to Cuba branches off here. The next noteworthy town is *Waldo* (84 miles from Fernandina), at the junction of the Southern and Central Division of the Florida Railway and Navigation Company. The climate here is dry and the air balsamic, and the region is regarded as particularly favorable to invalids suffering from lung-diseases. The *Waldo House* is a highly comfortable hotel, and board may be had in private families for from $15 to $25 a month. The woods in the vicinity of the village abound in deer, ducks, quail, etc.; and about 2 miles distant is *Santa Fé Lake*, which is 9 miles long and 4 wide, and affords good facilities for boating and fishing. The streams in the neighborhood are filled with trout and perch. The Santa Fé River disappears underground a few miles from Waldo, and after running underground for 2 miles rises and continues to its discharge into the Suwanee River. **Gainesville** (98 miles) is the principal town on the line of the road. It has 5,000 inhabitants, 4 churches, 4 hotels (*Arlington House*, the *Rochemont*, the *Alachua House*, the *Magnolia*, the *Seminole*, and the *Park House:* terms $1.50 to $3 a day, $25 and upward a month), and 2 newspapers. Owing to its favorable situation in the centre of the peninsula and in the midst of the pine-forests, which clothe this portion of Florida, Gainesville is much frequented by consumptives and other invalids. The surrounding scenery is very beautiful, and the vicinity abounds in natural curiosities. The town was destroyed by fire early in 1884, but has been substantially rebuilt since. The woods are alive with game; and oranges, lemons, limes, grapes, and peaches grow in abundance. The *Alachua Sink* teems with fish of various kinds, and with alligators. **Cedar Keys** (the *Suwanee, Gulf House, Magnolia,* and *Bettelin's Hotel*), the Gulf terminus of the railway, is a thriving village of about 700 inhabitants, pleasantly situated on a large bay, which affords excellent facilities for bathing, boating, and fishing. The chief commerce of the place is in cedar and pine wood, turtles, fish, and sponges, the sponging-grounds being about 60 miles distant. The climate of Cedar Keys is blander than that of Jacksonville, and is beneficial to rheumatism as well as consumption; but there are as yet no adequate or proper accommodations for invalids. From Cedar Keys a steamer sails on Mondays and Thursdays for *Tarpon Springs*, at the head of Anclote River, a voyage of eight hours. Eighteen miles west of Cedar Keys, the *Suwanee River*, navigable to Ellaville, enters the Gulf; and the *Withlacoochee River*, 18 miles south. Lines of steamships ply regularly between Cedar Keys and New Orleans, Key West, Tampa, and Manatee, and others connect it with the country on the Suwanee River. **Southern** Division.—This division of the Florida Railway and Navigation Company diverges at *Waldo* (p. 15) in a direction nearly southeast, crossing at *Hawthorne* the track of the Florida Southern R. R. *Citra* and *Anthony* are passed on the way to *Silver Spring* junction, whence a branch two miles long leads to *Silver Springs* (p. 20). *Ocala* is a vigorous little city of 3,000 inhabitants, and the *Ocala House* can accommodate 400 guests. Sixteen miles south is the *Lake Weir* country, and 10 miles farther is *Wildwood* (whence a branch line runs to Leesburg), to Plant City, where connection is made with the South Florida R. R. At Tavares (22 miles from Wildwood) is the terminus of this division, where connections are made with *Sandford*, on the St. John's River (p. 20), and Orlando. **Western Division.**—From Baldwin (p. 15) this branch runs to *Olustee, Lake City*, the site of the Florida Agricultural College, and Welborn, the nearest point to the *White Sulphur Spring*. At *Live Oak* the Florida branch of the Savannah, **Florida & Western** R. R. intersects. *Ellaville* and *Madison* **are** reached before arriving at *Ancilla* (131 miles), **the** nearest point to the mythical "Florida Volcano," **which** is said to be marked by **a pillar of smoke.** *Monticello* is seated on **a** high ridge, is well shaded, and possesses **a refined** society, numerous churches and schools, and a large, well-conducted hotel. Then the traveler enters *Tallahassee* (p. 22), and, passing through *Quincy*, strikes the Chattahoochee River at the western terminus of the road, *River Junction*.

B.—JACKSONVILLE, TAMPA & KEY WEST RAILROAD.

This great trunk line, starting from Jacksonville, follows the course of the St. John's River, passing through *Orange Park*, picturesquely seated on Doctor's Lake, to *Magnolia* (p. 16) and the favorite resort of *Green Cove Springs*. *Palatka* (56 miles) is the largest town on the river (p. 18). Twenty-eight miles from Palatka is *Seville*, an enterprising town with a good hotel. From *Astor Junction* a branch line of 6 miles connects with the St. John's & Lake Eustis R. R. Passing through the Spring Garden Grant, the line reaches *De Land Junction*, whence a branch line (3 miles) runs to De Land, a place of 2,500 inhabitants, with four good hotels. Passing Orange City, the line enters Enterprise (121 miles from Jacksonville), whence a branch runs to the Indian River region, while the main line crosses the St. John's River by a bridge 3,500 feet long to the terminus at *Sanford* (p. 20), whence the South Florida R. R. extends to the Gulf coast at *Tampa*.

C.—SOUTH FLORIDA RAILROAD.

From *Sanford* this line passes *Belair*, where is situated the fruit-farm of General Sanford, to *Maitland*, a colony of Northern families, and the rising resort, **Winter Park,** beautifully situated on Lake Osceola, five miles in circumference. A new hotel, *The Seminole*, will accommodate 400 guests. There is here always a large winter population. Passing *Orlando*, with 3,500 inhabitants and numerous good hotels and boarding-houses, the road reaches *Kissimmee City*, the headquarters of the Disston Land Improvement and Drainage Company, skirts the sparkling Lake Tohopekaliga, and continues through Lakeland and Plant City to *Tampa*.

D.—FLORIDA SOUTHERN RAILROAD.

This line extends from *Palatka*, crossing the Florida Railway and Navigation Company's line at Hawthorne to *Leesburg*, where it connects with the St. John and Lake Eustis branch. From Leesburg it is continued to Pemberton Ferry, Lakeland, and *Barton*, where it meets lines from Sanford, Orlando, and the St. John's River. From Barton trains run to *Punta Gorda*, on Charlotte Harbor, the most southern depot in the United States. Charlotte Harbor is a beautiful sheet of water, attracting the attention of sight-seers, sportsmen, and health-seekers. We have given a brief glance at the net-work of railroads which now place the hitherto inaccessible localities of Florida within thirty-six hours of New York. The same enterprise distinguishes the development of water communication.

The St. John's River.

The town of **Mayport**—the quarantine post and anchorage of Jacksonville—lies on the left of the river at its mouth. Opposite is Pilot Town and St. George's Island. Daily boats run from Jacksonville, passing over the site of the old Huguenot settlement under Landonnière, and the scene of the Menendez massacre. The exact spot is now, by a change in the river-bed, several yards from shore.

Jacksonville, reached 21 miles from Mayport, and of course the most important and conspicuous place on the river, has been already described. At this point the St. John's, after flowing north for 300 miles, turns eastward and empties into the Atlantic. Its whole course, which lies through an extremely level region, is about

400 miles, and throughout the last 150 miles it is little more than a succession of lakes, expanding in width from 1½ mile to 6 miles, and having at no point a width of less than ¼ mile. It is said that, with its navigable branches, the St. John's affords 1,000 miles of water transportation, and it is credited with carrying a larger volume of water than the Rio Grande. Its banks are lined with a luxuriant tropical vegetation, handsome shade-trees and orange-groves, and here and there are picturesque villages. "The banks are low and flat," says Edward King, "but bordered with a wealth of exquisite foliage to be seen nowhere else upon this continent. One passes for hundreds of miles through a grand forest of cypresses robed in moss and mistletoe; of palms towering gracefully far above the surrounding trees, of palmettos, whose rich trunks gleam in the sun; of swamp, white and black ash, of

Mouth of the St. John's.

magnolia, of water-oak, of poplar and of plane-trees; and, where the hummocks rise a few feet above the water-level, the sweet bay, the olive, the cotton-tree, the juniper, the red cedar, the sweet-gum, the live-oak, shoot up their splendid stems; while among the shrubbery and inferior growths one may note the azalea, the sumach, the sensitive-plant, the agave, the poppy, the mallow, and the nettle. The vines run not in these thickets, but over them. The fox-grape clambers along the branches, and the woodbine and bignonia escalade the haughtiest forest-monarchs. When the steamer nears the shore, one can see far through the tangled thickets the gleaming water, out of which rise thousands of 'cypress-knees,' looking exactly like so many champagne-bottles set into the current to cool. The heron and the crane saucily watch the shadow which the approaching boat throws near their retreat. The wary monster-turtle gazes for an instant, with his black head cocked knowingly on one side, then disappears with a gentle slide and a splash. An alligator grins familiarly as a dozen revolvers are pointed at him over the boat's side, suddenly 'winks with his tail,' and vanishes! as the bullet meant for his tough hide skims harmlessly over the ripples left above him.... For its whole length of 400 miles, the river affords glimpses of perfect beauty. One ceases to regret hills and mountains, and can hardly imagine ever having thought them necessary, so much do these visions surpass them. It is not grandeur which one finds on the banks of the great stream, it is Nature run riot. The very irregularity is delightful, the decay is charming, the solitude is picturesque."

Two fine steamers, the City of Palatka and the City of Monticello, ply twice a week from Charleston up the St. John's as far as Palatka, but it is usual to begin the up-river tour at Jacksonville. The steamers of the De Bary and People's Line leave Jacksonville daily at 3.30 P. M. for Sanford and Enterprise. Time, about 20 hours; fare, $7; round trip, $10. Returning, leave Sanford at 4.25 P. M., and reach Jacksonville next morning. Others make a daylight run, leaving Sanford at

5 A. M., and arriving at Jacksonville at 6.10 P. M. The following list of localities on the St. John's may prove useful to the tourist. The distances are from Jacksonville:

	Miles.		Miles.
Riverside	3	Welaka	100
Black Point	10	Beecher	101
Mulberry Grove	11	Orange Point	103
Mandarin	15	Mount Royal	109
Fruit Cove	18	Fort Gates	110
Hibernia	22	Georgetown	117
Remington Park	25	Lake View	132
Magnolia	28	Volusia	137
Green Cove Springs	31	Orange Bluff	140
Hogarth's Landing	36	Hawkinsville	160
Picolata	45	Cabbage Bluff	162
Tocoi	52	Lake Beresford	165
Federal Point	60	Blue Spring	172
Orange Mills	64	Emanuel	184
Dancy's Wharf	65	Shell Bank	193
Whitestone	66	Sanford	199
Russell's Landing	69	Mellonville	200
Palatka	75	Enterprise	205
Rawlestown	77	Cook's Ferry and King Philip's Town	224
San Mateo	80	Lake Harney	225
Buffalo Bluff	88	Sallie's Camp	229
Ocklawaha River	100	Salt Lake	270

Fourteen miles above, on the east bank, is *Mandarin*, one of the oldest settlements on the St. John's. It is the winter home of Mrs. Harriet Beecher Stowe, whose cottage is situated near the river, a few rods to the left of the shore-end of the pier. She owns about 40 acres of land, three or four of which are planted with orange-trees. *Magnolia* (28 miles), on the J., T. & K. W. R. R., and which has already been described, is situated on the west bank, and is considered one of the most desirable resorts in Florida for consumptives. It has a sandy soil, covered with beautiful groves of pine and orange trees, and there are no dangerous hummock-lands near by. The *Magnolia Hotel* ($4 a day) is one of the best on the river, and has several cottages attached. A little to the north of the point Black Creek, a navigable stream, up which small steamers make weekly trips as far as *Middleburg*, empties into the St. John's. The bank swarms with alligators, which are apt to be mistaken at times for logs, which are floated down this stream in large quantities to market. Three miles above Magnolia are the *Green Cove Springs*, one of the most frequented resorts on the river, but now more easily reached by rail from Jacksonville, as is fully stated in the tracing of the Jacksonville, Tampa, & Key West R. R. line. The spring discharges about 3,000 gallons a minute, and fills a pool some 30 feet in diameter with greenish-hued crystal clear water. The water has a temperature of 78° Fahr.; contains sulphates of magnesia and lime, chlorides of sodium and iron, and sulphuretted hydrogen; is used both for bathing and drinking; and is considered beneficial for rheumatism, gouty affections, and Bright's disease of the kidneys. Attached to the springs are comfortable bathing-rooms, and close by are several hotels. There are also good private boarding-houses. About 10 miles above, on the same side, is *Picolata*, the site of an old Spanish settlement, of which no traces now remain. Two hundred years ago it was the main depot for the supply of the Spanish plantations of the up-country, and it then contained a splendid church and several religious houses of their order built by the Franciscan monks. On the opposite side of the river are the ruins of a great earthwork fort of the time of the Spanish occupation. Tocoi (52 miles) is of some importance as the point where connection is made with the St. John's Railroad to St. Augustine, 15 miles distant. *Palatka* occupies a fine, high plateau with a wide-reaching view up and down the river. It is the head of navigation for steamships, 75 miles from Jacksonville by the river and 36 by railroad. It has railway connection with Gainesville and Ocala *via* the Florida Southern R. R. It has a population of nearly 5,000, and is admirably located on high ground on the west bank of the river, where the surface-land is for the most part sandy. It is the county-seat of Putnam County, and is at the head of a large bay, the plateau on which it stands being so high and broad as to afford a fine view up and down the river. The soil is rich, and yields abundant crops. Vast quantities of vegetables and small fruits are sent from this point every year to the North. In the vicinity are many old productive and valuable orange-groves; and on the opposite side of the river, reached by ferry, are the famous groves of Colonel Hart, where the finest fruits of the tropics may be seen in their different stages of growth. The Hart plantation is one of the show-places of the country adjacent to Palatka. The city contains numerous well-stocked shops, packing-houses, warehouses, hotels, several handsome churches, good schools, and public buildings. The streets are wide and neatly kept, and are generally shaded with large oaks and orange-trees. Tastefully constructed residences line them, and about them are usually ample and well-shaded grounds. Thrift, prosperity, and enterprise are everywhere manifest. The Florida Southern Railway Company, one of the most extensive corporations in the State, has its headquarters here, including car-shops, storehouses, depots, wharves, and general offices. In the winter season, from December till May, Palatka swells itself to the proportions of a fashionable winter city. The wonderful blandness of its climate renders Palatka peculiarly favorable to consumptives, and it offers advantages in the way of churches, schools, postal and telegraph facilities, etc., not possessed by many of the interior resorts. It has five good hotels: the *Putnam House*, the *Phœnix House*, the *St. John's Hotel*, the *Hotel Palatka*, the *Graham House*, and the *Palatka House*. Rates at these houses are from $2 to $4 per day. There are several private boarding-houses where board may be had at from $10 to $15 a week. Palatka is steamboat headquarters for the upper St. John's and its tributaries; and the steamers *en route* for Sanford discharge and receive freight. Those who make this place their point of departure for the hunting and fishing regions of the upper St. John's and the Indian River region, and do not come supplied with equipment, can purchase at Palatka to advantage.

An Orange Grove on the St. John's.

Steamers run from Palatka up the Ocklawaha River to Silver Spring, and a railroad—the St. Augustine & Palatka Railway—offers facilities for reaching the sea. Trains run the distance in 65 minutes, and leave each point twice daily.

Above Palatka the vegetation becomes more characteristically tropical, and the river narrows down to a moderate-sized stream, widening out at last only to be merged in grand Lake George, Dexter's Lake, and Lake Monroe. The steamers make the run from Palatka to Sanford in about 12 hours. Five miles above Palatka, on the opposite bank, is *San Mateo*, a pleasant hamlet situated on a high ridge overlooking the river. **Welaka** (25 miles above Palatka), above the entrance to Dunn's Lake, and opposite the mouth of the Ocklawaha River, is the site of what was originally an Indian **village**, and afterward a flourishing Spanish settlement. On the Ocklawaha is the famous *Silver Spring*, the largest and most beautiful of the springs of Florida, navigable by steamers of several tons' burden. This spring is said to be the "fountain of youth" of which Ponce de Leon dreamed, and for which he vainly searched. The clearness of its waters is wonderful; they seem more transparent than air. "You see on the bottom, 80 feet below, the shadow of your boat, and the exact form of the smallest pebble; the prismatic colors of the rainbow are beautifully reflected; and you can see the fissures in the rocky bottom through which the water pours upward like an inverted cataract." Just above Welaka the river widens into *Little Lake George*, 4 miles wide and 7 miles long, and then into **Lake George,** 12 miles wide and 18 miles long. This is one of the most beautiful sheets of water in the world, being considered by many tourists equal in attractions to its namesake in the State of New York. Among the many lovely islands which dot its surface is one called *Drayton*. It is 1,700 acres in extent, and contains one of the largest orange-groves on the river. All along the lake the eye is delighted and the ear charmed by the brilliant plumage and the sweet song of the southern birds. One finds here the heron, the crane, the white curlew, the pelican, the loon, and the paroquet; and there are many varieties of fish. *Volusia* (5 miles above Lake George, 137 miles from Jacksonville) is a wood-station, with a settlement of considerable size back from the river. An ancient Spanish town used to stand here, this formerly being the principal point on the line of travel between St. Augustine and the Mosquito Inlet country. A fort was erected here during the Seminole War, and from this fort General Eustis, in command of the left wing of the army, set out to cross the country to the Withlacoochee to join General Scott. After a fruitless campaign of three months, the latter and his army crossed the river here on their way to St. Augustine. Thirty-five miles above Volusia is *Blue Spring*, one of the largest mineral springs in the State. It is several hundred yards from the St. John's, but the stream flowing from the spring is large enough at its confluence with the river for the steamers to float in it. One can look over the side of the steamer into the crystal-clear water below, and observe every movement of the families of the finny tribe as they flit about in the stream. Pursuing its voyage to the south, and passing several unimportant landings, the steamer speedily enters *Lake Monroe*, a sheet of water 12 miles long by 5 miles wide, teeming with fish and wild-fowl. On the south side of the lake is **Sanford,** the metropolis of South Florida, with wide streets, fine churches, schools, stores, and hotels (*Lake View House, Sanford House, San Leon Hotel*), a young but rapidly growing city, which has sprung into existence within the last few years. It is situated at the head of navigation for large steamers on the St. John's, and is the principal avenue of entrance to Orange County, whither so many of the new settlers are going. The South Florida R. R. extends S. W. to Tampa, opening up an excellent country, and passing the growing towns of Maitland, Osceola, Interlaken, Orlando, the county-seat of Orange County, Kissimmee City, and Lakeland. Near Sanford are a number of fine orange-groves. On the opposite side of the lake from Sanford is **Enterprise,** by rail but a few hours' ride from Jacksonville, and one of the most popular resorts in Southern Florida for invalids, especially for those suffering from rheumatism. The climate is warmer than that of Jacksonville and Magnolia, but it is said to have invigorating qualities which speedily convert invalids into successful fishermen and hunters. The *Brock House* is famous among travellers, and reasonable board may be had in private houses. A mile N. of the town is the *Green Spring*, a sulphur-spring, with water of a pale-green hue, but quite transparent. It is nearly 80 feet in diameter, and about 100 feet deep.

Although Sanford is the head of large steamboat navigation on the St. John's, there is for the sportsman still another hundred miles **of narrow river,** deep lagoons, gloomy bayous, and wild, untrodden land, where **all sorts of** game, such as bears, wild turkeys, deer, and ducks, are plentiful, while the waters teem with innumerable varieties of fish. Small boats can be obtained to run during the winter through Lake Harney to *Salt Lake*, the nearest point to the Indian River from the St. John's; and a small steamboat makes frequent excursions through **Lake Jessup** to *Lake Harney*, for the benefit of those who wish to try their hand at the exciting sport of alligator-shooting, or of those who wish simply to enjoy the charming scenery. The trip to Lake Harney and back is made in 12 hours. Lake Jessup is near Lake Harney; it is 17 miles long and 5 miles wide, but it is so shallow that it cannot be entered by a boat drawing more than three feet of water. The St. John's rises in the elevated savanna before mentioned, fully 120 miles south of Enterprise, but tourists seldom ascend farther than Lake Harney. About 20 miles southeast of Enterprise (reached by stage) is the ancient town of *New Smyrna*, located on Halifax River, south of the Mosquito Inlet. New Smyrna was settled in 1767 by Dr. Turnbull and his colony of 1,500 Minorcans, and was named by his wife, who was a native of Smyrna. The colonists cultivated indigo with much success, but, not being dealt with according to contract, they abandoned the settlement in 1776, and established themselves in and near St. Augustine, where their descendants now reside. A large canal, draining the Turnbull Swamp into the Hillsboro' River, at New Smyrna, is the only permanent monument the founder of this colony has left to posterity. Near New Smyrna, on the Halifax and Hillsboro' Rivers, are the flourishing settlements of Daytona, Port Orange, Holly Hill, Blake, and Oak Hill; and the adjacent region is rapidly filling up.

Indian River.

At Enterprise Junction the Indian River Division of the Jacksonville, Tampa, & Key West Railroad offers transportation by steel rails and parlor-coaches to a region which has heretofore filled the tourist with tantalizing longings, and which has really seemed "so near and yet so far." It is a region teeming with the world's luxuries, and yet, because of its inaccessibility, they have lain hidden in forest and lagoon. It is now, however, by a pleasant ride past Osteen, Oak Hill, Minis, and La Grange to Titusville, brought in easy reach of Jacksonville. Its oysters—the finest in the world—may now, like its other productions, be landed in Jacksonville in six hours after being taken from their briny beds.

Indian River is a long lagoon or arm of the sea, beginning near the lower end of Mosquito Inlet (with which it is connected by a short canal), and extending southward along the east side of the peninsula for a distance of nearly 150 miles. It is separated from the Atlantic by a narrow strip of sand, through which it communicates with the open water by the Indian River Inlet (latitude 27° 30' N.) and by Jupiter Inlet; and for more than 30 miles of its northern course the St. John's River flows parallel with it, at an average distance of not more than 10 miles.

The water of the lagoon is salt, though it receives a considerable body of fresh water through Santa Lucia River, an outlet of the Everglades; there are no marshes in the vicinity; the adjacent lands are for the most part remarkably fertile, producing abundantly oranges, lemons, limes, bananas, pineapples, guavas, grapes, sugar-cane, strawberries, blackberries, and all varieties of garden vegetables; and the river itself teems to an almost incredible degree with fish of every kind, including the pompano, the mullet, the sheepshead, turtles, and oysters of the most delicious flavor. Along the shore of the lagoon toward the Atlantic is a belt of thick, evergreen woods, which, breaking the force of the chilling east winds that sometimes visit these latitudes in winter, renders the climate of the Indian River country peculiarly favorable to consumptives and rheumatic patients. At *Fort Capron*, near the Indian River Inlet, a series of meteorological observations, taken during a series of years, shows a singularly equable temperature, with comparative dryness; the winter months having a mean temperature of 63° 20' Fahr., and there being 217 fair-weather days for the year. The westward side of the lagoon presents a sad panorama of ruined sugar plantations and houses, and of superb machinery lying idle. This is all that remains of the once prosperous and famous Turnbull colony.

The Indian River orange is, perhaps, more than anything else, what has rendered the name of the river so familiar to the outside world. A recent writer in *Blackwood's Magazine* says of it: "They have produced an orange which is not to be mentioned in the same breath with ordinary oranges. It is a delicacy by itself, hitherto unknown to the world, and which Spain need never attempt to rival. Between an Indian River orange and the coarse-grained, spongy, bitter-sweet product of the Mediterranean, there is nothing whatever in common." The Dummitt grove at the head of the river gave the Indian River orange its earliest fame; but there are now superb groves at other places along the river—at La Grange, City Point, Rockledge, Turkey Creek, and elsewhere.

Game is very abundant, except where the country is thickly settled. In the marshes all manner of ducks abound, and include the teal, mallard, wood, red-heads, coot, blue-bill, and canvas-back. Deer in some places are found in large numbers. Bears are found, particularly in summer, when with the turtle they roam the Atlantic beach, it may be almost said, in company—the turtle to deposit its eggs, the bear to eat them. Either of them—bear or turtle—may be counted good game. Otter, wildcat, panther, catamount, foxes, squirrels, raccoons, opossums, wild-turkey, quail, marsh-hen, plover, pheasant, snipe, cranes, egrets, curlews, and almost innumerable smaller birds may be found in the hummocks and about the lagoon.

Merritt's Island, a body of about 58,000 acres of land, lies in the Indian River, opposite Cape Canaveral. It is beautifully situated, and has already a large population, with churches and post-offices. It is widely noted for its extensive pineapple plantations. At its northern end the Indian River connects by a canal with the Mosquito Lagoon, which is also known as the Hillsboro' River; and at the northern end of Mosquito Lagoon the Halifax River comes in, which begins about 40 miles south of St. Augustine. The principal settlements are *New Britain*, *Daytona*, and *Port Orange*, on the Halifax River; *New Smyrna*, on the Hillsboro' River (see p. 21); and *Titusville* (formerly Sand Point) and *Rock Ledge*, on the W. bank of the Indian River.

The Tallahassee Country.

"Middle Florida," in the midst of which Tallahassee lies, differs from the rest of the State in that its surface is more broken and undulating, reaching here and there an elevation of from 300 to 400 feet. The hills are singularly graceful in outline, and the soil is exceedingly fertile, producing all the characteristic products of the Southern States, including tobacco and early garden vegetables. The vegetation is less tropical in character than that of Eastern and Southern Florida, but it is very profuse, and comprises many beautiful evergreens. Tallahassee, the capital of the State and county-seat of Leon County, is situated 165 miles west of Jacksonville, and 21 miles north of the Gulf of Mexico, in lat. 30° 25′ N. It has a population of about 5,000. It is beautifully located on high ground, and is regularly laid out in a plot a mile square, with broad streets and several public squares, shaded with evergreens and oaks. The abundance and variety of the shrubs and flowers give it the appearance of a garden. The business portion of the city is of brick. The public buildings are the *Capitol* (commenced in 1826), a large three-story brick edifice, with pillared entrances opening east and west; and the *Court-House*, a substantial two-story brick structure. There are several free public schools, two weekly newspapers, telegraph and express offices, and Baptist, Episcopal, Methodist, Presbyterian, and Roman Catholic churches. The car and machine shops of the railroad company are located here; also the only cotton-factory in the State. The society of Tallahassee is distinguished for its intelligence and refinement, and the old-time hospitality has survived the ravages of the war. The climate is delightful, the heat of summer and the cold of winter being tempered by the breezes from the Gulf; but consumptives should bear in mind that, as the site is higher than that of Jacksonville, the air is more likely to prove trying to weak lungs, unless proper precautions are taken as to clothing, etc. In the immediate neighborhood of Tallahassee are *Lake Bradford*, *Lake Jackson* (17 miles long), and *Lake Lafayette* (6 miles long)—the second named after General Jackson and the last after the French marquis.

The hotels of Tallahassee are a source of pride to its citizens and of comfort to the large numbers of people who annually visit the city. The new **Leon** has accommodations for 125 guests, is complete in appointments, and well conducted.

The *City Hotel* is the oldest in the State, and has a reputation honorable and widespread. It is now known as "*The Morgan*," having been renovated, remodelled, and rechristened. The *Whitaker* and *St. James* are smaller, but popular, houses.

Quincy, 24 miles farther west, is a charming little mountain village, and one of the oldest towns in the State. It was incorporated in 1828. The surrounding country, like all Middle Florida, is hilly and picturesque, constantly reminding one of Kentucky, Tennessee, or Virginia, and, like those States, excels in the cultivation of tobacco. This entire section is a constant surprise to the stranger, and affords unfailing delight to those familiar with its attractions.

Monticello (33 miles east of Tallahassee) is an important town of about 2,000 inhabitants. It contains Baptist, Episcopalian, Methodist, and Presbyterian churches, several schools, and a weekly newspaper. The hotels are the *Monticello* and the *Florida*, and board may be had in private families. In the vicinity of Monticello is *Lake Miccosukie*, whose banks are noted as the camping-ground of De Soto, and as the field of a bloody battle between General Jackson and the Miccosukie Indians.

Madison (22 miles east of Monticello), the capital of the county of the same name, is an attractive town of about 800 inhabitants, containing Baptist, Methodist, and Presbyterian churches, and several good boarding-houses. Near by is the Suwanee River, and in the county are the beautiful *Lakes Rachel, Mary, Francis,* and *Cherry* —all of which abound in fish.

The next point of interest is **Pensacola**, the terminus of the Pensacola & Atlantic Railroad. It is the principal city of West Florida, and is situated on the N. W. side of the bay of the same name, about 10 miles from the Gulf of Mexico. The adjacent country is sandy and covered with pines. The town itself, although a place of considerable political and commercial importance during the Spanish and English occupation, had, until a year or two prior to the civil war, presented a decayed appearance. At that time a large accession both to its trade and population took place, in consequence of the approach to completion of the railroad connecting it with Montgomery. Since the war it has had considerable commerce, and its population now numbers 12,000. The principal public buildings are a Custom-House, a new Court-House, and Roman Catholic, Episcopalian, Presbyterian, Methodist, and Baptist churches, and several fine hotels. There are several schools and academies, and two weekly newspapers. The remains of the old forts, San Miguel and St. Bernard, relics of the Spanish occupation, may be seen in the rear of the city. The climate of Pensacola is exceedingly healthful, the winter temperature being remarkably equable and bland. The entrance is defended by *Fort Pickens* on the east, situated on the extreme point of the long, low island of Santa Rosa, and *Fort McRae* on the west, situated on the mainland. About 1½ mile to the north, and immediately in front of the entrance, stands *Fort Barrancas*. Near this fort are extensive barracks, a *Light-house*, and the *Naval Hospital*. About a mile above the hospital (7 miles from Pensacola) is the *Navy-Yard*, situated on Tartar Point. The villages of *Warrington* and *Woolsey* lie immediately adjacent to the walls of the navy-yard. The Pensacola R. R. (44 miles long) connects at Pensacola Junction with the Louisville & Nashville R. R., and brings Pensacola into connection with the general railway system of the country. From New York and the North there are three main routes to Pensacola—one *via* Atlanta, West Point, and Montgomery; another *via* Macon, Columbus, and Montgomery; and a third *via* New Orleans and Mobile. The Perdido Railway is a short line of 9 miles, connecting Pensacola with *Millview*, on Perdido Bay, where there are extensive lumber establishments.

Returning to Tallahassee, we cannot resist the temptation of a trip over the *St. Mark's Branch* of the F. R. & N. system. It is but 21 miles long, and runs through a flat, uninteresting portion of country; but it leads up 16 miles from Tallahassee to **Wakulla**, which is the nearest station to the celebrated *Wakulla Spring*. This wonderful natural curiosity lies in the midst of a dense growth of hummock forest. Sidney Lanier says of it: "About 15 miles from Tallahassee is one of the most wonderful springs in the world—the Wakulla—which sends off a river from its single outburst.... Once arrived and floating on its bosom, one renews the pleasures enjoyed at Silver Springs. Like that, the water here, which is similarly impregnated with lime, is thrillingly transparent; here one finds again the mosaic of many-shaded green hues, though the space of the spring is less broad and more shadowed by trees than the wide basin of Silver Spring."

The **St. Mark's River** is very picturesque, and is supposed to rise from the great Miccosukie Lake, which communicates underground with the "sink," where the river begins its course. It is navigable to the **Natural Bridge**, 18 miles from Tallahassee, where the stream disappears to reappear fifty feet below. Here took place the only battle of the civil war in Middle Florida.

The Wakulla River is also picturesque and beautiful, and a trip from St. Mark's up to the spring is something the tourist should not omit. At its mouth stand the remains of the ancient Spanish fortress of San Marco.

Western Florida.

That portion of the State lying west of the Appalachicola River is usually spoken of as "West Florida," and by Nature belongs rather to Alabama than to Florida. Its population is very scanty, and, being less accessible than any other part of the State, it is seldom visited by either tourists or invalids. Its coast-line is indented with many beautiful bays, and the country is watered by numerous creeks and rivers, down which is floated the lumber which constitutes the chief staple of its industry. Leaving the line of the Florida Railway and Navigation Co. at River Junction (p. 16), the line of the Pensacola & Atlantic R. R. traverses that portion of the State which lies between the Chattahoochee and Appalachicola Rivers. *Marianna (Milton House)*, the first place of importance in our westward course, is picturesquely situated in the midst of a fine fertile agricultural section. **De Funiak Springs**, midway between the Chattahoochee and Perdido, is classed among the most popular winter resorts of Florida. It is a circular lake, or spring without visible outlet or source of supply. It is one and one fourth mile in circumference, round as if drawn by Nature's compasses. A branch "Chautauqua," known as the "Florida Chautauqua," has selected this place for its annual assemblies, which are held

A River Post-Office.

in winter, beginning in February and closing April 1st. A large assembly hall the Tabernacle, capable of accommodating 1,000 listeners, and provided with a large, commodious stage, organ, etc., stands on the shores of the lake. The *Hotel Chautauqua* is a large and exceedingly handsome structure, which last year was unable to meet the demands of the public. It has been enlarged during the present summer to double its former capacity.

Up the Ocklawaha.

In the earlier days of Florida travel, a trip up the Ocklawaha to the famous Silver Spring was the ultimatum of the tourist's ambition; but times have very much changed in this as in other respects. The Silver Spring is now reached (if one so chooses) in a Pullman drawing-room or a Mann boudoir, and, if the tourist misses the chance of "roughing it," he finds all the advantages of civilization, comfort, and even luxury, following him into the depths of primeval Nature. The old mode of travel, however, still possesses its charms, and a recent writer, in describing a trip of but a few months ago, says that "no visitor to Florida who values his peace of mind will leave the State without having made the trip up the Ocklawaha to Silver Spring." The Ocklawaha boats start from Palatka at nine o'clock in the morning. The trip occupies all of one day and one night, and until an early breakfast hour of the second day. The rude, awkward, nondescript craft which waited for passengers in the winter mornings of a few years ago, is passed away, and now the Ocklawaha River boats are five in number, all of them models of comfort, yet adapted to a nicety to their peculiar service. They are all stern-wheelers, and all carry Indian names. The first three hours of the trip is occupied in going up the St. John's to *Welaka*, a point just opposite the mouth of the Ocklawaha. The scenery immediately changes when the mouth of the river is entered. The channel is narrow and tortuous in the extreme, and winds through a dense cypress swamp. The giant trees on each side meet and interlace overhead, and the route among them seems more like entering and traversing a forest aisle. The whole trip is most interesting, but becomes especially so after dark, when the pathway of the steamer is illuminated by the dancing glow of a light-wood fire suspended in iron fire-pans or cages on the corners of the pilot-house. These are constantly fed with resinous or "fat" pine-knots. The effect of this glaring flame, bursting out of blackest darkness, it is impossible to describe. The glinting water, the giant trees, the over-hanging, dreary-

The Lookout.

looking moss, the very emblem of desolation, the fantastic forms of twisted water-oaks, the glimpses of lazy-looking alligators, the cry of birds startled by the light—all combine to make an experience that may be counted an event in any life. Often, at the most opportune moment, a banjo is heard from the lower deck, giving out weird, uncanny minor tones; it is soon accompanied by untrained but singularly melodious voices, in some jingle so meaningless in its diction as to seem an impromptu rhyme, yet in the whole a marvellous preservation of the unities, perfect in its harmony with the surroundings. The scene is complete. Nothing could be added that would make it more intensely picturesque. About midnight the boat passes through "The Gateway of the Ocklawaha," as it is called. This is formed by two immense cypress-trees, growing so close to each other that scarcely enough room is left to allow the boat to pass. About daylight the boat turns suddenly to the right, and the celebrated "Run" is entered. Here the stream becomes a river 100 feet in width, and runs with a swift current, against which these diminutive steamers make laborious way for nine miles. The "Run" is the crowning marvel of the river. Its waters are so clear that it can be compared to nothing but a river of glass with emerald banks. Its bottom is of white sand, and so transparent are its waters that mosses and grasses growing on the bottom, 100 feet below, can be seen distinctly. As they move in the current, it is difficult to dispel the delusion that they are waving in the wind. At the end of the "Run" the boat crosses the "Silver Spring" and anchors at a wharf on its farther shore. The proper thing to do next is to take a seat in the row-boat awaiting the tourist, and explore the wonderful spring at leisure. It is about 60 feet in depth, and sends up thousands of gallons of water without producing a ripple on the surface. The water is so smooth and so translucent that it seems to possess a marvellous power of reflection. Floating on its surface in a small boat, the traveller may fancy himself afloat in a balloon, so faithfully are all the objects of the upper world duplicated in the water beneath him. The most surprising effect is produced when the boat floats from shadow out into sunshine, for then it seems, by some miraculous power, to be suspended in mid-air, between two worlds of clearest ether; while, "glancing downward," says a graphic writer, "on the sanded bottom is seen a sharp, clear *silhouette* of man, boat, and paddle." Facing the wharf, an elegant hotel, with all modern appliances, awaits the traveller's emergence from the wild wood, and is ready to welcome him to comfort and rest. Several home-like cottages will also, for moderate compensation, refresh and entertain him for any period of time. Here, too, he finds the parallel rails and the iron horse ready to return him to Palatka in a few hours, if he prefers that to a return trip on the boat. A little steamer, the "Emma," plies upon the spring and down the "Run." By this means invalids and other travellers, who do not desire the fatigue of the trip from the mouth of the Ocklawaha, can come to the hotel by rail, and in this little steamer can cross the spring, enter the "Run" from the spring, and traverse its nine miles and return.

The Gulf Coast.

It has already been remarked, in the general description of the State, that much the larger part of the coast-line of Florida is washed by the Gulf of Mexico; but this immense stretch of sea-front is almost inaccessible on account of shallow soundings, and has few good harbors. The principal towns on the coast—Pensacola, Appalachicola, and Cedar Keys—have already been described. Steamers make semi-weekly trips between Cedar Keys, Tampa, Manatee, Key West, and Havana, touching at intervening points, which are flourishing farming or lumbering settlements, offering great attractions to sportsmen, but scarcely interesting to the tourist or invalid. **Tampa**, the first noteworthy point below Cedar Keys, is situated near the centre of the western coast, at the head of the beautiful Tampa Bay (formerly Espiritu Santo Bay). The bay is about 40 miles long, is dotted with islands, and forms a splendid harbor for the largest vessels. Its waters swarm with fish and turtle, the former being so numerous in some places as to impede the passage of boats; and there is an abundance of sea-fowl, including the beautiful flamingo-bird. Deer swarm on the islands. The surrounding country is sandy, and for miles along the shore there is a luxuriant tropical vegetation. Large groves of orange, lemon, and pine trees are everywhere to be seen. The village is growing rapidly, and is probably destined to become one of the chief cities and health-resorts of Florida. There are good hotels (the *H. B. Plant*, the *St. James*, the *Orange Grove*

Hotel, the *Palmetto Hotel*, and the *Collins Hotel*), and board may be had in private families. The South Florida R. R., which is a part of the Savannah, Florida & Western R. R. system, connects Tampa with river-travel on the St. John's at Sanford. The Jacksonville, Tampa & Key West R. R. also contributes to make this town an important point. The Florida Southern Railway connects with the St. John's River steamers at Palatka, and with the Jacksonville, Tampa & Key West R. R. for Ocala, Leesburg, etc. A steamer leaves Tampa twice every week for Key West and Havana. The through fast mails from the North and East to Cuba are now carried by this route. A steamer leaves Tampa every Wednesday and Saturday for **Tarpon Springs** (12 hours), which can also be reached from Cedar Keys. The *Tarpon Springs Hotel* is kept in first-class style; the *Tropical Hotel* and the *Fernald House* are cheaper. Camp-life is a feature of Tarpon Springs, and every facility is offered for it. **Manatee** is a small village situated on the Manatee River about 8 miles from its mouth. There are two or three boarding-houses here, where fair accommodations may be had at $2 a day or $40 a month. **Charlotte Harbor**, or *Boca Grande*, south of Sarasota, is about 25 miles long and from 8 to 10 miles wide, and is sheltered from the sea by several islands. The fisheries in and around the harbor are very valuable, the oysters gathered here being remarkably fine and abundant. The entrance to the harbor between Boca Grande Key and Gasparilla is 6 fathoms deep and $\frac{3}{4}$ of a mile wide. **Punta Rassa** is a small hamlet near the mouth of the Caloosahatchee River, chiefly noteworthy as the point where the Cuban telegraph-line lands, and as a U. S. Signal Service station. The thermometrical observations recorded here are interesting as indicating the climate of all this portion of the coast. North and west of Tampa Bay is Clear Water Harbor, a sheet of water about which it is becoming a common, as it is a very natural, thing for visitors to become rapturous. Its shores are high and bluff-like in character, its waters are deep, and their appearance is aptly set forth in its name. Two miles out of Tampa, on the South Florida R. R., is the mushroom of Florida. It is Ybor City, a town of cigar-makers.

Key West.

Key West, the largest city in Florida, next to Jacksonville, is situated upon the island of the same name, off the southern extremity of the peninsula, and occupies the important post of key to the Gulf passage. The island is 7 miles long by from 1 to 2 miles wide, and is 11 feet above the sea. It is of coral formation, and has a shallow soil, consisting of disintegrated coral, with a slight admixture of decayed vegetable matter. There are no springs, and the inhabitants are dependent on rain or distillation for water. The natural growth is a dense, stunted chaparral, in which various species of cactus are a prominent feature. Tropical fruits are cultivated to some extent, the chief varieties being cocoanuts, bananas, pineapples, guavas, sapodillas, and a few oranges. The air is pure and the climate healthy. The thermometer seldom rises above 90°, and never falls to freezing-point, rarely standing as low as 50°. The mean temperature, as ascertained by 14 years' observation, is, for spring, 75.79°; for summer, 82.51°; for autumn, 78.23°; for winter, 69.58°. The city has a population of about 7,000, a large portion of whom are Cubans and natives of the Bahama Islands. They are a hardy and adventurous race, remarkable for their skill in diving. The language commonly spoken is Spanish, or a *patois* of that tongue. The streets of the town are broad, and for the most part are laid out at right angles with each other. The residences are shaded with tropical trees, and embowered in perennial flowers and shrubbery, giving the place a very picturesque appearance. The buildings, however, are mostly small, and are constructed of wood, except the Western Union telegraph-office, those belonging to the United States Government, and one other, which are of brick. The public buildings are the **Custom-House**, Naval Storehouse, **Marine** Hospital, **County Court-House**, County Jail, **a Masonic** Hall, and an **Opera-House**. Near the Naval Storehouse is a monument **of dark-gray** granite, **erected in** 1866 to the memory **of the** sailors and soldiers who died in **the** service on **this station** during the civil **war**. Key West has a fine harbor, and, being the key **to the best** entrance to the Gulf **of Mexico**, it is strongly fortified. The principal work of defense is *Fort Taylor*, built on an artificial island within the main entrance to the harbor. It mounts nearly 200 guns, and there are several sand-batteries. The *Barracks* are large and commodious, and are garrisoned by 60 men. There is a *U. S. Dock*, with cisterns to catch rain-water, a condensing and distilling apparatus, and a machine-shop and foundery. Among the principal industries of Key West are turtling, sponging, and the catching of mullet and other

Key West.

fish for the Cuban market. The value of sponges annually obtained is about $100,000. Upward of 30 vessels, with an aggregate of 250 men, are engaged in wrecking on the Florida Reef, and the island profits by this industry to the amount of $200,000 annually. The manufacture of cigars employs about 800 hands, chiefly Cubans, and 25,000,000 cigars are turned out yearly. An establishment for canning pineapples—the only one in the United States—is also in successful operation. The city contains Baptist, Episcopal, Methodist, and Roman Catholic churches, two public and eight private schools, a convent, and two weekly newspapers (one Spanish). There are a number of charming drives on the island, and the fishing and boating are unsurpassed. Within the past year Key West has been visited by fire, which nearly swept the island, and all but blotted the town from the map of the United States. It was a staggering blow, from which she is but slowly and painfully recovering.

Steamers leave Key West occasionally for the Dry Tortugas, a series of desolate, barren rocks at the extreme end of the Florida Keys. During the war these islands were used as a penal station for Confederate prisoners, and several of the conspirators concerned in the assassination of President Lincoln were confined there.

South Florida.

PERHAPS no portion of the United States has, for the past two years, attracted so much attention as the 28,000 square miles which compose the region known as South Florida. By this name is known all that portion of the State south of the 29th parallel of latitude. It includes regions as utterly unknown and unexplored as were the most interior recesses of the Dark Continent before Livingstone or Stanley were born. Other portions of it are crossed and recrossed by lines of steel rails, and embryo cities and busy towns record a doubling of their population annually.

In some parts of it are New England hills, lifting their heads in Florida sunshine, and within its borders lies also that shoreless, inland sea of solitude, the great, dismal, mysterious *Okeechobee*—vast saw-grasses, marshes, and cypress-sentineled swamps. This region includes some of the finest locations and richest lands in the State, and Polk, Hernando, and Hillsboro' Counties are receiving an almost steady stream, not of visitors only, but of sturdy American citizens, who come to stay. They are rapidly settling up; Orange, Sumter, and Brevard have reputations already that are almost world-wide. The first effort to explore the Okeechobee was made about five years ago by a canoeist of much reputation (Mr. C. K. Munroe, of New York), who, following the coast from the mouth of the Suwanee to the Caloosahatchie, entered the latter, and, ascending the stream, worked his gradual way into the wide and desolate Okeechobee Lake. Here it is said that, solitary and alone, he made an eight days' search for the mouth of the Kissimmee, the northern tributary of the lake. Unable to find it, he returned to the Gulf by the route through which he had entered it. A year or two later, Mr. Williams, of the New Orleans *Times-Democrat*, with a considerable party, entered by the Kissimmee, explored the lake, and made exit through the Caloosahatchie. In 1881 Hamilton Disston, of Philadelphia, purchased from the State of Florida 4,000,000 acres of land, of which a large tract borders on Lake Okeechobee and the Everglades. A few months later the Drainage Company, organized by Mr. Disston, commenced the cutting of the canal which now connects the Okeechobee with the head-waters of the Caloosahatchie. By it the lake has been bailed out, so to speak, and miles and miles of country have been drained. These reclaimed lands are found to possess an exceptional fertility.

Hints for Sportsmen.

Probably every portion of the United States, off the beaten lines of travel, has been in turn described as "a paradise for sportsmen"; but it is literal truth to say that there is at the present time no place on the continent like Florida for both game and fish. In the immediate vicinity even of such centres of population as Jacksonville, St. Augustine, and Tallahassee, there is excellent sport for either the angler or the huntsman, and it is only necessary to penetrate a short distance into the country in any direction in order to find game incredible in quantity and variety. One great advantage which Florida offers to sportsmen is that, owing to the extreme mildness of its climate, what is called "roughing it" is a much less trying process than perhaps anywhere else in America. By taking only the most obvious precautions as to clothing, etc., even invalids may camp out for weeks with substantially no risk; and, so much of the locomotion being by water, there is comparatively little likelihood of exhausting fatigue.

As for game, there is an inexhaustible variety from which to choose. Of quadrupeds, there are the bear, the panther, the lynx, the gray wolf, the gray fox, the raccoon, the Virginia deer, the Southern fox-squirrel, the gray squirrel, the gray rabbit, and the opossum. The game-birds include the wild-turkey, the Canada goose, the mallard, the canvas-back, the teal, the black duck, the scaup-duck, the red-head duck, the wood-duck, the ruddy duck, the raft-duck, the green wingtail, the blue wingtail, quail, black-billed plover, golden plover, piping plover, snipe, yellow-legs, godwits, curlew, black-necked stilt, rails, herons, cranes, and ibis. The fish include the pompano (most delicious of American fish), the sheepshead, the red-fish or channel bass, the black bass, the sea-bass, the mullet, the trout, the salt-water trout, the drum, the whiting, the red snapper, the "grouper," the cavalli, the crab-eater or sergeant fish, the hogfish, the catfish, the "tarpum," the bream, the sunfish, and several varieties of perch. Sharks are numerous in all the sea-coast waters, and alligators and other reptiles abound in all the inland streams.

We have already remarked that there is no portion of the State where sufficient sport cannot be had to satisfy a reasonable amateur's appetite; but those who are especially in search of game should go to Mosquito Inlet, to the Indian River, to the Upper St. John's, to the Upper Ocklawaha (Leesburg), or to the points mentioned in the preceding section on the "Gulf coast." The southwest coast, in particular, is comparatively little visited.

GEORGIA RESORTS.

GEORGIA, the last settled of the "original thirteen States," and long regarded as the "Empire State" of the South, lies just north of Florida, between lat. 30° 21' and 35° N. and long. 80° 48' and 85° 40' W., having an extreme length north and south of 320 miles, and an extreme breadth east and west of 254 miles, with an area of 59,475 square miles. The sea-coast, extending about 100 miles along the Atlantic, is similar to that of Florida and the Carolinas, being very irregularly indented, and skirted by numerous low islands, which extend parallel to the shores, from which they are divided by narrow lagoons or sounds. The famous Sea-Island cotton is grown on these islands, and wild-fowl are abundant in all varieties. The State presents a great variety of surface. Along the coast and the Florida line it is low and swampy, while a little farther back occur parallel ranges of sand-hills, 40 or 50 feet high. Near the southeast corner is the Okefinokee Swamp, or rather series of swamps, about 180 miles in circuit, filled with pools and islands, covered with vines, bay-trees, and underwood, and teeming with alligators, lizards, and other reptiles. The elevation for 20 miles inland rarely exceeds 40 feet, and averages 10 to 12 feet above the sea. Then the land suddenly rises by a terrace 70 feet higher, and this table-land continues nearly level about twenty miles farther inland, when another rise of 70 feet leads to a third tract, which continues to ascend toward the north, till at the distance of about 150 miles from the sea the elevation is about 575 feet. From the central portion of the State, the surface becomes more elevated, the hills increasing in size toward the north, till, at last, they verge upon the great hill-region traversed by the Appalachian or Alleghany Mountains. These noble ranges occupy all the northern counties, and present to the charmed eye of the tourist scenes of beauty and sublimity not surpassed in any part of the Union. The soil of the coast-islands is light and sandy, but the mainland consists of rich alluvions, producing corn and cotton in abundance, while the tide-swamps of the rivers are fertile in rice. Back from the coast is a stretch of sandy land, chiefly valuable for its timber and naval stores. The southwest portion of the State is light and sandy, but yields good crops

Cotton Picking.

of cotton, corn, tobacco, sweet-potatoes, sugar-cane, fruits, etc. The "northern" region contains much fertile land, particularly in the valleys, yielding grain, fruits, potatoes, and other vegetables, but is not so well suited to cotton. Near the coast the growth along the banks of the streams is of canes, cypress, *magnolia glauca*, and *grandiflora*, gums of different species, oaks, tulip, ash, sweet-bay, and many other genera; while back upon the sandy lands pines and scrub-oaks are almost the only trees. Several species of palmetto give a tropical aspect to the sea-islands, and the magnificent live-oaks largely obtained in the vicinity of Brunswick furnish the most valuable ship-timber grown in the United States. One of the most charming features of Georgia vegetation is that, in the larger portion of the State, tropical fruits, and flowers, and shrubbery, grow side by side with those characteristic of the more northern States. There are many fine rivers in Georgia; but, as with the watercourses of the South generally, they are often muddy, and their only beauty is in the luxuriant vegetation of their shores, with here and there a bold, sandy bluff. The Savannah, which divides the States of Georgia and South Carolina through half their length, has a course, exclusive of its branches, of about 450 miles. The Chattahoochee pursues a devious way through the gold-region westward from the mountains in the northeastern part of the State, and forms the lower half of the dividing line between Georgia and Alabama; at the point where it enters Florida it is joined by the Flint River, and the united waters are thenceforward called the Appalachicola. The Oconee and Ocmulgee combine to form the Altamaha, which, next to the Savannah, is the largest river falling into the Atlantic. Other important streams are the Ogeechee, the Santilla, and the St. Mary's.

The **climate** of Georgia, like that of California, presents much variety. In the lowlands in summer it is hot and unhealthy, and malarious fevers are prevalent; but in the pine-lands farther back the air is salubrious, while in the northern portion of the State the summers are always cool and healthful. The winter climate is delightful, especially in the eastern and southern districts; the days are bright and sunny, with little variation in the temperature, and the atmosphere is dry and balmy. The following table embodies the results of meteorological observations made at Augusta and Savannah, under the direction of the chief Signal-Officer of the United States, for the year ending September 30, 1872:

MONTHS.	MEAN THERMOMETER.		TOTAL RAINFALL, INCHES.		PREVAILING WIND.	
	Augusta.	Savannah.	Augusta.	Savannah.	Augusta.	Savannah.
October	66°	68°	1.62	3.55	S. E.	N. E.
November	54	59	7.78	2.22	W.	S. W.
December	47	51½	4.98	1.59	N. W.	S. W.
January	41	46	5.20	2.09	N. W.	N. W.
February	46	50	5.87	4.65	W.	N. W.
March	50	52½	10.88	10.18	N. W.	N. W.
April	66	67	2.95	2.75	S.	E.
May	74	76	5.36	5.22	W.	S. W.
June	79	80	4.77	9.52	S. E.	S. W.
July	81	83	6.87	4.26	S.	S. W.
August	80	84	4.10	12.31	E.	E.
September	75	76	1.34	3.52	W.	S. E.
Year	63.3	66.2	61.75	61.96	W.	S. W.

Many consumptives and others who find it necessary to winter in a southern climate remain at Savannah, Augusta, Charleston, or Aiken, in preference to going to Florida. Here they find comforts, and conveniences, and social attractions, which, of course, cannot be secured in comparatively remote and unsettled regions; and the climate is scarcely less propitious. Out of 13,606 deaths in Georgia in 1870, only 875 were from consumption, and of these the majority occurred among visitors from the Northern States. The pine-woods of Georgia, beginning about 70 miles from the coast and extending through the eastern and central sections of the State, are considered highly beneficial to consumptives, and are resorted to in increasing numbers. In addition to the dryness and mildness of the atmosphere, the terebinthine odor of the pine is thought to exercise a curative and healing influence peculiar to itself. Malarial and pulmonary diseases are unknown in these woods; and, according to Dr. Howe, " invalids with troublesome coughs and shortness of breath rapidly improve after a short residence, and some far advanced in tubercular disease recover their health completely."

Savannah.

How to reach.—From New York, Savannah may be reached by steamer sailing three times a week, Tuesday, Thursday, and Saturday, from Pier 35 North River, at 3 P. M. Time, about 60 hours; fare (cabin), $20. There are also steamers to Savannah from Philadelphia (Pier 41) every Saturday at noon, and from Baltimore semi-weekly. By rail reached by the coast line, *via* Richmond, Wilmington and Charleston; or by way of Richmond, Danville, Atlanta and Augusta. From Cincinnati, St. Louis, and the West, it is reached by the Louisville & Nashville R. R. and branches *via* Chattanooga and Atlanta, and thence by Central R. R. of Georgia; and from New Orleans by Savannah, Florida & Western R. R., " Waycross Short line."

Hotels and Boarding-Houses.—The principal hotels are the *Screven House*, on Johnson Square; the *Pulaski House*, on Bryan St., Johnson Square; the *Marshall House*, in Broughton St.; and the *Harnett House*. The rates at these hotels, several of which are of a high class, range from $2 to $3.50 per day. *McConnell's* and *Bresnan's* are kept on the European plan. Excellent board may be had in private families in all parts of the city and also in the suburbs for from $5 to $10 a week.

Location, Climate, and History.—Savannah, the chief city of Georgia, is situated on the south bank of the Savannah River, 18 miles from its mouth. The site was selected by General Oglethorpe, the founder of the colony of Georgia, who made his first settlement at this point in February, 1733. The city occupies a bold bluff about 40 feet high, extending along the river-bank for a mile, and backward, widening as it recedes, about 6 miles. The river making a gentle curve round Hutchinson's Island, the water-front of the city is in the shape of an elongated crescent about 2½ miles in length. The corporate limits extend back on the elevated plateau about 1¼ mile, the total area of the city being 3¼ square miles. In its general plan, Savannah is universally conceded to be one of the handsomest of American cities. Its streets are broad and beautifully shaded, they cross each other at right angles, and at many

Savannah.

of the principal crossings are small public squares or parks, from 1½ to 3 acres in extent. These parks, 24 in number, located at equal distances through the city, neatly inclosed, laid out in walks, and planted with the evergreen and ornamental trees of the South, are among the most characteristic features of Savannah; and, in the spring and summer months, when they are carpeted with grass, and the trees and shrubbery are in full foliage, afford delightful, shady walks, and playgrounds for the children, while they are not only ornamental, but conducive to the general health by the free ventilation which they afford. Upon the large "trust-lots," four of

Public Square, Savannah.

which front on each of these squares (two on the east and two on the west), many of the public edifices and palatial private residences of the city are built. The residences are mostly surrounded by flower-gardens, which bloom throughout the year; and among the shrubbery, in which the city is literally embowered, are the orange-tree, the banana, the magnolia, the bay, the laurel, the cape-myrtle, the stately palmetto, the olive, the flowering oleander, and the pomegranate. Flowers are cultivated in the open air throughout the year, many choice varieties (queen among them all the beautiful *Camellia japonica*, which flourishes here in the greatest perfection, the shrub growing to a height of from 12 to 15 feet) blooming in mid-winter.

Being in lat. 32° 5′ north, and so near the Gulf Stream as to be within the influence of its atmospheric current, the climate of Savannah has all the mildness of the tropics in winter, without the intense heat in summer, the mean **temperature** being 66° Fahr., very nearly the same as that of Bermuda. The winter months are particularly genial and equable, the days being bright and sunny, with no marked or sudden changes of temperature. (For details, *see* meteorological table on page 31). In point of health, the mortuary statistics of Savannah will compare favorably with those of any other city of the same population in the United States, the locality being comparatively free from the fevers of the lower latitudes, and almost entirely exempt from the pulmonary affections so prevalent farther north. Great numbers of consumptives and other invalids prefer remaining here, where all the comforts and conveniences of a city can be secured, to going to the sanitary retreats farther south.

Savannah was founded, as we have seen, in February, 1733, by General Oglethorpe. In 1776 the British attacked it and were repulsed; but on December 29, 1778, they reappeared in overwhelming force and took possession of the city. In October, 1779, the combined French and Americans attempted to recapture it, but were unsuccessful, and Count Pulaski fell in the engagement. Savannah received a city charter in December, 1789. In November, 1796, a fire destroyed property to the amount of $1,000,000; and in January, 1820, another conflagration occurred, involving a loss of $4,000,000. During the civil war the city was occupied as a Confederate military port and depot. It was the point on the sea to which Sherman's march from Atlanta was directed, and by December 10, 1864, he had fairly invested it. The capture of Fort McAllister on December 13th sealed the fate of the city, and on the night of the 20th General Hardee evacuated his lines and left it to the possession of the Union forces. In 1850 Savannah had a population of 15,312; in 1860, 22,292; and in 1870, 28,235. By the census of 1880 its population was 30,681. It recovered rapidly from the effects of the civil war, and its commerce has since about doubled. The chief business of the place is the receipt and shipment of cotton, though the trade in lumber is also considerable.

Presbyterian Church.

Points of Interest. — The great warehouses of the city are located on a narrow street at the steep foot of the steep bluff; they open below on the level of the piers, and from the uppermost story on the other side upon a sandy area 200 feet wide and divided by rows of trees. This is called the *Bay*, and is the great commercial mart of Savannah. The principal business streets are *Congress, Broughton, Whitaker,* and *Bay* Sts., and the favorite promenade is Bull St. to Forsyth Park. Among the noteworthy public buildings are the new granite *Custom-House*, which also contains the *Post-Office*, corner Bull and Bay Sts.; the *City Exchange*, in front of which General Sherman reviewed his army after the capture of Savannah, January 7, 1865; the *Court-House, U. S. Barracks, Police Barracks, Artillery Armory,* and *Jail. St. Andrew's Hall* and the *Chatham Academy* are conspicuous buildings. From the tower of the Exchange the best view of the city and neighborhood is to be had. The building on the northeast corner of Bull and Broughton Sts., known as the *Masonic Hall*, is interesting as the place where the Ordinance of Secession was passed, January 21, 1861. Four years later (December 28, 1864), a meeting of citizens was held in the same apartment to commemorate the triumph of the Union arms. Among the interesting relics of the past history of Savannah are the building in which the Colonial Legislature held its sessions, in South Broad St. near Drayton, and the mansion of the Governor of Georgia during the occupation of the city by the British, which stands in Boughton St. The Georgia Historical Society has a large hall, in which are a fine library and some interesting relics, and the new *Telfair Academy of Arts* contains a collection of casts. Of the church edifices, the Episcopal Churches of *St. John's* and *Christ's* are the most striking. The former is in the Gothic, the latter in the Ionic style. The lofty spire of the *Independent Presbyterian Church* is much admired. This church is built of Quincy granite, and cost $130,000. *Trinity Church* stands in Johnson Square, near the spot where John Wesley delivered his famous sermons. The new *Catholic Cathedral* is an imposing structure.

The most attractive place of public resort is **Forsyth Park**, an inclosure of 40 acres in the south part of the city. It is shaded by some venerable old trees, is laid out in serpentine walks, and ornamented with evergreen and flowering trees and shrubs. In the centre is a handsome fountain, after the model of that in the Place de la Concorde, Paris, and a fine *Confederate Monument* stands in the new portion. In Johnson or *Monument Square*, near the centre of the city, is a fine Doric obelisk, erected to the memory of General Greene and Count Pulaski, the corner-stone of which was laid by Lafayette, during his visit in 1825. The **Pulaski Monument** stands in Monterey Square, and is one of the most perfect specimens of monumental architecture in the United States. The steps are plinths of granite; the shaft is of marble, 55 feet high, and is surmounted by an exquisitely-carved statue of Liberty, holding the national banner. The monument appropriately covers the spot where Pulaski fell,

Monument to General Greene.

during an attack upon the city while it was occupied by the British, in 1779. It was constructed by Launitz, of New York, at a cost of $22,000, gold.

Though built upon a sandy plain, Savannah is not without suburban attractions, there being several places in its vicinity whose sylvan character and picturesque beauty are in keeping with the "Forest City" itself. Thunderbolt, Isle of Hope, Beaulieu, Montgomery, and White Bluff are all rural retreats on "The Salts," within short driving-distance of the city, where, in the summer months, bracing sea-breezes and salt-water bathing may be enjoyed. The great drive is to **Bonaventure Cemetery**, which is situated on Warsaw River, a branch of the Savannah, about 4 miles from the city. The scenery of Bonaventure has long been renowned for its

Arcadian beauty. A hundred years ago the seat of the Tatnalls, a wealthy English family, the grounds around the mansion were laid out in broad avenues, and planted in native live-oaks. These trees, long since fully grown, stand like massive columns on either side, while their far-reaching branches, interlacing overhead like the fretted roof of some vast cathedral, the deep shade of their evergreen foliage shutting out the sky above, and the long, gray moss-drapery depending from the leafy canopy, silent and still, or gently swaying in the breeze, give to the scene a weird and strangely sombre aspect, at once picturesque and solemn. A more beautiful or more appropriate home for the dead than in the shades of these green forest-aisles cannot well be imagined. On the road to Bonaventure the *Catholic Cemetery* is passed; the municipal cemetery, *Laurel Grove*, lies northwest of the city, near Forsyth Park. *Thunderbolt*, a popular drive and summer resort, is on the Warsaw River, a mile beyond Bonaventure. According to local tradition, this place received its name from the fall of a thunderbolt. A spring of water which issued from the spot upon that event has continued to flow ever since. *Jasper Spring*, 2½ miles west of the city, is the scene of the famous Revolutionary exploit of Sergeant Jasper, who, with only one companion, successfully assailed a British guard of eight men and released a party of American prisoners. *White Bluff*, 10 miles out, is another favorite resort of the Savannah people, and the road to it is one of the most fashionable drives.

Augusta.

How to reach.—From Savannah, Augusta is reached either by steamer on the Savannah River or by the Central Railroad (135 miles), or by Savannah, Charleston, & Port Royal R. R. (141 miles). From Charleston, *via* the South Carolina R. R. (137 miles). From the North through Washington, Danville, and Charlotte, or by the Coast-Line through Washington, Richmond, and Wilmington.

Hotels and Boarding-Houses.—The leading hotels are the *Central*, the *Planters'*, the *Globe*, and the *Augusta Hotel*. Rates, from $2 to $3 per day. Good board may be had in private families at from $5 to $10 a week.

Location, Climate, and History.—Augusta, one of the most beautiful cities in the South, and the third in population and importance in Georgia, is situated on the eastern boundary of the State, upon the banks of the Savannah River, 230 miles from its mouth, and at the head of its navigable waters. The river is wide at this point, and the shores picturesque. Along the high banks upon which Augusta is built are rows of old mulberry-trees, the trunks of which are covered with warts and knots, and the roots exposed by the washings of many freshets. Facing these trees are many pleasantly-situated cottages and villas, with very charming prospects of the river and the green slopes of the opposite shore. The area embraced by the city proper is 2 miles in length and about a mile in width, but it is rapidly spreading itself over the level lands westward. It is very handsomely laid out, with wide streets crossing each other at right angles. These avenues may well claim the palm for beauty among city thoroughfares. The principal one—Greene Street—is 168 feet wide, and lined with elegant mansions; tall, spreading trees not only grace the sidewalks, but a double row, with grassy spaces between, runs down the centre of the ample roadway. *Broad Street*, the main thoroughfare of the city, is another noble avenue, 165 feet wide and 2 miles long. In the centre of Broad Street stands the *Confederate Monument* (the handsomest in the South). It consists of an obelisk 80 feet high, surmounted by a statue of a soldier, and the 4 corner pedestals contain statues of Lee, Jackson, T. R. R. Cobb, and W. H. T. Walker. This is the Broadway of Augusta, wherein all the shopping and promenading are done, and where the banks and hotels and markets are to be found. Other streets will attract the visitor's notice, and the entire city is embowered in foliage.

The *climate* of Augusta is very similar to that of Aiken (from which it is only 17 miles distant). It is slightly cooler than that of Savannah, but is marked by the same genial equability, the same bright, sunny winter days, and the same dry and balmy atmosphere. (For details, *see* meteorological table on page 31.) The mean temperature in December and January is about 50° Fahr.; in midsummer it is 80°. Many consumptives find Augusta more beneficial than the warmer resorts farther south; and the climate is thought to be peculiarly invigorating to persons suffering from overwork and nervous exhaustion. A good many invalids, after spending the first part of the winter in Savannah or in Florida, come to Augusta to remain during February, March, and April, which are here especially delightful.

Augusta was laid out by General Oglethorpe only two years after the settlement of Savannah (1735), and became an important point in military operations during the Revolutionary War, being alternately in the possession of the royal troops and the Americans. The city was incorporated in 1798, and the chief magistrate bore the appellation of Intendant until 1818, when the first mayor was elected. It escaped the ravages of the civil war, and the population increased from 12,493 in 1860 to 15,386 in 1870. In 1886 the population is about 28,000.

Points of Interest.—There are a few fine public buildings in Augusta, among them a *Masonic Hall* of massive and imposing architecture, a handsome *Odd-Fellows' Hall*, and an *Opera-House* of good dimensions and considerable beauty. The City Hall, completed in 1824 at a cost of $100,000, is a really fine building of venerable age, set in an ample green amid tall trees, and having about it an air of quiet dignity and repose. On the green in front of the hall stands a granite monument 45 feet high, erected by the city in 1849 to the memory of the Georgian signers of the Declaration of Independence. The *Medical College* and the *Richmond Academy* have neat buildings; and an *Orphan Asylum*, 178 feet by 78, has been recently completed at a cost of $150,000. The churches are about 25 in number, and of all denominations. *St. Patrick's*, constructed in 1863 at a cost of $42,000, is a fine edifice. The *Market-Houses* are on Broad St., and are ¾ of a mile apart. The rapid development of the up-country of Georgia, within a few years, has brought down to Augusta great commercial prosperity; and the water-power, secured by means of the *Augusta Canal*, which brings the upper floods of the Savannah River to the city, at an elevation of 40 feet, is enriching it by extensive manufactures. This canal, 9 miles in length, was constructed in 1845. The *City Water-Works* were completed at a heavy cost in 1861; the water is drawn from the canal and forced into a tank, holding 185,000 gallons, in a cylindrical brick tower standing 115 feet above the general level of the city. There is a *City Cemetery*, which exhibits the taste and care that, in America, are now so commonly bestowed upon "God's acre." Just outside of the city, and east of the cemetery, are the **Fair-Grounds** of the Cotton States Mechanics' and Agricultural Fair Association, which were opened in 1870. Situated upon a plain, level as the sea, they are especially adapted to the uses which they serve. They embrace about 47 acres, and are laid out in attractive walks and drives.

An excellent view of Augusta and its environs may be had from **Summerville**, a suburban town of handsome villas situated on high hills about 3 miles from the city. A line of horse-cars runs from the town to the summit of the range. Here are situated many villas and cottages, embowered in trees, with broad verandas, handsome gardens, and many signs of wealth and culture. The scene is more Northern in its general features than Southern; the houses are like those of the North, and the gardens not essentially different, although the Spanish-bayonet— that queer horticultural caprice, with its bristling head of pikes—shows a proximity to tropical vegetation. These heights form a part of the famous red sand-hills of Georgia, and a characteristic feature are the rich red tints of the roadways. Among the objects of interest at Summerville, are the *United States Arsenal*, built in 1827, and the long range of workshops built and used by the Confederates during the war. The latter extend upward of 500 feet in length, are substantially built, and present an imposing effect. Returning to the city by leaving the main road to the left, a short distance from the Arsenal, the traveler can get a view of the *Powder-Mill* and *Cotton Factories* immediately on the outskirts of the city. These latter are very extensive, and give constant employment to 700 operatives. There are other pleasant drives along the banks of the Savannah, particularly below the city; and across the river at *Hamburg* there are some beautiful wooded and grassy terraces, known as Schultz's Hill, and much resorted to as a picnic-ground.

The river-voyage between Augusta and Savannah is a very pleasant one, presenting to the eye of the stranger many picturesque novelties in the cotton-fields which lie along the banks through the upper part of the passage, and in the rich rice-plantations below. Approaching Savannah, the tourist will be particularly delighted with the mystic glens of the wild swamp-reaches, and with the luxuriant groves of live-oak which shadow the ancient-looking manors of the planters. A few miles above the city of Savannah he may visit the spot where Whitney invented and first used his wonderful cotton-gin.

Thomasville.

How to reach.—Thomasville is on the line of the Savannah, Florida & Western R. R., 200 miles from Savannah, 58 miles from Albany *via* the Albany Division of that road, and 36 miles from Bainbridge, on the Flint River, where there is connection by steamer with Columbus, Ga., and Appalachicola, Fla. Thirty-eight hours from New York by Atlantic Coast-Line route. Same time from Chicago *via* Nashville and Albany.

Hotels and Boarding-Houses.—The *Mitchell House* is one of the most spacious, well-equipped, and well-kept hotels in the country outside of the great cities. A rival fully worthy of it, called the *Piney Woods Hotel*, has also been completed. Cheaper hotels are the *Gulf House* and the *Harley*. Besides the above hotels, many private families receive boarders on moderate terms.

Across the southern portion of Georgia, from east to west, extends a broad belt of primitive pine-forest. Its width is about 75 miles, and the surface of the country is almost a dead level. No underbrush grows, and no other tree besides the tall, spindling, long-leaved pine. The ground is carpeted with a green growth of weeds, and so open is the forest that were it not for the fallen trunks of dead trees a horseman might ride through it at a gallop. At the northern verge of this forest-wilderness, on the highest ground between Savannah and the Flint River, stands Thomasville, a pretty town of 5,000 inhabitants. It has broad, well-shaded streets, has Episcopal, Methodist, Baptist, Presbyterian, and Roman Catholic churches. The city is 330 feet above the level of the sea, and 200 miles distant from the Atlantic, and about 60 miles from the Gulf of Mexico. Every sea-breeze that reaches it must pass through miles of pine-forest. It is the centre of a pleasingly undulating country, well farmed, and abounding in rivulets of pure water. There is an artesian well 1,900 feet deep, which supplies the town with water, a careful analysis of which shows to be equally pure and to possess the medicinal virtues of the famous Waukesha water.

The following is a consolidated meteorological report, for the last four years, by Prof. L. S. McSwain, Volunteer Observer U. S. Signal Service at Thomasville: Latitude, 30.50; longitude, 84.10; altitude, 330 feet; average temperature, about 55° Fahr.

MONTHS.	Temperature.	Relative Humidity.	MONTHS.	Temperature.	Relative Humidity.
November	58.63	67 per cent.	February	55.87	62 per cent.
December	58.40	64 "	March	61.51	61 "
January	54.89	65 "	April	67.85	60 "

Mineral Springs.

There are numerous mineral springs in various portions of Georgia, the best known and most frequented being the Warm Springs, in Meriwether County, 36 miles northeast by stage from Columbus. Nearer railway points are Lagrange, on the Atlanta & West Point R. R.; and Geneva, on the Southwestern R. R. The Springs discharge 1,400 gallons of water per minute, of 95° Fahr. The waters are used for both bathing and drinking. Their effect is tonic and alterative, and they have acquired considerable reputation for the cure of rheumatism, gout, cutaneous affections, and other chronic diseases for which such waters are commonly employed. The springs are pleasantly situated in a picturesque and salubrious district near the Pine Mountains, and the accommodations (*Warm Springs Hotel*) are good. Besides the warm springs proper there is in the immediate vicinity a cold spring containing iron and a large proportion of free carbonic-acid gas; and another containing sulphates of soda and magnesia, and a large quantity of sulphuretted hydrogen. The *Chalybeate Springs*, in Talbot County, 7 miles south of the Warm Springs, have fine tonic properties, and are picturesquely located. They are reached by a stage-ride of about 20 miles from Geneva, on the Central R. R. of Georgia. The Indian Springs, *Indian Springs Hotel* and *Elder House*, in Butts County, are sulphurous waters, with a reputation for the cure of rheumatism and diseases of the liver. Their virtues were known to the Indians, and they have long been a place of popular resort. The springs are reached by stage from Forsyth, a town on the Central R. R. of Georgia, 26 miles from Macon. Among the attractions in the vicinity are the beautiful *Falls of the Towaligo*, consisting of a series of cascades, cataracts, and rapids, where the river runs for about a quarter of a mile down a series of rocky ledges and shoals. Gainesville, on the Atlanta and Charlotte Air-Line R. R., 51 miles from Atlanta, is a centre from which several mineral springs may be visited. About a mile distant (reached by horse-cars) is the *Gower Springs Hotel*, and 2 miles east are the *New Holland Springs*, a favorite resort. About 28 miles north are the *Porter Springs*, attractively situated among the mountains, and much frequented in summer. The *Madison Springs*, in Madison County, are a pure and excellent chalybeate, having wide reputation as a tonic. They are reached by stage from Athens, on the Athens branch of the Georgia R. R. The *Red Sulphur Springs* (or "Vale of Springs") are at the base of Taylor's Ridge, in Walker County, the northwest corner of the State. No less than 20 springs are found here in the space of half a mile—chalybeate, red, white, and black sulphur, and magnesia. In the vicinity are Lookout Mountain and other beautiful scenery. The *Catoosa Springs* are in Catoosa County, 4 miles from Ringgold on the Western & Atlantic R. R. The waters are a saline chalybeate, and the springs are much resorted to in the watering-season. *Rowland's Springs*, in Bartow County (6 miles from Cartersville on the Western & Atlantic R. R.), and *Gordon's Springs*, in Murray County, are chalybeate, and have begun to attract the attention of invalids. The *Thundering Springs* are in Upson County; the nearest railway-station is Forsyth, on the Central Railroad. The *Powder Springs*, sulphur and magnesia, are in Cobb County, 20 miles above Atlanta.

Mountain Region and Scenery.

Throughout all Northern Georgia the traveler will find a continuation of that charming Blue Ridge landscape which constitutes the chief beauty of the scenery of Virginia and Western North Carolina. Here are the famous gold-lands, and in the midst of them *Dahlonega*, which contains a branch of the United States Mint, and which is beautifully situated on a high hill commanding a magnificent view of the mountain scenery of this lovely region. The most frequented if not the finest scenes in this neighborhood are in the northeast, as the wonderful falls of Tallulah and Toccoa, the valley of Nacoochee and Mount Yonah, in Habersham County, the Cascades of Eastatoia, and the great Rabun Gap in Rabun; all within a day's ride of the Sable Mountain, Cæsar's Head, Jocasse, the Whitewater Falls, and other wonders of South Carolina, described in the chapter on that State. Farther west are the Falls of Amicalolah, the Cahutta Mountain, the Dogwood Valley, and Lookout Mountain. This region was the hunting-ground of the Cherokees, before the final removal of the tribe to new homes beyond the Mississippi.

The point of rendezvous for the exploration of the mountain region is Clarksville, a pleasant village in Habersham County, much resorted to in summer by the people of the "Low Country" of Georgia. It is reached by stage from Toccoa or Mount Airy, on the Richmond & Danville (Piedmont Air Line) R. R.; or by stage from Walhalla (on the Greenville & Columbia Railroad) to *Clayton*, which is still nearer the mountains. Fair accommodations for travelers may be had at Clarksville, and also horses or wagons for the exploration of the surrounding country. The Toccoa Fall is reached from Toccoa, or by railway from Rabun Gap. A narrow passage leads to the foot of the falls. Before the spectator rises a perpendicular rock resembling a rugged stone-wall 180 feet high, and over it

"The brook comes babbling down the mountain's side."

There are picturesque legends connected with this winsome spot; one of which narrates the story of an Indian chief and his followers, who, bent upon the extermination of the whites, and trusting to the guidance of a woman, were led by her over the precipice. The **Cataracts of Tallulah** are 12 miles from Clarksville, by a road of very varied beauty. They are reached directly by the Northeastern R. R. of Georgia from Athens, a distance of 72 miles. There is a comfortable hotel near the edge of the gorges traversed by this wild mountain-stream, and hard by its army of waterfalls. The Tallulah, or *Terrora*, as the Indians more appositely called it, is a small stream, which rushes through a chasm in the Blue Ridge, rending it for several miles. The ravine is 1,000 feet in depth, and of an equal width. Its walls are gigantic cliffs of dark granite. The heavy masses, piled upon each other in the wildest confusion, sometimes shoot out, overhanging the yawning gulf, and threatening to break from their seemingly frail tenure, and hurl themselves headlong into its dark depths. Along the rocky and uneven bed of this deep abyss the infuriated Terrora frets and foams with ever-varying course. Now, it flows in sullen majesty, through a deep and romantic glen, embowered in the foliage of the trees, which here and there spring from the rocky ledges of the chasm-walls; anon, it rushes with accelerated motion, breaking fretfully over protruding rocks, and uttering harsh murmurs as it approaches the verge of a precipice, and plunges in a broad sheet into the loud-resounding gorge below. The most familiar point of observation is *The Pulpit*, an immense cliff which projects far into the chasm. From this position, the extent and depth of the fearful ravine and three of the most romantic of the numerous cataracts are observed. At various other localities fine glimpses down into the deep gorge are afforded, and numerous other steep paths lead to the bottom of the chasm. At the several cataracts—the *Lodore*, the *Tempesta*, the *Oceana*, the *Serpentine*, and others—the picture is ever a new and striking one—which the most striking and beautiful, it would be very difficult to determine. The natural recess called the *Trysting-Rock*, once the sequestered meeting-place of Indian lovers, is now a halting-spot for merry groups as they descend the chasm, just below the Lodore Cascade. From this point, Lodore is upon the left, up the stream; a huge perpendicular wall of party-colored rock towers up in front and below; to the right are seen the foaming waters of the Oceana Cascade, and the dark glen into which they are surging their maddened way. Tempesta, the Serpentine, and other falls, lie yet below. The wild grandeur of this mountain-gorge, and the variety, number, and magnificence of its cataracts, give it rank with the most imposing waterfall scenery in the Union. The **Valley of Nacoochee** (or the Evening Star) is a pleasant day's excursion from Clarksville. The valley is said by tradition to have won its name from the story of the hapless love of a beautiful Indian princess, whose sceptre once ruled its solitudes; but with or without these associations it will be remembered with pleasure by all whose fortune it may be to see it. *Mount Yonah* looks down into the quiet heart of Nacoochee, lying at its base; and if the

Falls of Toccoa.

tourist should stay overnight in the valley, he ought to take a peep at the mountain panorama from the summit of Yonah. Another interesting peak in this vicinity is *Mount Currahee*, which is situated south of Clarksville, a few miles below the Toccoa Cascade. The traveler, fresh from the lowlands, always finds this a scene of much interest.

The Falls of **the Eastatoia** are about 3 miles from *Clayton* (see page 39), in Rabun, the extreme northeastern county of Georgia. Clayton may be reached easily from Clarksville, or by a ride of 12 miles from the cataract of Tallulah. The falls lie off the road to the right, in the passage of the Rabun Gap, one of the mountain-ways from Georgia into North Carolina; they would be a spot of crowded resort were they in a more thickly-peopled country. The scene is a succession of cascades, noble in volume and character, plunging down the ravined flanks of a rugged mountain-height. From the summit of one of the highest of the falls, a magnificent view is gained of the valley and waters of the Tennessee, north of the village of Clayton, and of the hills which encompass it.

Union County, adjoining Habersham on the northwest, is distinguished for natural beauty, and for its objects of antiquarian interest. Among these latter is the *Track Rock*, bearing wonderful impressions of the feet of animals now extinct. *Pilot Mountain*, in Union, is a noble elevation of some 1,200 feet. The *Hiawassee Falls*, on the Hiawassee River, present a series of beautiful cascades, some of them from 60 to 100 feet in height. The much-visited Falls **of Amicalolah** are in Lumpkin County, 17 miles west of the village of Dahlonega, near the State road leading to East Tennessee. The name is a compound of two Cherokee words—" Ami," signifying *water*, and " Calolah," *rolling or tumbling ;* strikingly expressive of the cataract, and affording us another instance of the simplicity and significant force of the names conferred by the untutored sons of the forest. The visitor should rein up at the nearest farm-house, and make his way thence, either up the Rattlesnake Hollow to the base of the falls, or to the summit. The range of mountains to the south and west, as it strikes the eye from the top of the falls, is truly sublime ; and the scene is scarcely surpassed in grandeur by any other, even in this country of everlasting hills. The view of the falls from the foot is much more striking than the view from above ; both, however, should be obtained, for here we have a succession of cataracts and cascades, the greatest not exceeding 60 feet in height, but the torrent, in the distance of 400 yards, descending more than as many hundred feet.

Nickajack Cave extends into the Raccoon Mountains, near the northwest extremity of the State, for several miles, with a portal 160 feet wide and 60 feet high, through which flows a stream, up which boats can pass for 3 miles to a cataract. The cave is said to have been the headquarters of the leader of a band of negro outlaws. He was known by the name of "Nigger Jack ; " hence the name of the cave.

SOUTH CAROLINA RESORTS.

South Carolina, one of the original thirteen States of the Union, is situated between lat. 32° and 35° 10' north, and lon. 78° 25' and 83° 19' west. It has the form of an irregular triangle, with the coast-line for its base, and Georgia and North Carolina for its converging sides. Its extreme length from east to west is 275 miles, and its greatest breadth from north to south 210 miles; area about 34,000 square miles. The topography of the State resembles that of Georgia. The coast for about 100 miles inward is flat and sandy, with a light soil, covered by pitch-pine forests, traversed by sluggish streams, and interspersed with numerous swamps. This portion of the State is of alluvial formation. Beyond this plain is a belt of low sand-hills, called the "middle country," which is moderately productive. West of the middle country is a belt called the "ridge," where the land rises abruptly, and thence continues to ascend, exhibiting beautiful alternations of hill and dale, till it terminates at the extreme northwest part of the State in the Blue Ridge, the highest peak of which in South Carolina is Table Mountain, 4,300 feet above the Atlantic. The coast presents numerous inlets, bays, shallow sounds and lagoons, and a few good harbors; small islands skirt the southern portion, shut off from the mainland by narrow channels, which afford "inside" steamboat communication between Charleston and Savannah. These islands are low and flat, and produce sea-island cotton. Rice is also produced in large quantities, and tropical fruits flourish. The natural scenery of the State is exceedingly varied: on the seaboard of the south, broad savannas, and deep, dank lagoons, covered with teeming fields of rice, and fruitful in a thousand changes of tropical vegetation; in the middle districts, great, undulating meadows, overspread with luxuriant maize, or white with snowy carpetings of cotton; and, again, to the northward, bold mountain-ranges, valleys, and waterfalls.

There is very little waste-land in South Carolina, and the soil is generally fertile, producing in abundance cotton, rice, tobacco, maize, oats, rye, barley, wheat, all kinds of garden vegetables, and numerous varieties of fruit. Of forest-trees, on the islands are found the live-oak, pine, palmetto, and laurel; in the lower and pine-barren districts, pitch-pine; and in the middle and higher regions, oak, hickory, and pine. The palmetto is the most characteristic of the vegetable productions, and it grows in such abundance, especially in the southern districts, that South Carolina is known throughout the Union as the "Palmetto State." The State is remarkably well watered, and almost every county abounds in good water-power. Among the more important rivers are the Savannah, the Great Pedee, the Santee and its affluents, the Congaree and Wateree, the Salada and the Broad, the Edisto and the Combahee, together affording an inland navigation of 2,400 miles.

Of the climate of South Carolina, Dr. Joseph W. Howe, of New York, who has made a special study of its adaptation to invalids from the North, says: "In many respects it has a climate resembling Southern Europe, without any more sudden variations in the daily temperature than are noticed there. Both the Carolinas are good winter resorts, but they are objectionable in the summer months. . . . During the winter there is very little rain; the days are usually cloudless and warm. The diurnal thermal variations are greater than in Florida. Between the day and night temperature there is often a difference of 20°. Hence, invalids must pay great attention to their clothing, and provide suitable winter dress for day and evening wear. Consumptives generally improve faster in the highlands of the western part of the State than in the counties bordering on the Atlantic. However, there are some who prefer the moister and lower lands, and who do well there. Rheumatic and gouty patients may reside anywhere in the neighborhood of the mineral springs. Those afflicted with malaria will do well to seek a residence in some other State, but they may derive benefit from the climate of the northern slope of the Blue Ridge Mountains. The fall and spring months are the best seasons to reside in South Carolina. The latter part of December, January, and February, consumptives who are beyond the incipient stages will do well to go farther south into Georgia or Florida. March and April are exceedingly mild in South Carolina, and very free from disagreeable variations." For details as to thermometrical range and mean temperature, consult the following articles on Charleston and Aiken. Out of 7,380 deaths in the State in 1870, 657 were from consumption; there being 11.2 deaths from all causes to one from this disease. Pneumonia caused 709 deaths out of the total number, or 10.4 deaths from all causes to one from this disease.

Charleston.

How to reach.—From New York, Charleston is reached direct *via* "New York and Charleston Steamships," leaving Pier 29, East River, at 3 P. M. on Tuesdays, Thursdays, and Saturdays. Time, about 60 hours; fare (cabin), $20. From Philadelphia, *via* steamer leaving Pier 4 every Friday. Time, about 60 hours; fare, $15. From Baltimore by steamer every 5 days. Time, about 50 hours; fare, $15. From either of the above cities, and from the North generally, it may be reached by the Atlantic Coast-Route, through Washington, Richmond, and Wilmington, and from the West by railroads from Chattanooga and Atlanta. For fares by rail from

CHARLESTON.

New York, see Table of Railway Fares. From Savannah, Charleston may be reached by Charleston & Savannah R. R.

Hotels, Boarding-Houses, etc.—The leading hotel is the *Charleston Hotel*, centrally located in Meeting Street, between Hayne and Pinckney Streets. It is noted for its great stone colonnade and piazza, reaching from pavement to roof. The *Mills House*, also in Meeting Street, is a private boarding-house. The *Pavilion Hotel*, corner of Meeting and Hasel Streets, and the *Waverley House*, in King Street, near Hasel, are good houses. The prices at these hotels vary from $2 to $4 per day. Board may be had in different parts of the city at from $5 to $12 a week. There are few *restaurants* in Charleston—almost none deserving the name—though there are "lunch-rooms" with bars attached. The best of these are in Bay Street, near Broad, and in King Street, near Wentworth.

Location, Climate, and History.—Charleston, the chief commercial city of South Carolina, is picturesquely situated at the confluence of the Ashley and Cooper Rivers, in lat. 32° 45′ north, and lon. 79° 57′ west. The rivers run a parallel course for nearly 6 miles, widening as they approach the sea, and thus gradually narrowing the site of the city to a peninsula. The harbor is a large estuary, extending about 7 miles to the Atlantic, with an average width of 2 miles. It is landlocked on all sides

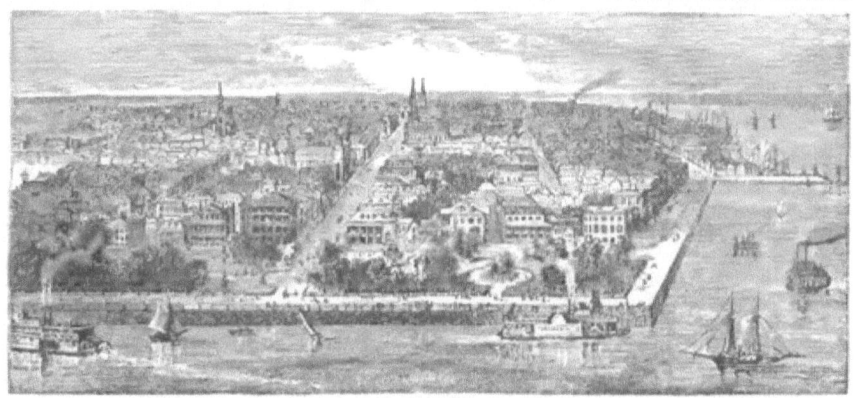

Charleston.

except an entrance of about a mile in width. The passage to the inner harbor is defended by four fortresses. On the right at the entrance is Fort Moultrie, on Sullivan's Island, occupying the site of the fort which, on June 28, 1776, beat off the British fleet of Sir Peter Parker. On the left, raised upon a shoal in the harbor and directly covering the channel, is Fort Sumter, rendered famous by the part played in the opening scenes of the civil war. Immediately in front of the city, and but one mile from it, is Castle Pinckney, covering the crest of a mud-shoal, and facing the entrance. A fine view of the city is obtained in entering the harbor from the sea; and, as it is built on low and level land, it seems to rise from the water as we approach, whence it has been called the "American Venice." The corporate limits of Charleston extend from the Battery or White Point, on the extreme southern verge of the city, to an arbitrary line on the north, about 3 miles above. Within this area the city is laid out with tolerable regularity, the streets generally crossing each other at right angles. On the 31st of August, 1886, and for some time afterward, Charleston experienced a succession of earthquake-shocks which destroyed many of the older buildings. They are now being replaced by newer but less picturesque erections. There are few regular blocks or rows of buildings, and no uniformity; but with the fine gardens, shade and fruit trees, creepers, vines, the magnolia, the oak, the cedar, and the pride of India, the effect is highly picturesque.

The *climate* of Charleston is very similar to that of Savannah, and differs but little from that of the most favored localities in Southern Europe. The genial contrast which its mildness in winter presents to the fierce rigors of the Northern States, is yearly drawing to it more and more visitors, and increasing its claims to be numbered among the popular winter resorts. The mean temperature of Charleston is: for spring, 65.8°; for summer, 80.6°; for autumn, 68.1°; for winter, 51.7°; for the year, 66.6°. The average rainfall is: spring, 8.60 inches; summer, 18.68; autumn, 11.61; winter, 9.40; year, 48.29. Prevailing wind, southwest. From careful observations taken during the year 1872 it was found that the mean temperature of January was 45°; of February, 48.5°; of March, 51°; of April, 65.6°; of May, 74.9°; of June, 79.7°; of July, 84.1°; of August, 81.8°; of September, 77.8°; of October, 69°; of November, 59°; of December, 49°. There is comparatively little rainfall in winter; the days are bright, sunny, and cheerful; and it is seldom that even invalids are compelled to remain in-doors on account of the inclemency of the weather. As in the case of Savannah and Augusta, many consumptives and other invalids prefer remaining in Charleston—where they can enjoy all the comforts, conveniences, luxuries, facilities, diversions, and social attractions of a large city—to going to the sanitary resorts farther south. Charleston is especially attractive to those who, without being sick, desire to escape the rigors of a Northern winter.

Charleston was settled in 1679 by an English colony under William Sayle, who became the first Governor. It played a conspicuous part in the Revolution, having been the first among the chief places of the South to assert a common cause with and for the colonies. It was thrice assaulted by the British, and only yielded to an overwhelming force, May 12, 1780. It was the leading city, both in the Nullification movement during Jackson's Administration and in the incipient stages of Southern secession. Open hostilities in the civil war began at Charleston, with the bombardment of Fort Sumter on April 12, 1861; and for the next four years it was one of the chief points of Federal attack, without being lost by the Confederates, however, until Sherman's capture of Columbia on February 17, 1865. During the war many buildings were destroyed by shot and shell, and in 1861 a great fire desolated a large part of the city. Since the close of the war rapid progress has been made in rebuilding, and Charleston is now more prosperous than ever. The growth of population has been as follows: In 1800, it was 18,711; in 1850, 42,985; in 1860, 40,519; in 1870, 48,956; and in 1880, 49,999. The commerce of the city is large, the chief exports being cotton, rice, naval stores, and fertilizers. The manufacture of fertilizers from the valuable beds of marl and phosphate, discovered in 1865, is now a leading industry; but there are also flour and rice mills, bakeries, carriage and wagon factories, machine-shops and cotton-mills.

Modes of Conveyance.—Two lines of *horse-cars* traverse the city, and afford easy access to the chief points of interest (fare 5c.). They pass through the principal streets, from the Exchange and the Battery to the upper ends of Rutledge Ave. and Meeting St. *Omnibuses* are in waiting at the depots and landings on the arrival of trains and steamers, and convey passengers to any portion of the city (fare 50c.). *Livery-stables* are attached to the different hotels, and, though the charges are not uniform, they are usually moderate.

Streets and Drives.—The two principal streets are King and Meeting, which run north and south, nearly parallel, the whole length of the city, but converge to intersection near the northern limits. King St. contains the leading retail stores, and is the fashionable promenade. The jobbing and wholesale stores are chiefly in *Meeting St.*; and the banks, and brokers' and insurance offices, are in *Broad St.* The Battery is a popular promenade, lying near the water's edge, and commanding an extensive view of the bay; it is surrounded by fine private residences. Fine residences are also found in Meeting St. below Broad, in Rutledge St. and Ave., and at the west end of Wentworth St. The roads leading out of the city along the Ashley and Cooper Rivers are singularly beautiful, and afford interesting drives. They are all richly embowered in loveliest foliage; pines, oaks, magnolias, myrtles, and jasmines, vying with each other in tropical luxuriance and splendor. There are also fine drives on Sullivan's Island (reached by ferry).

Public and Prominent Buildings.—Several of the most important of these are clustered at the intersection of Broad and Meeting Sts. On the northeast corner is the

City Hall, an imposing building, entered by a double flight of marble steps, and standing in an open square. The Council-Chamber is handsomely furnished, and

Live-Oak on the Ashley.

contains some interesting portraits. On the northwest corner is the *Court-House*, a structure of brick, faced so as to resemble stone. On the southeast corner stands St. Michael's Church, the body of which suffered much from the earthquake; and on the southwest corner is the *Guardhouse*, or Police Headquarters, a plain brick building, with a colonnade extending over the sidewalk in Broad St. The force is semi-military in organization, and is composed about equally (or was until recently) of whites and negroes, who drill with Winchester rifles. At the foot of Broad St. stands the *Post-Office*, a venerable structure, dating from the colonial period, the original material having been brought from England in 1761. It was much battered during the war, but has since been renovated. The new *Custom-House*, which has been building for several years and is now completed, is situated just south of the Market-wharf, on Cooper River. It is of white marble, in the Roman-Corinthian style, and will be the finest edifice in the city. A noble view is obtained from its graceful Corinthian portico. The *U. S. Court-House* is an elegant building in Meeting Street, between Broad and Tradd, with a pretty garden in front. It was erected before the war, by the Carolina Club (which was broken up by the war), and is now used by the United

States Courts. The *Chamber of Commerce* occupies the 2d and 3d floors of a handsome building at the corner of Broad and East Bay Sts.; it has a good reading-room and a restaurant for the use of the members. The *Academy of Music*, cor. King and Market Sts., is one of the finest theatres in the South. It is 60 by 231 feet, and cost $160,000. Besides the theatre, with accommodations for 1,200 persons, it contains two large halls for concerts, lectures, etc. The *Masonic Temple* is a large but fantastic building, at the cor. of King and Wentworth Sts. The old **Orphan-House**, standing in the midst of spacious grounds, between Calhoun and Vanderhorst Sts., is the most imposing edifice in the city, and one of the most famous institutions of the kind in the country. John C. Fremont, once a candidate for the presidency, and C. C. Memminger, Confederate Secretary of the Treasury, were educated there. A statue of William Pitt, erected during the Revolution, stands in the centre of the grounds. The *College of Charleston*, founded in 1788, has spacious buildings, located in the square bounded by George, Green, College, and St. Philip Sts. It has a library of about 6,000 volumes, and a valuable museum of natural history. The *Medical College*, cor. Queen and Franklin Sts., and *Roper Hospital*, cor. Queen and Logan Sts., are large and handsome buildings, the latter especially so. On the same square with these two are the *City Hospital* and the *County Jail*. The *Workhouse*, near by, in Magazine St., is a spacious castellated structure in the Norman style. The *Charleston Library*, founded in 1748, has a plain but commodious building at the cor. of Broad and Church Sts. It lost heavily in the fire of 1861, but now contains about 17,000 volumes. The *South Carolina Society Hall*, in Meeting St. near St. Michael's Church, is a substantial structure, with colonnade and portico, and a fine interior. **Market Hall**, in Meeting St. near the bay, is a fine building, in temple form, standing on a high, open basement, having a lofty portico in front, reached by a double flight of stone steps. In rear of this building are the markets, consisting of a row of low sheds supported by brick arches, and extending to East Bay St. Between 6 and 9 A. M. these markets present one of the most characteristic sights that the stranger can see in Charleston, and should by all means be visited.

Churches.—There are at least two churches in Charleston that no stranger should fail to visit—St. Michael's and St. Philip's—both Episcopal. **St. Michael's** is at the southeast corner of Broad and Meeting Sts. It was built in 1752, it is said from designs by a pupil of Sir Christopher Wren. The tower is considered very fine, and the situation of the church made the spire a conspicuous object far out at sea. Its chimes are celebrated for their age and sweetness. During the siege of Charleston, in the late war, the spire was a mark for the Federal artillerymen; but, though persistently shelled, it was struck but a few times, and then only with slight injury. The view from the belfry is very fine, embracing the far stretch of sea and shore, the fortresses in the harbor, the shipping, and nearer at hand buildings as ancient as the church itself. **St. Philip's**, in Church St. near Queen, was the first church establishment in Charleston; but the present structure, although of venerable age, is yet not quite so old as St. Michael's. The view from the steeple is fine; but there is a keener interest in the graveyard than even in the old church itself, for here lie South Carolina's most illustrious dead. In the portion of the graveyard that lies across the street is the tomb of John C. Calhoun. It consists of a plain granite slab, supported by walls of brick, and for inscription has simply the name of "CALHOUN." *St. Finbar's Cathedral* (Roman Catholic), or rather the ruins of it (for the building was destroyed in the great fire of 1861), is at the cor. of Broad and Friend Sts. It was one of the most elegant edifices in Charleston, and the walls, turrets, and niches, still standing, are highly picturesque. The *Citadel Square Baptist Church*, cor. Meeting and Henrietta Sts., is a fine building, in the Norman style, with a spire 220 feet high. The *Central Presbyterian*, in Meeting St. near Society, has an elegant Corinthian portico with 8 columns. The *Unitarian Church*, in Archdale St. near Queen, is a fine specimen of the perpendicular Gothic style, and has a very rich interior. The new *German Lutheran Church*, in King St. opposite the Citadel, is a handsome building, in the Gothic style, with lofty and ornate spire. *Grace Church* (Episcopal), in Wentworth St., is the most fashionable in the city. The old *Huguenot Church*, corner Church and Queen Sts., is worthy of a visit, if for no other purpose, to see the quaint and elegant mural entablatures with which its walls are lined.

Suburbs.—Just outside of the city, on the northern boundary, is *Magnolia Cemetery* (reached by horse-cars). It is embowered in magnolias and live-oaks, is tastefully laid out, and contains some fine monuments, of which the most noteworthy are those to Colonel Wm. Washington, of Revolutionary fame, Hugh Legaré, and W. Gilmore Simms, the novelist. In a vault repose the remains of Lieutenant Van-

Scene in Magnolia Cemetery.

derhorst, whose coffin, shrouded with the Union Jack, may be seen through the lattice-door of the tomb.—Of the old planters' houses that stood along the Ashley, but one remains, and that is abandoned. *Drayton Hall* is a large brick mansion, standing in the centre of grounds of a park-like character. The rooms are wainscoted from floor to ceiling, the fireplaces are lined with old-fashioned colored tiles, and the mantels are richly carved; but the building was never entirely finished, for the owner lost the bride for whom it was designed, and since then it has stood in its incompleteness a memorial of his loss. A few miles farther up the river, on a slight elevation, are the ruins of the celebrated *Middleton Place*, once one of the most beautiful plantations in South Carolina. The scenery, the flowers, hedges, and shrubbery, the undergrowth and noble oaks, the ponds and lakes, the picturesque old tombs—these still remain, but it is melancholy to contemplate that all the ruin which one sees around him was caused by the unsparing hand of war. Visitors frequently make a pilgrimage to the spot in order to gratify their curiosity, and, if reports are true, the house has suffered greatly from their unscrupulous desire for relics. A steamer makes regular excursions to this place during the winter.—Perhaps the most interesting spot in the neighborhood of Charleston is the old **Church of St. James** on Goose Creek (reached by carriage, or by Northeastern R. R. to Porcher's station, 15 miles). It is situated in the very heart of a forest, is approached by a road little better than a bridle-path, and is entirely isolated from habitations of any sort. The church was built in 1711, and was saved from destruction during the Revolutionary War by the royal arms of England that are emblazoned over the pulpit. The floor is of stone, the pews are square and high, the altar, reading-desk, and pulpit, are so small as to seem like miniatures of ordinary church-fixtures, and on the walls and altar are tablets in memory of the early members of the congregation. One dates from 1711 and two from 1717.—A short distance from the church, on the other side of the main road, is a farm known as *The Oaks*, from the magnificent avenue of those trees by which it is approached. The trees are believed to be nearly 200 years old; they have attained great size, and for nearly ¼ of a mile form a continuous arch over the broad road.

Not the least interesting of the "sights" of Charleston, even to a casual tourist, will be a visit to the "*Phosphate Mines*," as they are called, along the Ashley River or on Bull River. The phosphates overlie the extensive marl-beds of the South Carolina lowlands, which have long been known, and cover almost the entire peninsula between the Ashley and Cooper Rivers. To the unscientific eye they appear to be merely stones or nodules of various shapes, and ranging in size from a walnut to a bowlder. Since the Eocene period there they have lain, richer than a gold-mine, awaiting the test of the exploring chemist who was to develop the fact that they contained from 40 to 70 per cent. of phosphatic strength; that every ton was worth sixty dollars in the market for fertilizing purposes; and that every acre of land, previously owned as almost valueless, held, but a few inches below its surface, thousands upon thousands of dollars in actual, tangible wealth. This test was applied in 1865 by one of the resident chemists—and so poor was he at the time that he could not afford to hire a horse with which to pursue his investigations. He endeavored to borrow money in Charleston, and to organize a company for the purchase of some of these lands, but failed. The capitalists looked on him as a theorist. A friend loaned him money enough to reach Philadelphia. There he exhibited his specimens, explained the character of his discovery, and with three or four gentlemen inaugurated the enterprise. In a little while they owned 20 square miles of the richest phosphate-lands around Charleston. A great factory was built for the manipulation of the article, which consists—1. Of its removal from the earth and transportation. 2. Washing, or burning, and drying. 3. Grinding to powder and mixing with sulphuric acid. It is then ready for use as a pure phosphate, or may be still further combined with fish, guano, or other articles calculated to make it more valuable on certain soils. Since that time many companies have been formed, and it has been discovered that the entire coast, including the beds of the rivers, is covered with this valuable fertilizer. Fleets of English and Scotch vessels are to be seen at nearly all seasons of the year in Bull River, and at other points, loading with phosphate in its rough state just as it comes from the land or water. Its value in even this rude condition is six or seven dollars per ton. Employment is thus given to thousands of negroes, and much machinery has been invented and manufactured to aid in obtaining the article by the most speedy and economical means. Through the winter boats frequently run to these works with excursion-parties.

A day or two may be profitably spent in visiting the various points of interest in the harbor: *Fort Sumter*, which is now entirely rebuilt; *James Island*, with its ruined plantations and crumbling fortifications; *Mount Pleasant*, now a popular summer resort, frequented by parties from the city; and *Sullivan's Island* (*New Brighton Hotel*), which is becoming the "Long Branch" of South Carolina, and contains many handsome cottages and some attractive drives. A steamboat plies regularly every hour between the city, Mount Pleasant, and Sullivan's Island, and on the latter is a line of horse-cars. Many Notherners spend the winter on Sullivan's Island, the climate of which is favorable to consumptives, and peculiarly so to sufferers from rheumatism.

Summerville.

Summerville is a small town, 22 miles from Charleston on the South Carolina R. R., situated on a ridge which extends across from the Cooper to the Ashley River, which is covered with pine-woods, and is remarkable for its healthfulness. Its climate is very agreeable, especially in winter, when, being beyond the range of the east winds that frequently prevail on the coast, the temperature is extremely mild and equable. Many invalids who find the winter climate of Charleston too variable would derive benefit from a residence here, and its attractions as a health resort are rapidly becoming known. The village, though containing but a small population, spreads over a good deal of ground; the houses being built far apart, so that each one is perfectly private, and like a country residence. There is no hotel, but a number of good boarding-houses at which the charges are from $7 to $10 a week. Rents are cheap, there are several schools, and churches of nearly all the religious denominations, while the proximity of Charleston affords liberal supplies for the market. The South Carolina R. R. runs special trains for the accommodation of residents, who are thus enabled to enjoy all the advantages and attractions of the adjacent city. The country around abounds in game, and in the immediate vicinity of the village are many pretty walks and drives, while on the banks of the Ashley, about 4 miles distant, are some spots of great beauty. The most interesting of these is *Newington*, once an elegant country-seat, now a picturesque ruin. Approaching from Summerville by a rather uninteresting pine-land road, the scene suddenly changes and the visitor finds himself in the midst of a dense growth of live-oaks, magnolias, and other trees, denoting the neighborhood of the river. Passing through these he comes upon an open space in which stand the walls of the once splendid mansion, almost hidden by a dense growth of vines and creeping plants. There are remnants of several other fine seats in this neighborhood which were occupied by wealthy men in the days when this part of the country was more resorted to in summer than it is at present.

Aiken.

How to reach.—The Pennsylvania R. R. Co. sell unlimited tickets by 8 different routes to Aiken, as follows: 1. *Via* Baltimore, Norfolk. Wilmington, Columbia, and Graniteville (fare, $29.80); 2. *Via* Baltimore, Norfolk, Weldon, Raleigh, Charlotte, and Graniteville (fare, $31.85); 3. *Via* Baltimore, Norfolk, Wilmington, Florence, and Charleston (fare, $31.20); 4. *Via* Washington, Richmond, Greensboro', Charlotte, and Graniteville (fare, $26.80); 5. *Via* Washington, Richmond, Petersburg, Raleigh, Charlotte, and Graniteville (fare, $26.80); 6. *Via* Washington, Richmond, Petersburg, Wilmington, Columbia, and Graniteville (fare, 29.80); 7. *Via* Washington, Richmond, Wilmington, Florence, and Charleston (fare $31.20); 8. *Via* Washington, Lynchburg, Danville, Greensboro', Charlotte, and Graniteville (fare, $26.80). Limited tickets by all routes $23.65. A favorite route for invalids from the North is *via* steamer to Charleston or Savannah, and thence by rail, as a brief period of sea-air is found to be frequently beneficial to those not too far advanced in disease, and to prepare the way for the effect of the balmy air of the pine-lands.

Hotels and Boarding-Houses.—The *Highland Park Hotel*, the *Aiken Hotel*, and *Clarendon* are situated upon the edge of the plateau, and overlooking the broad intervales which drop off from the ridge upon which the town is situated. Near by, also upon the edge of the highland, is a group of neat cottages which are let to families who desire to escape the bustle of a great hotel. The *Highland Park Annex* is open when-over the Highland Park Hotel is too full for the convenience of its guests. There are many boarding-houses in and about the town, charging from $10 to $20 a week.

Location, Climate, and Characteristics.—Aiken, the most frequented winter resort in America, is situated on the line of the South Carolina R. R., 16 miles from Augusta, and 120 from Charleston. The land upon which it lies is an elevated, sandy plateau, some 600 or 700 feet above the sea, the water-shed of the Edisto and Savannah Rivers. The soil is an almost unmixed sand, covered by a scanty crust of alluvium which is so thin that a carriage-wheel easily breaks through. It bears but little grass, and hardly any of the minor natural plants; but the great Southern pine finds here a congenial habitat, and vast forests of it encircle the town on all sides. The streets of the town are remarkably wide, the main avenue being 205 feet wide, and the cross-streets 150 feet. The houses are generally large and pleasant, and very far apart. Within the town, the natural barrenness of the soil has been overcome by careful culture and a liberal use of fertilizers; and every house has its garden full of trees and Southern plants. Inside the white palings are dense thickets of yellow jasmine, rose-bushes, orange, wild-olive, and fig trees, bamboo, Spanish-bayonet, and numberless sorts of vines and creepers, to say nothing of the low bush and surface flowers that are common in the North. But, without the palings, the sand is as dry and white as it is upon the sea-shore.

The air of Aiken is remarkably pure and dry, and the balsamic odors of the pines endow it with a peculiar healing power. The winter climate is wonderfully mild and genial, consisting, as some one has described it, of "four months of June." From observations carefully recorded, it has been found that the mean temperature of Aiken in spring is 63.4°; in summer, 79.1°; in autumn, 63.7°; in winter, 46.4°; for the year, 63.1¼°. The average rainfall during the same period was, spring, 11.97 inches; summer, 13.89; autumn, 7.34; winter, 7.16; for the year, 40.36. The climate is not less beneficial to rheumatic and gouty patients than to consumptives; and many come here, who, without being sick, desire to escape the rigors of a Northern winter. It is said, too, that about one-fifth of the total population of 2,500 consists of Northerners who have taken up their permanent residence at Aiken. The ease and comfort with which Aiken may be reached (being only 36 hours from New York) render it especially available for patients recovering from typhoid fever and other exhausting diseases, the period of convalescence being greatly shortened by the change. In the following table is shown at a glance the relative dryness (or humidity) of the three leading Southern resorts:

Mean, Maximum, and Minimum of Relative Humidity.

MONTHS.	AIKEN, S. C.			ASHEVILLE, N. C.			JACKSONVILLE, FLA.		
	Mean.	Maximum.	Minimum.	Mean.	Maximum.	Minimum.	Mean.	Maximum.	Minimum.
January	61.80	91.20	16.40	61.06	88.05	36.01	67.08	94.00	23.00
February	64.30	94.10	19.30	62.00	93.01	36.05	70.04	94.00	19.00
March	51.80	91.40	13.20	56.00	89.02	25.05	69.02	95.00	19.60
April	55.80	96.20	17.90	58.01	86.01	35.08	67.00	94.00	20.00
May	61.70	94.70	32.00	72.03	91.00	43.03	65.03	90.00	31.90
June	68.40	95.00	32.40	76.08	96.96	58.00	68.06	95.00	29.00
July	67.10	65.00	41.80	82.05	97.00	71.06	68.05	96.00	26.00
August	79.50	95.00	41.80	81.07	95.01	71.08	75.97	95.00	40.00
September	69.50	94.80	39.70	79.08	97.00	67.01	74.08	95.00	34.00
October	63.20	97.30	10.60	64.00	87.08	31.03	73.04	95.00	26.00
November	71.20	96.70	21.90	72.03	93.03	41.06	78.09	95.00	23.00
December	68.90	97.10	4.20	74.05	98.00	27.06	71.01	94.00	19.00
Mean	64.04			70.10			69.72		

In our next table is shown the relative equability of Aiken as compared with that of some of the most important health-resorts in the United States. It is compiled from reports on file at the Signal-Office, Washington:

Table *comparing* the Mean of Variation in Twenty-four Hours at Aiken with that at other Health-Resorts.

HEALTH-RESORTS.	September.	October.	November.	December.	January.	February.	March.
Key West	10.00	8.87	8.43	8.54	8.95	9.83	9.18
San Diego	12.00	12.77	14.30	17.16	12.93	12.67	15.19
Aiken	10.03	17.03	18.26	18.06	12.45	19.14	17.64
Jacksonville	15.00	19.38	15.76	19.22	14.54	18.60	20.32
San Antonio	14.36	25.33	23.15	21.33	22.22	22.05	16.46
St Paul	19.00	16.41	14.46	17.61	20.09	20.82	19.00
Colorado Springs	25.50	24.22	27.85	26.98	31.87	24.28	25.22

It will thus be seen that, in the essential point of equability, Aiken is surpassed by but one health-resort of importance (San Diego, p. 85).

The best description that has been given of the surroundings of Aiken, and of the characteristic features of life there, is that which, under the title of "Spring Days in Aiken," was contributed, some years ago, by Mr. Albert F. Webster, to APPLETONS' JOURNAL. The substance of the sketch we shall reproduce in the following paragraphs: "The spirit of the town is a languid one. Apart from the ease and lassitude that naturally belong to the class of visitors, there is a contented leisure in all the people native to the place. No one seems anxious. No one hastens. The days and the seasons are long, and life seems endless. If a horse moves faster than a walk, he takes the 'lope'—a pace which is as lazy as the rocking of a cradle. You hear no rattle of hoofs, for the sand is so soft; the single railroad is hidden in a cut, and so there is no roar to the approaching trains; there are no factories in town, and therefore no clatter of machinery and no clangor of bells. Just without the town—indeed, encroaching upon its very streets—begin the true pine-woods. To the north, east, and south, the land is level, but to the west it falls away in deep gorges, and gives the shade and sunshine plenty of play. Through all the forests there run winding paths and a certain species of thoroughfares, known as 'neighborhood roads.' These are roads that lead from one house to another, across the country, and without respect to line or distance. This carelessness makes them charming. They are commonly hard and of gray-white sand, thickly sprinkled with pine-needles and fragments of bark, and they lose themselves like threads in a tangle. The moment that one strolls outside the town he discovers these foot-ways leading off here and there from the right and the left into leafy obscurities, half illuminated by the sun and half darkened by the shade of the lofty pine-plumes far above. Few birds are to be heard. Now and then a jay lifts up its short and somewhat querulous voice, but commonly all are silent. Where the ground is level, one may look far in advance and see among the brown tree-trunks another portion of the path he is treading; but upon the western side of the town, where the land is broken, the way loses itself at once up-hill and down-dale, and in winding turns in and out among the oaken copses.

"The landscape about Aiken never 'climbs the sky.' Looking off in any direction you find your eye to be on a level with the horizon. There are no hills, no elevations of any sort. The sky seems as vast as it seems at sea. The trees, notwithstanding their height and density, lie before you in long lines, with beautiful vistas between that run on to the right and left indefinitely, but never rise in those grand hill-side terraces that are so dear to Northern eyes. This flatness adds to the sense of tranquillity that you are sure to feel. There is nothing to clamber, nothing to ascend, nothing wherefrom you are tormented to take a view. To the west of the town there is a very charming region where the land sinks in a very irregular manner away from the high plateau, leaving many isolated hills, scarcely less in height than the table-land itself. Except at the very bottom of the ravines, the neighborhood is well wooded with pines of great size, together with a young growth of oaks. Among these trees, and perched upon nearly every point of vantage, are low, wide-porticoed houses, of the true Southern type. Roads turn and twist and turn again, past and about these dwellings, leading from grove to door and back to grove again, then losing themselves at once in the thicket. Every house has its formal paling, its fountain of roses, its shaded piazzas, its tilting-board, its quartet of chimney-stacks, its sunlit yard, and its look of welcome to the passer-by. Some face the east, some the west, and some have fronts for all points. From the windows of one you look down upon the roof of a second, and a little way below and across at porches of another, or upon the opposite border of the valley. Encircled with grand if not mournful woods, half enveloped in flowering vines, inviting the soft winds with their open doors, they completely fill one's notion of true country-homes. Among these hills are a few cultivated fields, with their red earths, and among their lanes a few spare cattle wander in search of a little more grass. Negro cabins stand upon many of the boldest spurs of the land, and the shabby white of their rough walls adds not a little to that that is picturesque. A little way off begins a strange valley, with wooded sides, running to the west, and along whose bottom trails the 'river of sand.' This river resembles almost any other, except in the fact that there is not a drop of water in it. The rains have brought down from the hill-sides thousands of currents of fine, clean earth, of a yellow shade, and have caused them to eddy about the trees and roots that have stood in the way, and to spread and disperse themselves in all the inequalities of the ground. Yet the torrents of water which have caused this have been instantly absorbed in the bed of their own making, leaving all the marks of their presence, indeed their fac-similes, upon the sand above. It is hereabout that the town-urchins, and industrious visitors as well, come to gather the colored earth for mementos of the place. It is not unusual to find before your hotel-door on a March morning a group of children of all shades of black, holding in their hands bunches of roses in full bloom, and tubes of glass filled with fifty specimens of tinted sands. The colors range from green to russet-red and chrome-yellow, and include chocolate and violet. Every stranger buys, and it is a thriving trade. The land in the region of this river is filled with springs of the softest water. They trickle out from the hill-sides, cut deep ravines for themselves in the soft ground, and flow away the veriest threads ten feet below the surface, and overshaded with grasses and ferns. In the town they cover the wells with pretty trellis-work, with pagoda-like roofs, and in a few places in the woods, where the head of water is quite strong, considerable care has been taken to make the streams approachable.

"The effect of a fair Aiken day upon one fresh from the bitter spring winds of the North is something wonderful. You descend from your chamber in the early morning, and find the doors and windows gaping wide, and a faint, fresh breeze stirring through the house. You perceive the scent of flowers, and you go out upon the veranda. The garden below you, with its soil of whitish-yellow sand, is over-crowded with verdure. The masses of leaves, so rich are they, seem to have been lately drenched with water. The white and red roses lift themselves with their own grace into the sweet air, and every interval in the cloud of green shows a handful of fragrant blooms. There is none of that earthy scent that one always perceives in Northern gardens in early morning; the air is dry, even though it is cool and fresh. Outside the white fence is the broad, deserted street, with a score of lofty, fine-leaved oaks growing hap-hazard in the centre of it. A thin sprinkling of grass covers the untraveled portion of the way, while the tracks in which the wheels run is of soft earth, ankle-deep. Beneath the shade of the oaks is a bench or two, where strollers sit when they are tired. Beyond the trees on the other side of the way are another paling, another garden, and another house with a pillared portico, perhaps, but all so distant that you look upon the demesne as a hermitage of some sad recluse—a place not to be thought of with familiarity, still less to be talked of. In another direction you see a negro's log-cabin built close on the highway, with its brown-mud chimney sticking close to its shabby end, and its little herd of children playing and falling about upon the door-step. Beyond this and beyond the trees, on every side, you catch glimpses of other huts and other houses: now a gable; now a gray roof; now another chimney-stack; and now more pillars and more piazzas. There seem to be plenty of suggestions of life and neighborhood, but you look in vain for a settlement, and you listen in vain for noises of bustle and traffic. You walk out into the sunlight at ten o'clock; you pass down the street, seeing no one and hearing nothing, except now and then, perhaps, the caroling of some canary-bird in some hidden parlor. You look up the street, and you see that it disappears at the distance of a quarter of a mile in a wood. You look down, and you see in another distance that it crosses a ravine by means of a brown bridge. If you wait a while, a negro will walk past; or a four-wheeled cart, drawn by two shaggy oxen, driven by a stolid, pale-faced countryman, will trail along through the tiresome sand upon the avenue.

"The pleasures to be had at Aiken are all of the minor sort. To walk, to ride saddle-horses in the afternoon, to visit the out-of-town farms and rose-gardens, to dance in the evening, are nearly the only means at hand to speed the days.... It is safe to assert that nine persons in every ten are cast down at the end of the third or fourth day of their stay in the town. They look out of their windows and see a scanty, silent settlement, a wide expanse of rich foliage, and an arid soil bedecked with flowers. And this is all. There seems to be nothing to entice or to stimulate them. They find themselves wholly without scenes that might awaken strong emotions. After a day or two of prostration, or perhaps of absolute *ennui* and disappointment, they begin, out of sheer compulsion, to search about among the small resources that do exist for satisfaction. And they succeed admirably. They become enamored of the solemn and limitless woods, and grow content to wander hour after hour in the companionship of their own spirits. Their yesterday cravings for the towering rocks of the great hills become satisfied with the colored sands that they uncover with their footsteps. They count the kinds, turn the pretty shades to the sun, and marvel at the profusion of hues. They get as much out of a handful as they used to get out of a whole landscape. If, in the depths of the groves, they find a spray of phlox, they gather it, and study it more than they ever studied the half-tropical verdure of Florida. When they come upon an old plantation, with its flat expanse of pale fields, its few verdant copses, its gray log-cabins, and its lonely dwelling, they stand and gaze at it, and find that it is overflowing with the most marvelous color. Thus, having been awakened, they grow content. It is a matter of fact that the rebound from their despair carries them up to the heights of elation. After five days in Aiken the visitor becomes happy. It is a place of rest. Every thing in Nature induces tranquillity, and so does every thing in the town. There is nothing to disturb, nothing to excite; a tired man may here fold his hands and forget the world. That this forgetfulness, combined with the comfort of warmth and the pleasure of beholding in the days of winter the glories of summer, is a gift of inestimable value, it needs no paper like this to prove. One has but to look closely at the pinched faces that he sometimes meets in his walks, to reckon how valuable these few conditions are in the tiresome struggles of a mortal for a little more time."

Mineral Springs.

The only mineral springs in South Carolina that are much visited are the *Glenn Springs* and the *Limestone Springs* near Spartanburg. **Spartanburg** is in the northern part of the State, 223 miles from Charleston and 93 miles from Columbia, and directly on the line of the Richmond & Danville R. R. (Piedmont Air-Line). It is also one of the termini of the Spartanburg & Asheville R. R. and the Spartanburg, Union & Columbia R. R. It is much resorted to in summer, and is also a good winter resort, the air being cooler than, but quite as dry as, that of Aiken. *Glenn's Springs* here are strongly impregnated with sulphur, and contain traces of sulphate of magnesia, with sulphate, percarbonate, and chloride of lime. The waters are considered efficacious in certain forms of rheumatism, scrofula, and dyspeptic affections. The *Limestone Spring* is a chalybeate, and possesses valuable tonic properties. Both are much visited. The scenery around Spartanburg is very attractive, and not far from the village is the memorable Revolutionary battle-field of the Cowpens, located on the hill-range called the Thickety Mountain. The battle was fought January 17, 1781, and resulted in the defeat of the British under Tarleton. In the olden time the cattle were suffered to graze upon the scene of the contest—whence its name. *Chick's Springs*, in **Greenville County**, on the **Ennoree** River, just below the mountains, are also a good deal visited. The springs are two in number. One is slightly sulphurous, and is used for hepatic and intestinal affections and cutaneous diseases; the other is a mild chalybeate, and is employed as a tonic. The *Williamston Springs*, near the railway between Anderson and Greenville, are represented as having valuable tonic and alterative properties.

The Mountain-Region.

The northern districts of South Carolina form, with the neighboring hill-region of Georgia and the western part of North Carolina, one of the most interesting chapters in the great volume of American landscape. In mountain surprises, picturesque valley-nooks, and romantic waterfalls, this region is nowhere surpassed. Beautiful and healthful villages, with high social attractions, afford most agreeable homes and headquarters to seekers after the picturesque. These villages are rapidly becoming favorite resorts of people from the lowlands of the State; and their elegant mansions and villas are every year more and more embellishing the vicinity. **Greenville**, on the Richmond & Danville R. R., 143 miles from Columbia and 271 from Charleston, lies at the threshold of the chief beauties of the mountain-region, and gives ready access to all the rest. The village is beautifully situated on Reedy River, near its source, and at the foot of the Saluda Mountain. It is a popular summer resort, and contains excellent hotels (*Exchange Hotel*, *Mansion House*), schools, and a university.

Twenty miles above Greenville is **Table Mountain**, one of the most remarkable of the natural wonders of the State, rising as it does 4,300 feet above the sea, with a long extent on one side of perpendicular cliffs, 1,000 feet in height. The view of these grand and lofty rocky ledges is exceedingly fine from the quiet glens of the valley below, and not less imposing is the splendid amphitheatre of hill-tops seen from its crown. Among the sights to be seen from Table Mountain is Cæsar's Head, a lofty peak with one side a precipice of great height, just back of which is a large hotel. It is the highest point in the vicinity, and the tourist will be well repaid for his visit. Cæsar's Head used to be the favorite summer resort of South Carolinians, and drew many visitors from all quarters. The *Stool Mountain*, which is prominent from the valley below, here dwindles to its proper height. The top of Table Mountain, which is comparatively level, is of great extent. In

The Cliffs.

many places the surface is stony, in others alluvial and covered with noble trees. Near the centre the remains of a hut exist; a building erected as the kitchen to a hotel, which it was once contemplated to erect on the rock. At the base of Table Mountain, in a romantic glen, are the famous **Falls of Slicking**, a wonderful series of cascades and rapids. Leaving the cabin at the base of the mountain, the tourist, in his ascent, soon finds himself following the windings of the river. After the passage of about one-quarter of a mile, he reaches the "*Trunk*," so called from its being the point of junction of two different branches of the river or creek; the distance between these streams, as the ascent continues, gradually increases, and, when near the summit, they are widely separated; they bear one name, and abound, each, in cascades. The right-hand branch is the more picturesque, and is the one by which the visitor is usually conducted. From the "*Trunk*," the gem of all this locality, and the Table Rock, is a charming view of the neighboring mountains of Cæsar's Head, Bald Mountain, the Pinnacle Rock, and other spurs. At the "*Trunk*," the two streams fall perpendicularly some seventy feet, mingling in one in the basin below. This basin is easily accessible, and nowhere is there a more secluded or more wildly picturesque spot. Save when in his meridian, the sun's rays seldom penetrate its solitude. On one side are the two cascades leaping in snowy masses from rock to rock, and on others are mighty bulwarks of venerable stone, here and there studded with an adventurous shrub, or overhung with rich foliage.

The **Keowee** is a beautiful mountain-stream in Pickens County, which, with the Tugaloo River, forms the Savannah. The route from Greenville to the valley of Jocasse lies along its banks, amid the most lovely scenery, and the entire region is full of romantic memories of the Cherokee wars. Jocasse Valley, near the northern boundary-line, is one of the most charmingly secluded nooks in the State, environed as it is on every side, except that through which the Keowee steals out, by grand mountain-ridges. The great charm of Jocasse is that it is small enough to be seen and enjoyed all at once, as its entire area is not too much for one comfortable picture. It is such a nook as painters delight in. White Water Cataracts are an hour's brisk walk north of Jocasse. Their chief beauty is in their picturesque lines, and in the variety and boldness of the mountain-landscape all around; though they would maintain their claims to admiration for their extent alone, even were the accessory scenes far less beautiful than they are. Adjoining this most attractive region of South Carolina, and easily accessible therefrom, are Tallulah, and Toccoa, and Yonah, and Nacoochee, and the other lovely spots described in the chapter on Georgia; also the beautiful scenes of Western North Carolina, to be described in the next chapter.

NORTH CAROLINA RESORTS.

NORTH CAROLINA, also one of the original thirteen States, lies just north of South Carolina, between lat. 33° 53' and 36° 33' north, and lon. 75° 25' and 84° 30' west, with an extreme length from east to west of 490 miles, and an extreme breadth from north to south of 185 miles; area, 50,704 square miles. The State may be physically divided into the coast and swamp-land section, extending from 80 to 100 miles inland; the middle section, extending to the foot of the mountains; and the mountain section, embracing the western part of the State. The first section abounds in valuable timber, and includes the turpentine region. The country is level, with many swamps and marshes, and the streams are sluggish and muddy. Much of the land is sandy, but a large portion of this region is very fertile, the swamps being generally so. Rice, cotton, tobacco, and maize flourish. The Great Dismal Swamp extends north from Albemarle Sound into Virginia, covering an area of about 150,000 acres. Between Albemarle and Pamlico Sounds is the Alligator or Little Dismal Swamp, which is about as large as the other. It is estimated that the swamps of the State altogether cover 3,000,000 acres. Parts of the Little

Dismal Swamp have been drained so as to make valuable rice and grain lands; and a considerable quantity of the swamp-land may be drained or reclaimed by embankment. The middle section is adapted to the production of the cereals, tobacco, and cotton. It possesses great mineral wealth, and abounds in streams affording extensive water-power. About 100 miles from the coast the land begins to rise into small hills, and a little farther westward is every variety of hills and dales consistent with a fertile country fit for cultivation. West of the Yadkin and Catawba Rivers is an elevated region from 1,000 to 2,000 feet above the sea; and still beyond this plateau the main range of the Appalachian Mountains traverses the State from northeast to southwest, reaching here its greatest altitude. The Iron or Smoky Mountains separate the State from Tennessee. Between these two ridges is a plateau whose altitude ranges from 3,500 to 4,000 feet, being the highest plateau of the same extent east of the Rocky Mountains. In the centre stands the symmetrical forest-crowned summit of the Sugar Mountain (5,312 feet high), and on its margin rises the Grandfather (5,897 feet), the highest summit of the Blue Ridge, though inferior in altitude to the adjacent peaks of the Black Mountains. The mountain-region presents much beautiful scenery, and affords rich grazing-lands and abundant water-power. The coast-line is nearly 400 miles long, and along its whole length are sandy, barren, desert islands, from $\frac{1}{2}$ to 2 miles wide, separated by numerous inlets, few of which are navigable. From these islands shoals extend far into the sea, which render the navigation of the coast extremely dangerous. Cape Hatteras forms the headland of the dangerous triangular island beach which separates Pamlico Sound from the ocean. Narrow, shallow lagoons, filled with constantly-shifting sand-bars, extend all along the coast south of Cape Lookout between the mainland and the sand-islands. In the northeastern part of the State, above Cape Lookout, are two extensive sounds, Pamlico and Albemarle, and a smaller one, Currituck, which are cut off from the ocean by the islands or sandbanks before referred to. Their waters are nearly fresh, and little affected by tides. The rivers of North Carolina are numerous, but have shifting sand-bars at their mouths, and rapids in their descent from the hilly regions. The principal are the Cape Fear (300 miles long), the Roanoke (250 miles long), the Neuse, the Tar, the Chowan, the Yadkin, and the Catawba. These all flow into the Atlantic. From the western slope of the Blue Ridge flow New River, the Little Tennessee, and several other streams, the waters of which, breaking through the Iron or Smoky Mountains, join those of the Ohio and Mississippi.

The soil of North Carolina is of every variety, from the sands and marshes of the coast to the rich alluvions of the river-bottoms. In the coast-regions the swamps when drained are fertile, and rice grows well. The pine-region is barren for the most part, while farther inland the soil improves, and is well adapted to wheat, rye, barley, oats, and flax. Cotton is chiefly raised in the counties along the southern border. Among the leading products are sweet-potatoes (of which North Carolina produced more in 1870 than any other State), tobacco, and Indian-corn. The forest-trees of the upland are oak, hickory, ash, walnut, and lime; in the low country, pine; and in the swamps, cedar, cypress, maple, oak, and poplar, with an undergrowth of vines. Among the fruits are apples, pears, peaches, plums, cherries, grapes, and strawberries. Grapes are especially abundant in the coast-region. The Scuppernong, which is a native of and peculiar to North Carolina, has attracted attention for its large size, luscious flavor, and excellent wine-making qualities. Cranberries are produced in abundance and are exported. The great characteristic product of the State, however, is spirits of turpentine, which is distilled from the sap of the pitch-pine, vast forests of which cover the middle section of the State. In Albemarle and Pamlico Sounds immense quantities of herring and shad are taken in season; and the estuaries and bays are favorite resorts of wild-fowl of every description. In the forest-country in the eastern part of the State, quail, partridges, and other game-birds abound; while in the mountainous region of the western portion deer are plenty, and bears and other wild animals are found.

The **climate** of North Carolina is very similar to that of South Carolina (see page

42), except that it is a trifle colder. In the low country, the atmosphere is warm and humid, and malarial and bilious diseases prevail. In the mountain-region it is cool, dry, and bracing, and remarkably healthy. The mean annual temperature at

Making Tar.

Raleigh, the capital of the State, is 60°. At Asheville, in the mountains, the mean temperature of spring is 53.1°; of summer, 71.70°; of autumn, 54.8°; and of winter, 38.2°. The rainfall in spring is 14.05 inches; in summer, 16.7; in autumn, 6.5; and in winter, 8.4. The winter climate of the mountain-section is peculiarly adapted to that class of consumptives who find a cold, dry climate more beneficial than a warm and moist one—to such, for instance, as go to Minnesota and Colorado. It has not the intense coldness of these, and is less marked by sudden variations of temperature. Asthmatics are also benefited by a residence here.

There are no places in North Carolina that have secured as yet any special reputation as "winter resorts," but the mountain-region is much visited in spring and fall by tourists on their way to or from more southern retreats, and further along we shall mention a few localities whose sanitary advantages are gradually becoming known.

The Mountain-Region.

Grand and impressive as is the mountain-region of South Carolina and Georgia, already described, that of North Carolina is vastly superior in extent and variety, and presents scenes of beauty and sublimity unsurpassed by anything east of the Rocky Mountains. Here the great Appalachian system reaches its loftiest altitude: here brawling mountain-streams dash down the precipitous mountain-sides in cascades and cataracts of incomparable splendor; and here the contrasted loveliness of smiling valley and rugged peak is brought out with a fullness scarcely equaled elsewhere. The region consists of an elevated table-land, 250 miles long and about 50 broad, encircled by two great mountain-chains (the Blue Ridge on the east and the Great Smoky on the west), and traversed by cross-chains that run directly across the country, and from which spurs of greater or lesser height lead off in all directions. Of these transverse ranges there are four: the Black, the Balsam, the Cullowhee, and the Nantahala. Between each lies a region of valleys, formed by the noble rivers and their minor tributaries, where a healthy atmosphere and picturesque surroundings are combined with a soil of singular fertility. The Blue Ridge is the natural barrier, dividing the waters falling into the Atlantic from those of the Mississippi, and its bold and beautiful heights are better known than the grander steeps of the western chain. This western rampart, known as the Great Smoky, comprises the groups of the Iron, the Unaka, and the Roan Mountains; and from its massiveness of form and general elevation is the master-chain of the whole Alleghany range. Though its highest summits are a few feet lower than the peaks

Mount Pisgah.

of the Black Mountain, it presents a continuous series of lofty peaks which nearly approach that altitude, its culminating point, *Clingman's Dome*, rising to the height of 6,660 feet. The most famous of the transverse ranges is that of the Black Mountain, a group of colossal heights, the dominating peak of which—*Mount Mitchell*—is now known to be the loftiest summit east of the Mississippi. With its two great branches it is over 20 miles long, and its rugged sides are covered with a wilderness of almost impenetrable forest. Above a certain elevation, no trees are found save the balsam-fir, from the dark color of which the mountain takes its name. Northward of the Black Mountain stand the two famous heights which Prof. Guyot calls "the two great pillars on both sides of the North Gate to the high mountain-region of North Carolina." These are the *Grandfather Mountain* in the Blue Ridge, and *Roan Mountain* in the Smoky. Both of these peaks command a wide view, but the Roan is especially remarkable for the extent of territory which it overlooks, comprising the seven States of North Carolina, Virginia, Tennessee, Kentucky, Alabama, Georgia, and South Carolina. Next to the Black, in the order of transverse chains, comes the Balsam, which in length and general magnitude is chief of the cross-ranges. It is 50 miles long, and its peaks average 6,000 feet in height, while, like the Blue Ridge, it divides all waters and is pierced by none. From its southern extremity two great spurs run out in a northerly direction; one terminates in the *Cold Mountain*, which is over 6,000 feet high, and the other in the beautiful peak of *Pisgah*, which is one of the most noted landmarks of the region. "Among the mountains which, seen from Asheville, lie in blue waves against the southern horizon, this commanding pyramid stands forth most prominently, and from its symmetrical outline, not less than from its eminence, attracts the eye at once."

The key of the mountain-region, and converging point of all the roads west of the Blue Ridge, is **Asheville** (*Grand Central Hotel, Eagle Hotel, Swannanoa*), in the valley of the French Broad River, surrounded by an amphitheatre of hills, and commanding one of the finest mountain-views in America. Just above its site the Swannanoa unites with the French Broad, charming natural parks surround it, and within easy

Asheville.

excursion-distance is some of the noblest scenery in the State. The town itself is adorned with many elegant private residences, the hotel accommodations are superior, and there are good churches, schools, banks, and newspapers. "Asheville Court-House stands nearly 2,250 feet above the sea; and the climate of all the adjacent region is mild, dry, and full of salvation for consumptives. The hotels and many of the cheery and comfortable farm-houses are in summer crowded with visitors from the East and West; and the local society is charmingly cordial and agreeable." Asheville is also an excellent winter home for those who are benefited by a cold, dry climate. (See tables on pp. 50 and 51.) A few miles from the town are some white sulphur springs; and 9 miles north are the so-called *Million Springs*, beautifully situated in a cave between two mountain-ranges, where sulphur and chalybeate waters may be had in abundance.

There are six routes by which Asheville may be reached, and, as each of them presents numerous attractions to tourists by the way, we shall describe them at some length:

1st Route.—From Salisbury, *via* Western North Carolina R. R., branch of the Richmond and Danville (Piedmont Air-Line). **Morgantown**, on this railway, 80 miles from Salisbury, is a popular resort, and well worth the attention of all lovers of mountain-scenery. It is a town of considerable age, and was named in honor of General Morgan, of Revolutionary fame. It is situated on the slopes of the Blue Ridge, 1,100 feet above the sea, and a very beautiful view may be obtained from any eminence in the vicinity. About 15 miles west of Morgantown are the *Glen Alpine Springs*, whose waters are of the lithia class, and are said to possess diuretic, tonic, and alterative properties. The springs have considerable local reputation, a good hotel, but their remoteness has prevented them from becoming widely known. In this neighborhood the *Hawk's Bill* and *Table Rock* are situated. The latter is a high, bleak rock rising out of the top of a mountain to the height of over 200 feet. It can easily be ascended, and upon the summit there is about an acre of rock with a smooth surface. About 25 miles from Morganton is the grand **Linnville Gorge**, where the Linnville River bursts through the massive barrier of the Linnville Mountains. The gorge is 15 miles in length, and the heights which overshadow it are not less than 2,000 feet high. The river plunges into its dark depths in a majestic fall, 100 feet high and 150 broad, and then rushes forward over a bed of rock. Cliffs, worn by the ceaseless action of the water into the most fantastic shapes, lean over it, detached masses of granite strew its channel, and the tumult of its fretted waters only ceases when it pauses now and then in crystal pools of placid gentleness. Beyond Henry's the route is very picturesque, crossing the Blue Ridge by the Swannanoa Tunnel (1,800 feet long and 2,700 feet above the sea), and descending gradually into the elevated basin in which Asheville lies. The latter part of the route lies along the banks of the Swannanoa, loveliest of North Carolina rivers.

2d Route.—From Spartanburg, South Carolina, by the Asheville & Spartanburg R. R.

3d Route.—From Charlotte, North Carolina, by railway to Statesville, on the Western North Carolina R. R.; or by stage from Shelby on the Shelby Division of the Carolina R. R. Near Shelby are *Wilson's Springs*, somewhat noted as a summer resort. This route lies through the famous **Hickory-Nut Gap**, the scenery of which has been declared by some European travelers to be equal in beauty and grandeur to any pass in the Alps. The entire length of the Gap is about 9 miles, the last five being watered by the Rocky Broad River. The gateway of the gorge on the eastern side is not more than half a mile wide, and from this point the road winds upward along a narrow pass, hemmed in on all sides by stately heights. From the summit of the Gap there is a most impressive view in all directions.

4th Route.—This route and the following are given for those who prefer to journey with less speed than the railroad, and to traverse more romantic scenery. By stage from Greenville, South Carolina (*see* page 54), *via* Saluda Gap, Flat Rock, and Hendersonville, to Asheville (60 miles). Some of the attractions of this route have already been described in the chapter on South Carolina, but the entire road lies through the most enchanting and picturesque scenery. **Flat Rock**, once the most frequented of Carolina resorts, has been shorn of its former glories, but the lovely valley still contains some noble mansions, surrounded by gardens filled with rarest and costliest of shrubbery and flowers.

5th Route.—By stage from Greenville, South Carolina (*see* page 54), *via* Jones's Gap and Cæsar's Head to Asheville (about 75 miles). *Cæsar's Head* is a bold and beautiful headland in South Carolina (*see* page 54), and will well repay a visit. Beyond Cæsar's Head the route passes near **Cashier's Valley**, famous for its salubrious climate, and so accessible from South Carolina that many gentlemen from the low country have erected summer residences there. It is more of a table-land than a valley, lying on the side of the Blue Ridge, so near the summit that its elevation above the sea cannot be less than 3,500 feet, and hemmed in on all sides by noble peaks, among which *Chimney-Top* stands forth conspicuously. On the southwestern edge of the valley is **Whiteside Mountain**, which is in many respects the most striking peak in North Carolina. Rising to a height of more than 5,000 feet, its southeastern face is an immense precipice of white rock, which, towering up perpendicularly 1,800 feet, is fully 2 miles long, and curved so as to form part of the arc of a circle. The face of the precipice is not altogether smooth, as one fancies when approaching it, but has been worn by the elements into wildly picturesque escarpments and cave-like recesses. The largest of these recesses is known as the *Devil's Supreme Court-House;* and according to Cherokee tradition the prince of the powers of darkness will on the day of doom erect his throne here and try all the spirits who fall under his jurisdiction. The approach to it at present is along a narrow and dangerous ledge, upon which only the most cool-headed should venture.

The Swannanoa.

The ascent to the summit of the mountain can be made partly on horseback and presents no difficulties, and the view is of surpassing grandeur. "To the northeast, as far as the eye can reach, rise a multitude of sharply-defined blue and purple peaks, the valleys between them, vast and filled with frightful ravines, seeming the merest gullies on the earth's surface. Farther off than this line of peaks rise the dim outlines of the Balsam and Smoky ranges. In the distant southwest, looking across into Georgia, we can descry Mount Yonah, lonely and superb, with a cloud-wreath about his brow; 60 miles away, in South Carolina, a flash of sunlight reveals the roofs of the little German settlement of Walhalla; and on the southeast, beyond the precipices and ragged projections, towers up Chimney-Top Mountain, while the Hog-Back bends its ugly form against the sky, and Cold Mountain rises on the left. Turning to the north we behold Yellow Mountain, with its square sides, and Short-Off. Beyond and beyond, peaks and peaks, and ravines and ravines! It is like looking down on the world from a balloon."

6th Route.—From the north, west, or southwest, Asheville may be reached *via* East Tennessee, Virginia & Georgia Railroads to Morristown, Tennessee; thence North Carolina Division, and West. N. C. R. R. through Warm Springs, up the valley of the French Broad to Asheville. The Warm Springs and the country thence to Asheville are described further along.

Having reached Asheville (*see* page 59) the tourist or invalid may spend days and weeks in visiting the many picturesque spots within an area of 35 or 40 miles, or in hunting, fishing, or exploring the caves, mines, and Indian mounds. The excursion which above all others he should not fail to make is that down the **French Broad River**, the supreme beauty of which has long been famous. Below Asheville

The French Broad.

the river flows through an ever-deepening gorge, narrow as a Western cañon and inexpressibly grand, until it cuts its way through the Smoky Mountains, and reaches Tennessee. For 36 miles its waters well deserve their musical Cherokee name (Tahkecostee, "the Racing River"), and the splendor of their ceaseless tumult fascinates both eye and ear. A fine highway follows its banks, and often trespasses upon the stream, as it is crowded by the overhanging cliffs. About 35 miles from Asheville, on the right of the road, is the famous rock, *Lover's Leap ;* and just below it, where the left bank widens out into a level plain, the **Warm Springs** nestle in a beautiful grove of trees. These springs are among the most noted mineral waters in the Southern States, and their virtues have been known for nearly a century. An analysis of the water shows that it contains free carbonic acid, free sulphuretted hydrogen, carbonic acid, and sulphuric acid, in combination with lime, and a trace of magnesia. Though quite palatable as a beverage, it is taken chiefly in the form of baths, for which there are excellent facilities, and is recommended for dyspepsia, liver-complaint, diseases of the kidneys, rheumatism, rheumatic gout, and chronic cutaneous diseases. The atmosphere is clear, cool, and invigorating, and is regarded as particularly beneficial in all pulmonary diseases. The hotel is spacious and comfortable, and is kept open winter and summer, as the place is a resort at all seasons. Five miles below the springs, on the Tennessee boundary, the road passes beneath the bold precipice of the *Painted Rocks*, a titanic mass over 200 feet high, whose face is marked with red paint, supposed to be Indian pictures. Near by are the *Chimneys*, lofty cliffs, broken at their summits into detached piles of rock bearing the likeness of colossal chimneys, a fancy greatly improved by the fireplace-like recesses at their base. *Mountain Island*, 2 miles above the Springs, is a hilly islet in the impetuous stream, its shores and slopes carpeted with evergreens, and rich in all the variegated colors of the North Carolinian flora.

Among the mountain-ascents that may be readily made from Asheville, those of Mount Pisgah and Mount Mitchell will best repay the trouble. *Pisgah* lies to the south, and commands an extensive view over Tennessee, South Carolina, and Georgia, as well as over the greater part of Western North Carolina. The excursion to **Mount Mitchell**, including the ascent of the peak and the return to Asheville, can be made in three days, and, though arduous, is entirely free from danger. There are three resting-places *en route:* one at "Patton's," which nestles at the base of the chain of peaks; another at the "Mountain-House," 4 miles from the foot; and another at the point where the Government once maintained an observatory, 3 miles from the topmost height. The summit of Mount Mitchell is the highest in the United States east of the Mississippi (6,701 feet), and affords the visitor a view of unsurpassed extent and grandeur. All Western Carolina lies spread below him, together with portions of Virginia, Tennessee, South Carolina, and Georgia. He can trace across the Old Dominion the long, undulating line of the Blue Ridge, which, entering North Carolina, passes under the Black, and thence runs southerly until it reaches South Carolina, when it turns to the west, and, making a curve, joins the Smoky near the northeast corner of Georgia. Overlooking this range, from his greater elevation, he sees every height in that part of North Carolina which lies east of it. Far away on the borders of the two Carolinas stands a misty mound, which is King's Mountain, of Revolutionary fame; and from this point the eye sweeps over an illimitable expanse, returning

Laurel Run, near Asheville.

to where the spurs of the Black cover the counties of Rutherford, Burke, and McDowell, with a network of hills.

"There is a greater attraction in the unknown than in the known, however," says a writer in APPLETONS' JOURNAL, "and the traveler who has followed the French Broad to where it surges around Mountain Island and sweeps beneath Paint Rock; who has stood on the hills of Asheville, and admired the gentle loveliness of the valleys which encompass it; who has tracked the Swannanoa to its birthplace in the ice-cold springs of the Black Mountain, and climbed to the summit of that Appalachian patriarch (Mount Mitchell)—it is natural that such a traveler, turning his back on these places, made familiar by exploration, should look with longing eyes at the dark chain of the Balsam, forming so lofty a barrier between himself and the still wilder, still more beautiful region that lies farther westward. If he possesses courage and resolution, if he does not shrink from trifling hardships, and if he can endure cheerfully a few inconveniences, let him resolve to scale those heights, and gaze at least upon all that lies beyond. There is very little difficulty in executing such a resolution, and nobody who can appreciate the sublime in natural scenery, or who likes the zest of adventure, will ever regret having executed it.

"As a first step, let him establish his headquarters at **Brevard**, a pleasant village of Transylvania County, lying in the matchless valley of the Upper French Broad. He will find here the most comfortable lodging and most admirable fare, together with that cordial hospitality which is ever ready to oblige the wayfarer and stranger. Should he possess the mountaineering spirit to which allusion has been made, he need not fear that time will hang heavily on his hands. There are speckled trout in the streams, there are deer in the coverts of the forests, and there are countless places of picturesque interest, many of which are within the easy range of a day's excursion. One of the most attractive of these excursions is to *Dunn's Rock*, a rugged cliff on the eastern side of the valley, from the summit of which a most charming view is to be had. Besides Dunn's Rock, there are many other eminences around Brevard, which repay a hundred-fold the exertion of ascending them; while down the glens of the hills impetuous streams come rushing in Undine-like cascades. Such are the lovely *Falls of Conestee*, of *Looking-Glass*, and of *Glen Cannon*. Into these enchanted recesses the lances of sunlight are scarcely able to pierce to find the laughing water, so luxuriant is the forest-growth, which forms depths of twilight obscurity where ferns and mosses and unnumbered bright, sweet flowers flourish.

"From Brevard the way to the **Balsam** is plain and short. Following the north fork of the French Broad into what is called the Gloucester settlement, the traveler will find himself at the foot of this range. Here he can readily secure a guide, and make the ascent of the peaks which attain their highest elevation at this point. Prof. Guyot has recorded his opinion that 'considering these great features of physical structure (the Balsam heights), and the considerable elevation of the valleys which form the base of these high chains, we may say that this vast cluster of highlands between the French Broad and the Tuckaseege Rivers is the culminating region of the great Appalachian system.' It is at least certain that their appearance impresses one with a deeper sense of grandeur and sublimity than even the Black Mountain. Immense ridges rise on all sides, lofty peaks lift their heads into the dazzling regions of the upper air, escarpments of rugged rock contrast with the verdure of the forest that clothes all other points, while trackless gorges and deep chasms, where the roar of unseen cataracts alone breaks the silence of solitude, are the characteristic features of the region. Leaving the domain of Gloucester, a traveler of faint heart and wavering courage may be struck with dismay at the wildness of the scenes into which he is led. The path is a trail, only visible to the eyes of a mountaineer, which plunges down precipitous hill-sides, winds along dizzy verges, where a single false step would send horse and rider crashing into the abyss below, and mounts ascents so steep that the saddles threaten to slip back over the straining animals, and a cautious rider will look well to his girths. Knob after knob is climbed, and yet the dominating heights, as one catches glimpses of them now and then, seem far away as ever. Nevertheless, it is evident that one's labor is not in vain. The air grows more rarefied, the horizon expands, the world unrolls like an azure scroll, and over it spreads the marvelous haze of distance.

"The tops of the Balsam peaks are generally bare of trees, and the Cherokees believe that these open spaces are the footprints of the devil, made as he stepped from mountain to mountain. They command singularly wild and impressive views, including no less than five great mountain-ranges. Looking to the west, we see on our left the Blue Ridge, on our right the Smoky, and in front the Cullowhee, with the Nantahala lying cloud-like in the far distance. Countless intervening chains spread over the vast scene, with graceful lines blending, and dominant points ascending, forming a whole of wondrous harmony. Near at hand the heights of the Balsam, clad in a rich plumage of forest, surround us in serried ranks—a succession of magnificent peaks, infinitely diversified in shape, but nearly approaching the same standard of elevation."

Brevard, which is described above, and is rapidly becoming a favorite resort, may be reached by rail *via* the Richmond & Danville R. R. to Charlotte, and thence *via* the Carolina Central R. R.

MINNESOTA RESORTS.

The State of Minnesota derives its name from its principal river, the Minnesota (St. Peter's), which, in the Sioux or Dakota language, means "muddy water." It is situated between lat. 43° 30' and 49° 24' north, and lon. 89° 39' and 97° 5' west, with an extreme length from north to south of 380 miles, and an extreme breadth from east to west of 337 miles; area, 83,531 square miles. Lying nearly at the centre of the continent, and occupying the most elevated plateau between the Gulf of Mexico and Hudson's Bay, Minnesota forms the water-shed of the three great river-systems of North America: that of the Mississippi, which flows south to the Gulf of Mexico; that of the St. Lawrence, which, connected with the great chain of Northern lakes, has an easterly direction to the Atlantic Ocean; and that of the Red River of the North, flowing north to Lake Winnipeg, which has its outlet in Hudson's Bay. A group of low sand-hills in the northeastern part of the State, formed by huge deposits of drift overlying a local outcrop of the primary and metamorphic rocks, and called *Hauteurs des Terres* (Heights of Land), forms the dividing ridge between the Mississippi and Lake Superior. These Heights of Land rise by scarcely perceptible slopes from the general level, in no instance higher than 1,680 feet above the sea, which is not more than 600 feet above the average elevation of the country. These hills are commonly flat at the top, varying in height from 85 to 100 feet above the surrounding waters. Generally the surface of Minnesota is an undulating plain, with an average elevation of nearly 1,000 feet above the sea, and presents a succession of small rolling prairies or table-lands, studded with lakes and groves, and alternating with belts of timber. Two-thirds of the surface slopes southeast with the waters of the Mississippi, the northern part of the State being nearly equally divided between the alluvial levels of the Red River valley on the northwest and the broken highlands of the northeast, which are mainly drained by the precipitous streams which flow into Lake Superior and the Rainy Lake Chain. The navigable waters of the State have a total shore-line of 2,746 miles, and comprise numerous rivers, of which the Minnesota, the Mississippi, the Red River of the North, the St. Croix, and the St. Louis, are the most important. A characteristic feature of the State is the number and beauty of its lakes, of which there are said to be upward of 10,000. They are from 1 mile to 30 miles in diameter, and many of them have an area of from 100 to 400 square miles. Their waters, generally sweet and clear, abound in fish. The largest are the Lake of the Woods, Rainy, Namekin, Bois Blanc, Vermilion, Swan, Sandy, Winibigoshish, Leech, and Mille Lacs, in the north and northeast; Red Lake, in the northwest; Big Stone, Benton, Sauk, and Swan, in the west and southwest.

The soil is fertile, two-thirds of the surface being well adapted to the cultivation of all the cereals and roots of the temperate zone. It is composed generally of a dark, calcareous loam, abounding in organic and saline ingredients, and is retentive of moisture. The country, especially above latitude 46°, is well-timbered; pine-forests extend far to the north, and birch, maple, aspen, ash, and elm abound. A large forest of hard-wood varieties, known as the Big Woods, extends over the central portion of the State west of the Mississippi, and covers an area of about 4,000 square miles. On the river bottoms are found basswood, elm, aspen, butternut, ash, birch, maple, linden, balsam fir, and some oaks; and in the swamps tamarack, cedar, and cypress. Among the wild animals are the elk, deer, antelope, bear, wolf, wolverene, otter, muskrat, mink, martin, and raccoon. Of birds, there are the golden and bald eagles, grouse, partridge, hawk, owl, quail, plover, lark, and many smaller kinds. There are also the pelican, tern, sheldrake, teal, loon, wild-geese, wild-ducks, and other water-fowl. The waters contain pike, pickerel, bass, whitefish, muskelonge, catfish, trout, and other varieties of fish. To the sportsman Minnesota offers greater attractions than any other State in the West.

The climate of Minnesota is very cold in the winter, but clear, dry, and equable, and is recommended for those invalids (such as are in the incipient stages of consumption for example) who are more benefited by a climate of this character than by one which is warmer and more moist. It is a well-ascertained fact that the *dryness* of the atmosphere is an even more important factor in the prevention and cure of consumption than its *warmth;* and, upon not a few consumptives, a climate which is warm without being dry has a peculiarly debilitating and unwholesome effect. For this class it is claimed that Minnesota presents greater advantages than any other locality in America. Though its winters are long, and the cold intense and continuous, yet the dryness of the atmosphere and the slight diurnal variations of temperature render the cold far less oppressive than in the Eastern Atlantic States, where the moist air and the rasping winds seem to tear weak lungs to pieces. There are few days of a Minnesota winter during which an invalid, if properly clad, cannot go out-of-doors for several hours at least; and the bracing air almost always has a decidedly tonic and exhilarating effect. The cold in winter and the heat in summer, though extreme, are subject to but slight variations in short periods, and all the seasons are remarkably free from those sudden changes that are so injurious to persons in delicate health. The following summary of meteorological observations, made at St. Paul during 1874, is reported by the United States Signal Bureau:

MONTH.	THERMOMETER.			Mean Barometer.	Total Rainfall, Inches.	Prevailing Wind.
	Maximum.	Minimum.	Mean.			
January	43.00	−23.00	13.85	30.073	0.49	Southeast.
February	36.00	−18.00	14.40	30.082	1.07	Southeast.
March	46.00	−5.00	23.66	30.030	2.24	Northwest.
April	71.00	7.00	37.52	30.003	0.95	North.
May	94.00	31.00	62.24	29.860	1.65	North.
June	94.00	42.00	68.70	29.797	11.67	Southeast.
July	90.00	53.00	74.72	29.842	1.94	Southeast.
August	91.00	54.00	70.54	29.892	3.90	Southeast.
September	92.00	37.00	60.95	29.908	5.76	Southeast.
October	71.00	21.00	49.36	30.003	3.21	Northwest.
November	72.00	−8.00	28.72	29.951	1.90	Southeast.
December	48.00	−20.00	18.81	30.848	0.72	Northwest.
Mean	71.67	14.25	43.62	30.490	35.50	Southeast.

These are the facts on which are based Minnesota's claims as a resort for invalids; and they are sustained by the record of vital statistics. While the rate of mortality from consumption is 1 in 254 in Massachusetts, 1 in 473 in New York, and 1 in 757 in Virginia, in Minnesota it is only 1 in 1,139. It is declared, moreover, on high authority, that there is no such thing as "Minnesota consumption," that is, consumption which has originated in the State itself. The recorded deaths from that disease are, in nearly every case, those of invalids from other States, in whom the disease had progressed too far for cure. It should be added, however, that the climate of Minnesota is thought to be unfavorable to sufferers from bronchitis or catarrh; and that of all those who have hitherto visited Minnesota with consumption, only 1 in 15 has recovered. Dr. Joseph W. Howe, an authority on the subject, says: "The cold, clear air of the State is undoubtedly beneficial to certain cases of consumption. None, however, should attempt the journey whose lungs are seriously diseased, or who have not the strength to take daily exercise in the open air. It is the open-air life after all that does the work of curing, and it is, therefore, little less than suicide for invalids to seek a home where they are compelled to shut themselves in-doors day after day."

Of the health resorts of Minnesota the most frequented are St. Paul, Minneapolis, and Winona; but there is really an unlimited range of choice, as any of the towns of the central, southern, or eastern portions of the State possess the advantages of climate already enumerated. Care must be taken, of course, that the local sanitary conditions are favorable, and a sheltered location is naturally best; but the visitor can hardly make a mistake in selecting any one of the more easily accessible towns.

St. Paul.

How to reach.—From Chicago, St. Paul may be reached *via* Chicago & Northwestern R. R. (distance, 409 miles; fare, $11.50); or *via* Chicago, Milwaukee & St. Paul R. R. (distance, 411 miles; fare, ($11.50). From St. Louis it may be reached *via* steamer up the Mississippi River. In the summer from Buffalo by steamer on Lakes Erie, Huron, and Superior, to *Duluth ;* thence *via* St. Paul & Duluth R. R. to St. Paul (155 miles). During the open season this last is a very pleasant route from the East.

Hotels and Boarding-Houses.—The leading hotels are the *Metropolitan*, in Third Street; the *Merchants' Hotel*, near the centre of the business quarter; the *Ryan*, cor. of 6th and Robert Sts.; the *Windsor Hotel;* and the *Clarendon*, centrally located near the parks and public buildings. The rates of these houses are from $2 to $3 per day. There are several smaller hotels and boarding-houses where board may be had at from $5 to $10 a week. In the summer, the suburbs are cooler than the city, but in winter the invalid had better seek a residence in the city.

Location, Climate, and History.—St. Paul, the capital of Minnesota, is a beautiful city of about 50,000 inhabitants, situated on both banks of the Mississippi River, 2,200 miles from its mouth. It was formerly confined to the left bank of the river, the site embracing four distinct terraces, forming a natural amphitheatre with a

St. Paul, Minnesota.

southern exposure, and conforming to the curve of the river. The city is built principally upon the second and third terraces, which widen into level, semicircular plains, the last, about 90 feet above the river, being underlaid with a stratum of blue limestone from 12 to 20 feet thick, of which many of the buildings are constructed. The original town is regularly laid out, but the newer portions are irregular. The streets are lighted with gas, and a system of sewerage is in progress. The water-works are supplied from Lake Phalon, 3 miles distant; and two lines of street-railway are in operation.—The climate of St. Paul has already been indicated in our general remarks on that of the State at large. The meteorological table on page 66 was compiled from observations made here. (See also comparative table on page 51). The city is a peculiarly favorable winter residence for consumptives because of its sheltered situation and the dryness of its soil. Tables of mortality show St. Paul to be one of the healthiest cities in the United States.—The first recorded visit to the site of St. Paul was made by Father Hennepin, a Jesuit missionary, in 1680. Eighty-six years afterward, Jonathan Carver came there and made a treaty with the Dakota Indians, in what is now known as Carver's Cave. The first treaty of the United States with the Sioux, throwing their lands open to settlement, was made in 1837, and the first claim was entered by Pierre Parent, a Canadian *voyageur*, who sold it in 1839 for $30. It is the present site of the principal part of the city. The first building was erected in 1838, and for several years thereafter it was simply an Indian trading-post. It was laid out into village streets in 1849, and a city government was obtained in 1854, when the place contained about 3,000 inhabitants. It derives its name from that of a log chapel dedicated to St. Paul by a Jesuit missionary in 1841.

Places of Interest.—The principal public buildings in the city are the *State Capitol*, a plain brick structure situated on high ground, and occupying an entire square; and the *United States Custom-House*, which also contains the Post-office. The principal place of amusement is the *Opera-House* in Wabashaw Street, near Third, a large and handsome building, with a fine auditorium seating about 2,300 persons. There are about 75 churches of all denominations in the city, some of them large and handsomely finished. There are 4 public and as many private circulating libraries, the former including the State Law Library, and those of the Historical Society and Library Association, comprising together about 24,000 volumes. The *Academy of Science* also contains 126,000 specimens in natural history. The public and private schools are noted for their excellence, the latter including several female seminaries of a high grade. There are 3 free hospitals, managed by the county and church organizations, and a Protestant and a Roman Catholic orphan asylum. *Carver's Cave* is a great natural curiosity, near the river, in Dayton's Bluff, on the east side of the city. It was named after Jonathan Carver; who, on May 1, 1767, made a treaty with the Indians, by which they ceded him a large tract of land. There is a lake in the cave, which may be crossed in a boat. *Fountain Cave*, about 2 miles above the city, was apparently hollowed out of the rock by a stream which flows through it. It contains several chambers, the largest being 100 feet long, 25 wide, and 20 high; and it has been explored for 1,000 feet without the termination being reached.

There are some beautiful drives in and around St. Paul, and many places in the neighborhood of the city which can be reached either by carriage or by rail. Of these the most popular is *White Bear Lake*, 12 miles distant, on the St. Paul & Duluth R. R. It is about 9 miles in circumference, with picturesque shores and an island in its centre. The lake affords excellent boating, fishing, and bathing. *Bald-Eagle Lake*, a mile beyond White Bear Lake, is noted for its fishing and picturesque scenery, and is a popular resort for picnic-parties. *Minnehaha Falls*, immortalized by Longfellow, are reached by a delightful drive past Fort Snelling. The Falls are picturesquely situated, but they hardly merit the prominence that Mr. Longfellow's poem has obtained for them. *Lake Como* is reached by a pleasant drive of 2 miles. The city park, comprising several hundred acres, is located on its shores.

Minneapolis.

The city of Minneapolis is situated on both sides of the Mississippi River, 10 miles above St. Paul, with which it is connected by three lines of railway. It is built on a broad esplanade overlooking the famous falls of St. Anthony and the river, which is bordered at various points by picturesque bluffs. The city is regularly laid out, with avenues running east and west, and streets crossing them north and south. They are generally 80 feet wide, with 20 feet sidewalks, and two rows of trees on each side. The *Court-House, City Hall, Chamber of Commerce, Lumber Exchange,* the *Minneapolis Exposition,* and the *Opera-House,* are noticeable structures; as are also the *West House,* the *Nicollet House,* and the *First National Hotel.* The Athenæum Library contains 8,000 volumes, and that of the University of Minnesota about 13,000. Besides the University, there are several other important educational institutions, and the public schools are numerous and good. The number of churches is 75, including all the denominations, and some of the church-edifices are elegant and imposing. The city is supplied with water by powerful works, the streets are lighted with gas, and a system of sewerage has been recently completed. Its situation being less protected than that of St. Paul, it is perhaps less desirable as a winter residence for invalids, but it is nevertheless much frequented. Population, 129,000.

A large part of the business prosperity of Minneapolis is owing to the *Falls of St. Anthony,* which afford abundant water-power for manufacturing purposes. The fall is 18 feet perpendicular, with a rapid descent of 82 feet within 2 miles. The rapids above the cataract are very fine, in fact much finer than the fall itself, the picturesqueness of which has been destroyed by the wooden "curtain" erected to prevent the wearing away of the ledge. The falls can be seen with about equal advantage from either shore, but the best view is from the centre of the suspension-bridge which spans the river above the fall. Minneapolis is the greatest centre of flour-milling in the world, and in its lumber interest it ranks second to Chicago only. The country around Minneapolis is remarkable for its beauty. Numerous lakes, of which the chief are *Lakes Calhoun, Harriet,* and *Cedar,* dot the landscape, particularly to the westward, and cultivated prairies roll off in every direction. The celebrated *Minnehaha Falls* are only 3 miles below, and the *Silver Cascade* and *Bridal Veil Falls* are within easy driving distance. *Lake Minnetonka* is 12 miles westward, and affords great attractions to the pleasure-seeker or the sportsman. Other attractive resorts render the neighborhood an especially alluring one for residents and tourists.

Winona.

Winona is a thriving little city of about 12,000 inhabitants, situated on the Mississippi 105 miles below St. Paul by river, and 215 miles by rail. It is built on a spacious plain, commanding a fine view of the river for several miles, and contains the State Normal School, several fine churches, and numbers of handsome stores and private residences. Being somewhat sheltered by the high bluffs which line the river above and below, it is thought to offer conditions favorable to consumptives and other invalids. About 20 miles below Winona is *Trempeleau Island* (sometimes called Mountain Island), a rocky island, 300 to 500 feet in height, and one of the most noted landmarks on the Upper Mississippi. About 12 miles above is the famous *Chimney Rock.* Good hotels are the *Huff House* and *Jewell House.*

Red Wing and Frontenac.

These lively little towns are situated on Lake Pepin, as it is called, respectively 40 and 51 miles below St. Paul. *Lake Pepin* is simply an expansion of the Mississippi, about 30 miles long and 3 miles in average width, and is considered by many the most beautiful portion of the river. The bluffs on either side present peculiar characteristics, which are found in such perfection nowhere else: grim castles seem only to want sentries to be complete, and all the fantastic forms into which the action of the weather can transform limestone cliffs are to be seen. For miles the bluffs are indented with huge natural amphitheatres, the land rising to the level of the projecting heights, which form the portals, the curve being apparently as true as that of any auditorium ever built. The forests reach to the river-bank, and the water is so beautifully clear that fish may be seen many feet below the surface. Red Wing (*St. James Hotel*) lies at the head of the lake, on a level plain, extending to the majestic bluffs, and is a well-built town of about 5,000 inhabitants. It is a favorite summer resort, and, being thoroughly protected by high hills, is also a desirable winter-residence. The La Crosse and St. Paul division of the Milwaukee

Lake Pepin.

& St. Paul R. R. connects Red Wing with St. Paul. **Frontenac** (*Lake Side Hotel*), in the centre of the region, is a favorite resort in summer on account of its fine scenery, and the hunting, bathing, fishing, and sailing, which it affords. Besides the sport furnished by Lake Pepin, there are fine trout-fishing in the streams and deer-hunting in the woods of Wisconsin, on the opposite side of the river, while prairie-chickens are found in abundance in the country back of the village. Frontenac offers the same advantages as a winter-residence as are possessed by Red Wing.

Faribault.

Faribault lies about 46 miles south of St. Paul, on the Iowa and Minnesota division of the Chicago, Milwaukee & St. Paul R. R. It is situated at the confluence of the Cannon and Straight Rivers, and is one of the most populous and thriving interior towns in the State. In 1853 it was the site of Alexander Faribault's trading-post; since 1857 its growth has been rapid, and the present population is estimated at 5,000. It is the seat of the State Asylum for the Deaf, Dumb, and Blind, and of an Episcopal academy, and contains several other schools, six or eight churches, two weekly newspapers, two national banks, and several flour-mills, saw-mills, foundries, etc. The *Arlington* and the *Barron House* are the leading hotels. For invalids, Faribault possesses all the characteristic advantages of the Minnesota climate.

ARKANSAS HOT SPRINGS.

How to reach.—The Hot Springs are reached from St. Louis *via* the St. Louis, Iron Mountain & Southern R. R. (distance, 413 miles; time, about 20 hours). Excursion tickets, good for 90 days, are sold from St. Louis for $28.30. Rates from New York by all railroads, $43.90, unlimited; $36.30, limited.

Hotels and Boarding-Houses.—The principal hotels are the *Arlington*, the *Avenue Hotel*, *Beldin House*, *New Sumpter House*, *New Waverly House*, *Windsor*, *Plateau Hotel*, *Southern Hotel*, *Haine Villa Hotel*, *Hay House*, *Clarendon*, and *Hôtel Josephine*. Rates at these houses range from $12 to $25 per week. Minor hotels are the *Branch House*, *Grand Central*, and the *Barnes Hotel*, where prices are from $8 to $15 per week. Besides these there are numerous other hotels and boarding-houses, where the charges are from $3 to $10 per week.

HOT SPRINGS, a town and capital of Garland County, Arkansas, is situated about 45 miles southwest of Little Rock, and 6 miles north of the Washita River, in a wild and picturesque mountain-region. It is built principally in the narrow valley of Hot Springs Creek, running north and south between the Ozark Mountains, and contains, besides the hotels, 3 schools, 5 churches, 2 weekly newspapers, and a permanent population of about 5,000. The town itself and the surrounding hill-sides are embowered in trees, and present a very picturesque and inviting appearance. The valley in which the town is situated is about a mile and a half long, and very narrow, and has an elevation of about 1,500 feet above the sea. In the middle of the day the sunbeams are like a blaze, but an almost constant cool and refreshing breeze renders the atmosphere cool and agreeable even in summer. The disappearance of the sun behind the mountain-tops is followed by a lovely twilight, such as is found in but few other places. The springs, 66 in number, issue from the western slope of the Hot Springs Mountain, which lies on the east side of the valley. They vary in temperature from 93° to 160° Fahr., and discharge into the creek upward of 500,000 gallons of water every 24 hours—about 350 gallons per minute. Fifty-four of the springs have been tested in temperature, but there are many under the roads and ledges that cannot be tested without too great labor. The largest spring discharges 60 gallons a minute at a temperature of 150°, which will cook eggs in 15 minutes. The water of the springs is very clear, pure, transparent, and almost tasteless, and does not deposit sediment by standing. It is taken both internally and externally, and a great number of bathing-houses have been constructed for the use of invalids. The *vapor-baths* stand at 112°; the *douche*, a spirit-bath, at 120°; and the *saving-bath* at 116°. The amount of hot water discharged into the creek renders it sufficiently warm for bathing purposes in midwinter. When taken internally, the waters of the springs have an aperient and tonic effect, are rapidly absorbed into the circulatory system, and are beneficial in nearly all diseases of the blood. Taken both internally and in the form of baths, they have performed many wonderful cures of rheumatism, rheumatic gout, stiffness of the joints, mercurial diseases (arising from the effects of mercury in the system), malarial fevers, scrofula, and diseases of the skin. Of the thousands suffering from these ills who flock to the Hot Springs yearly, many recover entirely, while those who do not achieve a cure experience great relief.

A heavy fog hangs continually over the springs and upon the sides of the mountains, giving the neighborhood the appearance, at a little distance, of a number of furnaces in active operation. Near the edges of the springs is found, luxuriantly growing, a species of green *algæ*, which seems to delight in these natural hot-beds; while the mountain-slopes are covered with luxuriant vines, whose growth is perpetually stimulated by the condensation of the vapor. The air is warm and very moist, *and for this reason the valley should be shunned by consumptives, and all who are suffering from pulmonary diseases.*

The United States Supreme Court decided in 1876 that the title to the "Hot Springs Reservation" was vested in the United States Government, and since March, 1877, a commission has been appraising its improved ground for the purpose of giving a clear title to the occupants.

COLORADO RESORTS.

COLORADO, one of the most recently admitted among the States of the Union, is situated between lat. 37° and 41° north, and lon. 102° and 109° west, forming nearly a parallelogram, with an average length east and west of 380 miles, and an average breadth north and south of 280 miles; area, 104,500 square miles. It has three great natural divisions: the mountain-range (including the park system), the foot-hills, and the plains. The mountain-ranges are so numerous, and cover such a large portion of the surface, that Colorado has been aptly called "the Switzerland of America." The State is intersected north and south, near the centre, by the *Rocky Mountains*, which here attain their greatest elevation; 200 peaks nearly 13,000 feet high, and about 25 of 14,000 feet and over, being visible from Mount Lincoln. Between latitude 38° and 40° this chain is about 120 miles broad, consisting of three parallel ranges running nearly northwest. The east one, called the Front, or Colorado range, as seen from Denver, appears to rise abruptly from the plain, stretching with snow-capped summits from Pike's Peak on the south to a group 20 miles north of Long's Peak, a distance of 120 miles. Six of its peaks are from 14,000 to 14,200 feet above the sea, viz., Long's Peak, Mount Torrey, Gray's Peak, Mount Rosa, Mount Evans, and Pike's Peak. West of this range lie the parks, separated from each other by comparatively low or broken cross-ridges; and parallel with it, and about 40 miles farther west, is the *Park Range*, forming the western boundary of North, Middle, and South parks. Its highest points are in the Mount Lincoln group, near the dividing ridge between South and Middle parks; 20 peaks exceeding 13,000 feet in height, while Mount Lincoln and Quandary Peak rise above 14,000 feet. West of the south part of the Park range is the Arkansas valley, and beyond this is the *National Range*, also called the Sawatch range, or Sierra Madre, dividing through nearly its whole extent the waters of the Atlantic from those of the Pacific. It is parallel with and about 16 miles west of the Park range, terminating some forty miles northwest of Mount Lincoln, in the Mount of the Holy Cross, about 13,400 feet high. The highest part of this range commences in the Grand Mountain (14,200 feet high), 20 miles south of the Holy Cross, whence for 50 miles farther south the whole range is 13,000 feet high, with 10 peaks rising to a height of from 14,000 to 14,400 feet. The principal summits are Mounts Elbert, La Plata, Harvard, and Yale. West of the National range, and connected with it, are the *Elk Mountains*, lying between the Grand River on the north and the Gunnison on the south. The most elevated peaks form a ridge about 30 miles long, nearly parallel with the National range, and 35 miles west of it. West of this group there are no high mountains, the ridges changing within 20 miles to plateaus, which fall off to the Colorado River. On the east side of the mountains, and parallel thereto, extending from the Black Hills on the north to the Wet Mountains on the south, are the *foot-hills*, having an average elevation of 8,000 feet. The *plains* constitute the geographical division of Colorado east of the mountain-belt, and embrace more than one-third of the entire territory. The surface of this section is not one continuous level, but a series of valleys separated by ridges and traversed by innumerable water-courses. The average elevation above tide-water is 6,000 feet. The most prominent feature of this vast plateau is the "divide," an elevation reaching a height of 7,500 feet above the sea-level, which separates the waters of the South Platte and the Arkansas, and supplies many of their affluents.

The most remarkable physical characteristic of Colorado is its system of great

Natural Parks, which consist of extensive irregular plateaus or basins, shut in on all sides by lofty mountain-ranges. The surface of these plateaus is diversified by numerous hills or ridges, and valleys, containing streams which form the headwaters of all the great rivers that rise in Colorado. These valleys are clothed with luxuriant grasses and flowering plants of various species, and possess an extremely fertile soil. The hills are covered with dense forests of pine, abounding in game, such as the bear, elk, and deer. The beds of the streams furnish many varieties of minerals and fossils, and afford a remarkable field for geological investigations. Mineral springs, with waters possessing rare medicinal properties, are numerous, while salt and coal beds seem to underlie the entire surface. The four principal parks are in the central portion of the State, and constitute the greater part of a

Gray's Peak.

belt running north and south between lon. 105° and 106°. They will be described in detail further on. The *river system* of Colorado embraces the principal tributaries of the **Rio Colorado**, Rio Grande, Arkansas, Platte, and Smoky Hill and Republican Forks of the Kansas. The Arkansas and the South Fork of the Platte drain the eastern part; the Bear River, the Bunkara, and the **Gunnison**, flow from the **western slopes of** the Rocky Mountains; the Rio Grande **rises in the** southern part of the State, and **flows** southward into the Gulf of Mexico. The Grand River, which unites with the Green to form the Colorado, flows through mountain-chasms of great depth; and the Colorado itself flows westward for hundreds of miles through a series of stupendous gorges or cañons which are among the wonders of the West, till it empties into the Gulf of California.

About one-third of Colorado is good agricultural land. In the plains and the parks the *soil* of the valleys is peculiarly fertile, and produces in abundance the hardier cereals and vegetables. The arid sands of the plains have been proved to be merely surface deposits, covering a soil of remarkable fertility when moistened. The necessary moisture is supplied by irrigating canals, which have already been constructed to a great extent. Vegetables reach an enormous size, and fruits of all kinds grow with remarkable luxuriance. Mining, however, is the principal industry, and the mineral deposits are among the richest in America. The principal varieties of *timber* are pine, hemlock, spruce, cedar, fir, cottonwood, box-elder, and quaking aspen. The sides of the mountain below the timber-line and the foot-hills are covered with forests of pine, larch, and aspen, which afford valuable timber and fuel. The *wild animals* are the bear, cougar, wolf, buffalo, elk, deer, antelope, mountain-sheep, lynx, wild-cat, badger, hare, fox, mink, beaver, and prairie-dog, the last resembling the fox-squirrel. Of game-birds there are the wild turkey, mountain-grouse, sage-hen, prairie-chicken, ducks, geese, swans, ptarmigan, etc.

The **climate** of Colorado is remarkably equable and healthy. The winters are mild, the days resembling those of a northern summer; and the summers are cool and bracing. Hot, sultry nights are unknown in summer, and in winter they are generally very cold. On the plains the temperature averages from 50° to 55°. At Denver the mean temperature for each month and the amount of rain and melted snow have been recorded as follows:

MONTHS.	TEMPERATURE.			Rain and Melted Snow, Inches.
	Maximum.	Minimum.	Mean.	
January	60°	5°	29.4°	1.15
February	64	1	35.5	1.70
March	67	—8	32.7	.70
April	80	16	48.1	2.80
May	86	40	56.1	.35
June	94	48	68.2	.52
July	98	53	74.2	.51
August	97	45	64.8	.12
September	89	40	60.1	2.85
October	83	27	47.8	.68
November	68	20	41.8	.54
December	60	—18	23	.73
Year			48.5	12.65

The average temperature for 1871 was 54.1°; rainfall, 12.35 inches. For 1872 the average temperature was 49.8°; rainfall, 18.77 inches. Among the foot-hills the average temperature is from 45° to 50°; in the mountains it is from 40° to 45°. On the summits of the mountain-ranges, and in the highest parks, the cold is often extreme; but in the mountain-valleys and foot-hills the thermometer seldom falls below zero, and in midwinter there is much delightful weather. The greatest extremes of cold and the most severe storms occur in November and December. In the mountains the greatest fall of snow occurs in September, October, and April; except on and near the summits, where the fall is considerable, it does not remain long on the ground. On the plains in the latitude of Denver, the fall of snow never exceeds 10 or 12 inches, and seldom remains longer than 24 hours. In the southern portion of the plains there is little snow, and the winters are extremely mild. There is no rainy season in Colorado. On the plains the rain generally falls in the spring and early summer, scarcely any falling in autumn or winter. In the mountains rains are frequent in the summer and autumn, but rain-storms of long duration are unknown. Heavy wind-storms are common in all parts of the State. The extreme rarity of cloudy weather and of mists and fogs is remarkable. The atmosphere is wonderfully clear and invigorating, and remarkably free from humidity. These characteristics of climate, together with the great altitude (4,000 to 10,000 feet), and the beautiful scenery, have made Colorado a popular resort for persons afflicted with throat and lung diseases. Consumptives who go there during the earlier stages of the disease are always benefited, and usually cured; but when hæmorrhages have supervened, the extreme thinness and dryness of the atmosphere are likely to aggravate them. Asthmatics can live comfortably in any part of the State; and rheumatism and gout are materially alleviated. Hay fever also is invariably cured.

Denver.

Denver, the capital and largest city of Colorado, is situated on the south bank of the South Platte River, at the junction of Cherry Creek, 15 miles from the eastern base of the Rocky Mountains, 922 miles from St. Louis *via* the Missouri Pacific and Kansas Pacific R. R., and 991 miles *via* the Atchison, Topeka & Santa Fé R. R., *via* Pueblo and Colorado Springs. It occupies a series of plateaus, facing the mountains, and commanding a grand and beautiful view. Through the clear mountain atmosphere may be seen Pike's and Long's Peaks, and the snow-capped range extending more than 200 miles. The city is the commercial centre of Colorado, and is compactly built, chiefly of brick manufactured in the vicinity. Its trade is very large, and five railroads radiate from it, which, with their stage connections, afford access to all parts of the State. There are upward of 30 hotels (of which the principal are the *Windsor*, the *St. James*, the *Markham*, the *Albany*, and *Charprot's*, European plan), numerous commercial buildings, a U. S. Branch Mint, several fine churches and school-houses, an *Opera House*, large manufactories and breweries, and some elegant private residences. The population of the city in 1880 was 35,630, and it is annually visited by a large number of tourists. The details as to its climate have been previously given. During the summer a residence in the suburbs is preferable to one in the city; but during the winter the invalid will find himself most comfortable in town. Whatever places in Colorado the tourist may wish to visit, Denver will be his natural starting-point.

Colorado Springs and Vicinity.

Colorado Springs (76 miles from Denver *via* the Denver & Rio Grande Narrow-Gauge R. R.) is an important centre for the tourist, being situated in close proximity to various points of interest; but its name is misleading, the Springs being 5 miles distant, and called Manitou. Colorado Springs is a city of 6,000 inhabitants, situated on the plains, with a fine view of the mountains, and with pleasantly shaded streets. *The Antlers* is a good hotel, thronged with guests from early fall till late spring. In no other part of the country is the precipitation of moisture so small as here, and as a winter resort *Colorado Springs* is growing rapidly into favor among those who seek relief from pulmonary troubles. Guides are at hand for the more distant points, and horses, etc., are easily procured.

The Manitou Springs are 5 miles from Colorado Springs, with which they connect by a branch railroad from Colorado Springs depot, and are so much resorted to as to be known as the "Saratoga of Colorado." They are situated among the foot-hills at the base of Pike's Peak, on the beautiful Fontaine Creek. The waters contain sulphur, soda, and iron, and are recommended for their tonic effects in all diseases of which general debility is a feature. Asthmatics and consumptives are generally benefited by a residence at Manitou; the former, always. There are several hotels (the *Mansion*, *Cliff House*, *Manitou House*, and the *Beebe House*), and the adjacent grounds are beautifully laid out and adorned. Within easy walking-distance of the hotel is the picturesque *Ute Pass*, through which the road runs to South Park. A short distance above the mouth of the Pass are *Ute Falls*, where the creek descends in an unbroken sheet over a precipice 50 feet high. In this vicinity is *Williams Cañon*, 15 miles long, with walls of rock rising 600 or 800 feet above a very narrow pass below. Manitou is on the road to **Pike's Peak**, the summit of which is only 11 miles distant, and may be climbed on horseback. This peak stands on the outer edge of the great mountain-range, and the view from its summit is magnificent, embracing many thousand square miles of mountain and plain. Here is a station of the Weather-Signal Bureau, which is occupied winter and summer.

Garden of the Gods is the fanciful title of a little mountain-valley lying 2 miles from Manitou. The road enters it through the "Beautiful Gate," a narrow passage-way between two towering but narrow ledges of cliffs, which is still further narrowed by a rock-pillar, 30 feet high, standing nearly in the centre.

Eroded Sandstones, Monument Park.

The Garden consists of a tract of land less than 500 acres in extent, hemmed in by mountains on the west and north, bordered by ravines on the south, and by Old Red sandstone-cliffs on the east, which shut it in entirely from the plains. Its features are a number of isolated rocks, upheaved into perpendicular positions, some of them rising to a height of 350 feet. The rocks are mainly of a very soft, brilliantly-red sandstone, although several ridges of cliffs are of a white sandstone. The foot-hills in the vicinity are many of them capped by similar upheavals, while all about the main cliff in the valley are numerous separate, spire-like columns. At the entrance to **Glen Eyrie** (1 mile from the Garden, and 3½ miles from Manitou) are similar formations, one of which stands like an immense tower, several hundred feet high, and not more than 7 or 8 feet in thickness. Glen Eyrie is a most picturesque mountain-gorge, closed in on either hand by frowning cliffs, and with a purling mountain-brook traversing it from end to end. Within it is the elegant summer-villa of General Palmer, President of the Denver & Rio Grande R. R., and the natural attractions of the place have been enhanced by art. Up the rugged *Queen's Cañon* is the Devil's Punch-Bowl, and a succession of picturesque rapids and cascades. The road to the Glen from Colorado Springs offers a succession of noble views.

Cheyenne Cañon, 9 miles from Manitou Springs, is a sequestered mountain-gorge, in which are some striking rock-formations and picturesque cascades. A tortuous trail leads from the mouth of the cañon in 3 miles to the first fall, which is 30 feet high, and extremely fine. From the ledge above the fall there is a view of a succession of falls, 6 in all, rising one above another at almost regular intervals, the remotest and highest being several miles away.

Monument Park, perhaps the most visited spot in Colorado, is 9 miles from Manitou Springs, and ¼ mile from Edgerton, a station on the railway above the Springs. The Park is very striking. "It is filled with fantastic groups of eroded sandstone, perhaps the most unique in the Western country, where there are so many evidences of Nature's curious whims If one should imagine a great number of gigantic sugar-loaves, quite irregular in shape, but all showing the tapering form, varying in height from 6 feet to nearly 50, with each loaf capped by a dark, flat stone, not unlike in shape to a college-student's hat, he would have a very clear idea of the columns in Monument Park."

Pueblo and the Boiling Springs.

Pueblo, at the junction of the Atchison, Topeka & Santa Fé R. R., the Denver & New Orleans R. R., and the Denver & Rio Grande R. R. (117 miles from Denver), is situated at the confluence of Arkansas River and Fontaine Creek. It is the centre of a vast and rich agricultural and grazing region, does a very large trade, and has a population of about 4,000. Pueblo enjoys a delightful winter climate, and its accessibility gives it many advantages for such invalids as cannot endure the fatigue of traveling to more remote points. *Las Animas* and *Trinidad* are other cities of Southern Colorado which offer great attractions to health-seekers in winter. They are reached *via* the Atchison, Topeka & Santa Fé R. R., from Pueblo 87 miles east to the former, and 98 south to the latter. Ten miles from Pueblo, near the foot of Pike's Peak, are the **Boiling Springs**, situated at an elevation of 6,350 feet above the sea.

Cañon City lies at the foot of the mountains, 41 miles from Pueblo by a branch of the Denver & Rio Grande R. R. It is a flourishing mining-town, and, besides mines, has in its vicinity coal-deposits, oil-wells, and mineral springs that are prized for their medicinal qualities. A short distance above Cañon City, the Arkansas River makes its exit from the mountains through the *Grand Cañon of the Arkansas*, a wild gorge of inconceivable majesty and grandeur. The site of the town is sheltered by the adjacent hills, and the winter climate is mild and delightful.

Among the features of Southern Colorado is La Veta Pass, by which the Denver & Silverton division of the Denver & Rio Grande R. R. crosses the Sangre di Cristo range. It is about 80 miles southwest of Pueblo, and the scenery amid which the road winds up for 14 miles is of unsurpassed grandeur and magnificence. Other wonders of natural scenery to be seen on this road are the *Los Pinos Cañon*, the *Toltec Gorge*, and the awe-inspiring *Phantom Curve*, where the road hangs over the stream 1,100 feet below. Five miles from South Arkansas are the *Poncha Hot Springs;* near Nathrop are the *Heywood Hot Springs*, and near Buena Vista are the *Cottonwood Hot Springs*. All these are near the line of the Denver & Rio Grande R. R.

Idaho Springs and Georgetown.

Visitors to Idaho Springs take the Colorado branch of the Union Pacific R. R. at Denver and travel to the Springs or to Georgetown by rail. The scenery along the route is exceedingly grand and picturesque. **Idaho Springs** (*Beebe House*) is beautifully situated in a lovely valley nestling among lofty mountain-ranges, at an elevation of 7,800 feet above the sea. The air is remarkably dry, pure, and invigorating, and the surrounding scenery is charming; but the chief attraction of the place is its hot and cold mineral springs. The waters contain soda, magnesia, iron, and lime, and have fine tonic properties. They are used chiefly for bathing, and there are extensive bathing establishments and swimming-baths, in which baths may be had at the natural heat of the water as it bubbles from the ground, or at a lower temperature. During the summer the little town is thronged with tourists, and its sheltered position makes it a desirable resort in winter. It is a favorite rendezvous for excursion-parties, and full outfits of carriages, horses, and guides, are here furnished to those desiring to visit Middle Park, the Chicago Lakes, Green Lake, the Old Chief, or the mining-regions. The most popular excursions are to *Fall River* (2½ miles), and to the lofty-lying *Chicago Lakes* (15 miles by trail). Invalids staying at the Springs in winter should be careful to select a residence in a protected situation, and to stay in-doors when the easterly winds are blowing.—Georgetown (the terminus of the Georgetown Branch R. R.) is 12 miles beyond Idaho Springs, is the centre of the silver-mining interests, and is situated on a broad plateau at the mouth of two or three cañons, walled in on three sides by Leavenworth, Republican, and Summit Mountains. It is a place of much commercial activity, and in point of climate resembles Idaho Springs. Many mountaineering tourists make Georgetown their base of operations during the season, and complete outfits and guides may easily be procured. The distance to the Hot Springs in Middle Park is 45 miles. Georgetown is also the starting-point for *Gray's Peak*, which every one who can should ascend. It is only 15 miles to the summit (14,200 feet above the sea), and the trip there and back can be made in a day. The mountain-view from Gray's Peak, except that it lacks the picturesqueness of the glaciers, has all the beauties of Alpine scenery. The best hotels at Georgetown are the *De Paris Hotel*, *Webb's Hotel*, and **Barton House**.

North Park, Middle Park, and the Hot Springs.

As we have already remarked in our general description of the State, the four great Natural Parks are perhaps the most characteristic feature of Colorado. **North Park**, lying in the extreme northern part of the State, has been less explored and settled than the rest, owing to its remote situation and colder climate. It offers, for these reasons, the greatest attractions for the sportsman and adventurer. The park embraces an area of about 2,500 square miles, and has an elevation of about 8,000 feet above the sea. Recent discoveries of gold and silver are attracting attention. It is best reached by stage from Fort Collins on the Colorado Central R. R., to *Mason City* (80 miles) and *Tyner* (125 miles). **Middle Park** lies directly south of North Park, from which it is separated by one of the cross-chains of the great mountain labyrinth. The snow-range, or continental divide, sweeps around on its eastern side, and it is completely encircled by majestic mountains. Long's Peak, Gray's Peak, and Mount Lincoln, from 13,000 to 14,500 feet high, stand sentinels around it. It embraces an area of about 3,000 square miles, extending about 65 miles north and south and 45 miles east and west, and is about 7,500 feet above the sea. It is drained by Blue River and the head-waters of Grand River, flowing westward to the Colorado. The portions of the park not covered by forest expand into broad, open meadows, the grasses of which are interspersed with wild flowers of every hue. There is game in abundance, including deer, mountain-sheep, elk, bears, and antelopes, and the waters teem with fish. The climate, notwithstanding the great elevation, is remarkably mild and equable, with cool nights in summer and warm days in winter. No one, of course, should attempt to winter here who cannot safely be cut off from many of the comforts and conveniences of life; but those who are able and willing to "rough it" will hardly find a place where they can do so under more favorable conditions.

The usual objective point of tourists who go to the Middle Park is **Hot Sulphur Springs**, which may be reached from Georgetown by the Berthoud Pass (45 miles); from Central City by the James's Peak trail (60 miles); and from South Boulder. The Colorado Company's large and comfortable four-horse stages leave the Barton House, Georgetown, every other day for the Springs. A pleasant way of making the journey is on horseback *via* the first-mentioned route. The Springs are situated on a tributary of Grand River, about 12 miles from the southern boundery of the park. Describing a visit to them in his "Switzerland of America," Mr. Samuel Bowles says: "On the hill-side, 50 feet above the Grand River, and a dozen rods away, these hot, sulphurous waters bubble up at three or four different places within a few feet, and, coming together into one stream, flow over an abrupt bank, say a dozen feet high, into a little circular pool or basin below. Thence the waters scatter off into the river. But the pool and the fall unite to make a charming natural bathing-place. You are provided with a hot sitz bath and douche together. The stream that pours over the precipice into the pool is about as large as would flow out of a full water-pail turned over, making a stream 3 to 5 inches in diameter. The water is so hot that you cannot at first bear your hand in it, being 110° Fahrenheit in temperature, and the blow of the falling water, and its almost scalding stream, send the bather shrieking out, on his first touch of them; but with light experiments—first an arm, then a leg, and next a shoulder—he gradually gets accustomed to both heat and fall, and can stand directly under without flinching; and then he has such a bath as he can find nowhere else in the world. The invigorating effects are wonderful. There is no lassitude or chill from it, as is usually experienced from an ordinary hot bath elsewhere. Though the water be 110° warm, and the air 30° to 40° cold, the shock of the fall is such a tonic, and the atmosphere, strictly, so dry and inspiring, that no reaction, no unfavorable effects are felt, even by feeble persons, in coming from one into the other. The first thing in the morning, the last at night, did we renew our trial of this hot bath during our brief stay in the neighborhood, and the old grew young, and the young joyous and rampant, from the experience." These baths have been found highly beneficial in cases of rheumatism, neuralgia, chronic diseases of the skin, and general debility. The accommodations for invalids are not first rate as yet, but sufficient, perhaps, for those who ought to venture upon the journey thither over the mountains. A small town is gradually growing up in the vicinity.

One of the pleasantest excursions in Middle Park is up the valley, 27 miles from the Springs, by a good road to *Grand Lake*, the source of the main fork of Grand River. The lake nestles close to the base of the mountains, precipitous cliffs hang frowning over its waters on three sides, tall pines come almost down to the white sand-beach, and its translucent depths are thronged with trout and other fish.

South Park and San Luis Park.

South Park, the best known and most beautiful of all the parks, lies next below Middle Park, from which it is separated by a branch of the Park range. It is 60 miles long and 30 wide, with an area of about 2,200 square miles, and, like the Middle Park, is surrounded on all sides by gigantic ranges of mountains, whose culminating crests tower above the region of perpetual snow. The maximum elevation of the park above the sea is 10,000 feet, while the average elevation is about 9,000 feet, and nearly all the land which it contains is well adapted to agriculture. The streams, which are supplied by melting snows from the surrounding mountains, are tributaries of the South Platte, and flow eastwardly through the park to the plains. The climate of the South Park is milder than that of either North or Middle Park, and its greater accessibility gives it peculiar advantages for such tourists and invalids as cannot endure much fatigue. *Fairplay* is the chief town of the region, and the best centre for excursions. The Park is traversed from north to south by the South Park Division of the Union Pacific R. R., which runs from Denver to Leadville, taking Morrison, Como, Fairplay, and Breckenridge *en route*. Portions of the scenery along this line are of incomparable grandeur and beauty. The visitor to Fairplay in summer should not fail to ascend *Mount Lincoln*, which is the highest in Colorado (14,296 ft.), and which affords a view that Professor Whitney declares to be unequaled by any in Switzerland for its reach or the magnificence of the included heights. The ascent may be made nearly all the way by wagon or carriage. The above-mentioned railroad runs southwest through South Park from Denver to *Leadville*, the great mining centre. Distance, 172 miles.

San Luis Park is larger than the other three combined, embracing an area of nearly 18,000 square miles—about twice the size of New Hampshire. It lies south of South Park, from which it is separated by the main range, which forms its northern and eastern boundary, while its western boundary is formed by the Sierra San Juan. It is watered by 35 streams descending from the encircling snow-crests. Nineteen of these streams flow into *San Luis Lake*, a beautiful sheet of water near the centre of the park, and the others discharge their waters into the Rio del Norte, in its course to the Gulf of Mexico. On the flanks of the great mountains dense forests of pine, spruce, fir, aspen, hemlock, oak, cedar, and piñon, alternate with broad, natural meadows, producing a luxuriant growth of nutritious grasses, upon which cattle subsist throughout the year, without any other food, and requiring no shelter. The highest elevation in the park does not exceed 7,000 feet above the sea, and this, together with its southern and sheltered location, gives it a wonderfully mild, genial, and equable climate. Thermal springs abound here, as in other parts of Colorado. The Denver & Silverton branch of the Denver & Rio Grande R. R. has rendered this vast and attractive region quite accessible.

[For further particulars concerning Colorado, especially the mountain ascents and scenery, *see* APPLETONS' HAND-BOOK OF AMERICAN SUMMER RESORTS.]

CALIFORNIA RESORTS.

The State of California extends along the Pacific coast of the United States, between lat. 32° 20' and 42° north, and lon. 114° 20' and 124° 25' west. Its outline is very irregular. Its general direction lengthwise is northwest and southeast, and a line drawn through its centre, following the curves of its eastern and western boundaries, would measure about 770 miles. The greatest breadth is about 330 miles, least breadth 150 miles, average about 230 miles. In size it is the second state in the Union, its area being 188,981 square miles, which is exceeded only by Texas; its population in 1870 was 560,247. The most striking feature in the physical geography of California is the existence of the two great ranges of mountains running northwest and southeast, and generally parallel, called the Sierra Nevada (snow range) and the Coast Range. The former is by far the more lofty and rugged of the two, its summit being generally above the region of perpetual snow, and having but few, and those very elevated, passes. In California it is 450 miles long and 80 miles wide, with an altitude varying from 5,000 to 15,000 feet above the sea. The sides of the mountains to a height of about 2,500 feet are covered with oak, manzanita, and nut-pine, above which, to a height of 8,000 feet, dense forests of coniferous trees appear, which are succeeded by naked granite and snow. From its western slope it sends off numerous spurs into the interior valley; and among these lies the great gold region discovered in 1848. The Coast Range, as its name indicates, runs along the coast, giving it a dangerous and forbidding rock-bound character. This range averages from 2,000 to 4,000 feet in height, and is divided in its length by long, narrow valleys: the Los Angeles; Salinas, Santa Clara, Sonoma, Napa, and others, and also by the Bay of San Francisco. The breadth of the coast mountains (from the Pacific to the great valley of the Sacramento and San Joaquin) does not exceed 40 miles in most parts of the entire length of the State. The mountains of this range are clothed throughout with luxuriant forests, and contain a great variety of minerals, of which some of the most valuable are found in abundance. Between the Coast Range and the ocean occur numerous minor ranges and isolated hills, frequently approaching the water's edge, and enclosing a succession of the most salubrious, beautiful, and fertile valleys. To the north, the Pacific is still more broken with low hills and mountains. The interlocking spurs of the Coast Range and Sierra Nevada cover the whole northern end of the State, and give it a very broken and rugged character. Between the Sierra Nevada and the Coast Range lies the great basin bearing the double name of the Sacramento and San Joaquin Valleys, although really but one geographical formation. This extends north and south about 400 miles, with an average breadth of from 50 to 60 miles, and presents evidences of having once been the bed of a vast lake. It is drained from the north by the Sacramento River, and from the south by the San Joaquin, which, after meeting and uniting in the centre of the basin, break through the Coast Range to the Pacific. Along the rivers the valleys are generally low and level, and extremely fertile, rising into undulating slopes and low hills as the mountains are approached on either side. At the northern end, between lat. 40° and 42°, is a high table-land or plateau, about 120 miles long, and 5,000 feet above the sea, lying between the main chain of the Sierra Nevada and a branch which extends northwest to Mount Shasta. This plateau is an independent basin; its waters do not leave it, but flow into a few lakes where they are absorbed in the sands. The great basin of Utah and the Colorado Desert, in the southeastern portion of the State, are barren and sterile tracts of land, with a sandy soil and scanty vegetation. The Sacramento and the San Joaquin are the most important rivers of California, and the only lakes worth mentioning are Donner Lake and Lake Tahoe, which lie together near the eastern boundary.

Its vast mineral wealth has hitherto attracted most attention to California; but it is no less remarkable for its vegetable productions. The soil of the valleys, both on the coast and in the interior, is generally fertile, consisting of a gravelly clay with a rich sandy loam. All the fruits and cereals of the temperate zone are produced in abundance throughout the State; while in the southern districts nearly all the most valuable products of the tropics are cultivated with success. In many of the southern counties two crops are taken annually from the same field. The production of fruits is unparalleled both in variety and amount, and includes apples, apricots, cherries, figs, grapes, lemons, oranges, plums, pears, peaches, nectarines, olives, pomegranates, pineapples, prunes, quinces, bananas, limes, citrons, raspberries, strawberries, blackberries, gooseberries, currants, raisins, almonds, walnuts, chestnuts, etc. Fruits generally attain a much larger size than in the Eastern States, and are brought to maturity with very little care. California is widely celebrated for

A California Vineyard.

its production of grapes and wines. The grape region extends from the southern boundary about 600 miles northerly, with an average breadth of about 100 miles, and includes three distinct wine-districts: the southern, or Los Angeles, making port and other sweet wines, together with some white wines; the Coast Range, producing white and red acid wines, hock, sauterne, claret, etc.; and the foot-hills of the Sierra Nevada, making dry wines of excellent quality, sherry, madeira, teneriffe, etc. Next to Australia, California is regarded as the best country in the world for sheep-raising; no shelter is needed for the flock, while the fleeces are remarkably heavy, and of superior quality. In the San Joaquin Valley and on the south coast are extensive ranges where large herds of cattle run almost wild, the animals being branded to indicate ownership.

The **climate** of California varies greatly in different parts, irrespective of the great range of latitude (9¼°) through which the State extends. It differs widely from that of the Atlantic slope in the same latitudes, and probably from that of any other country in the world. Properly speaking, California has several climates: the basin of the Sacramento and San Joaquin valleys having one; the western slope of the Coast Range north of lat. 35° another; and that portion of the State south of lat. 35° still another. The climate west of the Coast Range is different from that east of the same range, which is less than 60 miles in width. At San Francisco the mercury seldom rises above 80° in the dry, or falls below 40° in the wet season; the mean annual temperature is 56°, and the mercury seldom, if ever,

6

remains at the freezing-point 24 hours together. Snow very rarely falls there, and the winters bear a strong resemblance to the Indian summers of the Mississippi Valley. It is doubtful if any other country in the world has such warm winters and such cool summers as California; the mean temperature of the coldest month being only about 10° lower than that of the highest. The coolness of the summer nights is attributed to the extreme clearness of the atmosphere favoring radiation; and the warmth of winter to the influence of the great Japan Current, which performs the same functions in the Pacific as the Gulf Stream does in the Atlantic Ocean. The wind blows for a part of each day from the north and northwest along the coast nearly the whole year. During 8 months of the year the prevailing wind in San Francisco is southwest. This wind commences pouring through the Golden Gate toward noon, and increases in violence and chilliness till late at night. Heavy fogs occur during the night in the months of June, July, and August, but are of rare occurrence in winter, when the winds are not so strong. The numerous sheltered valleys near the coast are comparatively free from winds and fogs, and have a delicious and equable climate. In the interior the extremes are much greater, the mercury in the Sacramento Valley often rising in summer to 110° and 112°; but, owing to the extreme dryness of the atmosphere, this great heat is much less prostrating in its effects than even a considerably lower temperature on the Atlantic slope, and the nights are never so hot as to prevent sleep. In the Sacramento and San Joaquin basin the mean temperature of the winter is about 4° below that of the coast, and of the summer from 20° to 30° above. The greater heat of the summer is supposed to result from the absence of the ocean-breezes and fogs, and the cold of winter from the proximity of the snow-capped Sierra Nevada. Southern California is said to possess a better climate than Italy. South of San Francisco, and in the San Joaquin valley, frost is rarely known. Roses bloom throughout the winter, and many trees retain their foliage green the year round. The air, peculiarly *warm* and *dry*, is wonderfully healthful, and highly favorable to consumptives and persons subject to diseases of the throat. For this reason, San Diego, Santa Barbara, San Bernardino, Stockton, Visalia, and other places to be described further along, have become popular winter-resorts for invalids; and many cures, even of those in the last stages of consumption, have been recorded. The mean temperature for the year, and for the seasons, at various localities, is shown in the following statement:

PLACES.	Spring.	Summer.	Autumn.	Winter.	Year.
San Francisco	56.5°	60°	59°	51°	56.6°
Sacramento	56	69.5	61	46.5	58
Monterey	54	59	57	51	55.5
Santa Barbara	60.46	69.58	65.9	58.33	60.2
San Diego	60	71	64.5	52.5	62
Fort Yuma	72	90	75.5	57	73.5
Humboldt Bay	52	57.5	53	43.5	51.5

California has a rainy and a dry season, the former nearly corresponding to the winter, and the latter to the summer of the Atlantic region. The rains begin at the north early in autumn, but do not fall in the latitude of San Francisco in any appreciable quantity until about the middle of December, which is the month of greatest rain. The rainy season terminates toward the end of May. June, July, and August are dry, only 2.5 inches of rain having fallen in these months collectively in 17 years. It has been estimated that there are on an average 220 perfectly clear days in a year, 85 more or less cloudy, and 60 rainy. The average fall, in inches, for the seasons and the year, is as follows:

PLACES.	Spring.	Summer.	Autumn.	Winter.	Year.
San Francisco	6.64	.13	3.31	11.33	21.41
Sacramento	7.01	.00	2.61	12.11	21.73
Humboldt Bay	13.51	1.18	4.87	15.03	34.56
Fort Yuma	0.27	1.30	0.86	0.72	3.15
San Diego	2.74	0.55	1.24	5.90	10.43

Snow is very rare on the coast and in the valleys, and never remains for many days. A marked phenomenon of the climate is the comparative absence of thunder and lightning. During autumn many of the rivers sink in the sand soon after leaving the mountains in which they rise; the plains and hills are baked hard to the depth of many inches; and the grass and herbage, except near springs and in swampy ground, are dried up and burned as brown as the earth they grow upon. The climate is remarkably adverse to epidemic diseases, and California, as a whole, is one of the healthiest countries in the world.

San Francisco.

San Francisco is not considered a desirable residence for invalids, because of the prevalence of winds and fogs and its liability to sudden variations of temperature; but, whatever may be the ultimate destination of the tourist, this is likely to be his first resting-place and starting-point; and, as it is one of the most interesting cities in the United States, it is well worth a visit. Chicago, as being the great centre to which all principal railways from the east and south converge, may be regarded as the most important distributing point of Pacific coast travel. The journey from New York to San Francisco (3,378 miles) requires about 6 days. The fare, unlimited, is $94.90; limited, $80.50. Some invalids, however, find this journey very trying, and these should either break it at several points, or—better still—make the steamer-voyage from New York to San Francisco *via* Panama. The elegant steamers of the Pacific Mail Steamship Co. make the voyage in 15 days, with a railway journey of only 47 miles. Fare, $138, including stateroom and meals. The city of San Francisco is situated at the north end of a peninsula which is 30 miles long and 6 miles across at the city, and separates San Francisco Bay from the

City Hall, San Francisco.

Pacific Ocean. It stands on the eastern or inner slope of the peninsula, and at the base of high hills, the surface being very irregular. The business streets are built up densely, but beyond that the houses are scattered at considerable intervals, and the settled part of the city may be said to cover an area of 9 square miles. Of the hotels, the principal are the *Palace Hotel*, the largest and finest in the world; the *Baldwin House;* the *Grand Hotel;* the *Occidental;* the *Lick House;* and the *Russ House.* These hotels all rank among the best in the land. Rates, from $2 to $5 a day. The leading business streets are *Montgomery, Pine, Market, Battery,* and *Sanson. Kearney, Montgomery,* and *Mitchell* are the fashionable streets. The public buildings are the new *City Hall*, in process of erection in Yerba Buena Park, the *Custom-House*, the *U. S. Branch Mint*, the *U. S. Appraiser's Store*, the *Stock Ex-*

change, the *Merchants' Exchange*, and the building of the *Mercantile Library Association*. The *California Theatre*, the *Grand Opera House*, *Baldwin's Academy of Music*, *Woodward's Gardens*, and the Chinese theatres are the principal places of amusement; and the finest church edifices are *St. Ignatius's*, *St. Patrick's*, *Trinity*, *Grace*, *First Congregational*, the *First Unitarian*, and the synagogue of *Emanu-El*. The favorite drives are to the *Cliff House*, situated on the sea-shore, 6 miles from the city, and through *Golden Gate Park*. Across the bay at Alameda, Oakland, and Saucelito, are some large and beautiful public gardens.

Santa Barbara.

Santa Barbara, the best known and most frequented of the California health-resorts, lies in a sheltered nook of the shore of the Pacific, 275 miles S. S. E. of San Francisco (from which it is reached by steamer). Many of its climatic advantages are due to its peculiar situation. "Upon referring to a map of California," says a recent visitor, "the reader will see that, at Point Conception, the coast (previously running nearly north and south) makes a sharp and sudden turn to the east, and that it again turns, farther on, to the southward; also, that a range or succession of ranges of mountains, gradually gaining in altitude as they recede from the ocean, follows the general line. Between this range, which shuts off the force of the cold northwest winds which prevail upon the upper part of the California coast, and the sea, there lies that semi-tropical region that has of late years become noted as a place of refuge from Northern winters. In the midst of that region is Santa Barbara. The approach to it from the north and by sea is very pleasing, and disposes one pleasantly toward the town before it comes into view. The land terminates in abrupt cliffs, from 40 to 60 feet high, and at their bases there are long, smooth beaches, gently washed by the sea. From their tops the land recedes in low undulations, rich in pasturage, and the view terminates at the crests of high mountains about 20 miles farther inland. One perceives his approach to a settlement in the gradually increasing number of houses and farm-lands along the coast. Some of these houses are very fine, having balconies, broad piazzas, large gardens and groves, and the cultivated ground seems particularly rich and productive. Several hours before approaching this spot the traveler feels a very sensible change for the better in the temperature. Before turning Point Conception he shuddered with the cold, but now he is pleasantly warm, and he is tempted even to seek the shady side of the boat. . . . A sudden break in the coast-line discloses the town, lying upon a gently-rising plain facing almost south. It seems to be nearly encircled, first by low foot-hills, and then by lofty mountains in the rear. The plain is perhaps 3 square miles in extent, and over the greater part the town is distributed."

The town has grown out of an old Spanish mission which was founded in 1780, and which gradually drew around it the native cultivators of the adjacent lands. Its present population is about 6,000, half of whom are Americans, that have come here in search of health from the New England and Middle States; and, as most of these latter belong to what are called the "better classes," the society of the place is exceptionally pleasant and refined. There are several hotels (of which the best are the *Arlington* and the *Occidental*), many boarding-houses, banks, a college, good public schools, daily and weekly newspapers, and numerous churches. The town contains a "Spanish quarter" and a "Chinese quarter," both of which will prove interesting to strangers by their tumble-down picturesqueness; but the new or American part of the town, and especially the suburbs, are handsomely built. "Most of the cottages are really charming, and, if some of them are a little overdone in ornamentation, the trouble is balanced by the real beauty which Nature affords in the gardens. Every plot of ground, no matter how small, has its row of orange-trees, its exotics, and its bed of native perennials. Roses abound summer and winter. The verbena-beds are cut down like grass thrice yearly, and spring up again stronger

---

* All points in Southern California can be conveniently reached from the Middle and Southern States: 1. From Kansas City *via* Atchison, Topeka & Santa Fé R. R., and Southern Pacific, connecting at Florida Point, N. M.; 2. From St. Louis, Memphis, and New Orleans by the system of roads connecting with the Texas & Pacific, which last-named road connects with the Southern Pacific at El Paso, N. M. These lines constitute what is known as the Southern Transcontinental route.

than ever. Sago, palm, Japanese persimmon, cacti of the rarest and most curious sort, grow freely, and so do the calla, the Spanish bayonet, and the great white-plumed pampas-grass. Vines of every sort flourish luxuriantly. Heliotrope climbs 20 feet high. The two predominating native trees of the place are the live-oak and the sycamore. But the people plant a little shoot of the Australian blue-gum (*Eucalyptus globulus*), and in two years it becomes a shade-tree 15 or 20 feet high. One of these trees, having a graceful, green-brown foliage, will rise in five years above the surrounding verdure like a Lombardy poplar, and the rows which in Santa Barbara meet the eye everywhere are very marvels of rapid and healthy growth. A little apart from the town, and in all directions, there are large farms and ranches hundreds of acres in extent, and upon these are dwellings about as rich and tasteful as one sees in the suburbs of Boston. They are surrounded by a hundred umbrageous retreats, and are in all respects the results of the nicest taste."

The climate of Santa Barbara is extremely equable and mild. By reference to the table on page 82, it will be seen that the mean temperature for the year is $60.2°$; for the summer, $69.58°$; and for the winter, $53.33°$. The variations are very slight, the thermometer rarely rising above $80°$ in summer, and as rarely sinking to $40°$ in winter. The coldest day recorded during a period of 9 years was $42°$; and there are none of those sharp and sudden changes of temperature that are so trying to invalids. The air, too, is not only warm, but remarkably *dry*. The rainfall averages but 12 or 15 inches annually, and the days are nearly always brilliantly bright and sunny. The only serious drawback is the fogs which sometimes come in from the sea. Between May and September they average, perhaps, two a week; but they disperse at nine in the morning, and the succeeding weather is delightful. Mr. Nordhoff expresses the opinion that there were not "five days, either in Santa Barbara or San Diego, in December, January, and February of this year (1871), in which the tenderest invalid could not pass the greater part of the day out-of-doors with pleasure and profit. In Santa Barbara there were not a dozen days during the whole winter in which a baby I know did not play on the sea-beach. But in the evening you will sit by a wood-fire (mostly with the doors and windows open), and at night you sleep under blankets very comfortably." After reaching Santa Barbara it is necessary for the more delicate invalids to exercise some care in the selection of a residence. The air of the plateau near the *Old Mission* is thought to be drier than in the town itself, and in the valley back of the encircling foot-hills it is drier still. Sometimes a change of half a mile will make all the difference between discomfort and serene ease. Mr. Nordhoff recommends that persons who are very sensitive to damp should find lodgings in the upper part of the town, or in what is called *Montecito* (a little mountain), a suburb 2 or 3 miles distant, and sheltered from the sea-breeze by an intervening range of low hills. Near Montecito are the *Hot Sulphur Springs*, some containing sulphur and sulphureted hydrogen, and others containing iron, alumina, and potash. They are said to cure rheumatism and various diseases of the skin, but the waters should not be used by invalids except under the advice of a local physician.

The chief recreation at Santa Barbara is horseback-riding. Horses can be bought for from $20 to $50, and it costs very little to keep them. There are numberless attractive roads leading out in every direction, and a fine ocean-beach, on which the Spanish Californians in old times raced their horses. Besides the steamer-route, Santa Barbara is reached from San Francisco *via* the Southern Pacific R. R. to Newhall (438 miles), and thence by stage; or by Northern Division of the same road to Soledad, and thence by stage. From the south and east, Newhall may be reached by the Southern Pacific, and thence Santa Barbara by stage.

San Diego and Los Angeles.

San **Diego**, another favorite resort of health seekers, is the capital of San Diego Co., and lies on the northeast shore of a bay of the same name, about 460 miles southeast of San Francisco, and 15 miles north of the Mexican border (in lat. $32°\ 44'\ 41''$). Its harbor is, next to that of San Francisco, the best on the California coast, being well protected, capacious, and having a good depth of water. The town is more than 100 years old, having been founded by the Roman Catholic missionaries in 1769. Its growth during the last few years has been rapid, and it now has seven churches, two academies, three daily and two weekly newspapers, and good hotels and boarding-houses. Across the bay, 1½ mile distant, is Coronado Beach, a new resort. The climate of San Diego is remarkably equable. The average rainfall is only 10 inches per annum, and there is never enough at one time to render it muddy. From 1876 to 1885, both years inclusive, covering a period of ten years, and embracing a period of 3,653 days, there were 3,533 days on which the mercury did not rise above 80°, and only 120 days in ten years in which the thermometer marked a higher temperature than 80°. During the same ten years, containing 3,653 days, there were 3,560 days on which the mercury did not fall below 40°. On no day did the mercury remain at 40° more than one or two hours, and this between midnight and daylight; the lowest maximum for any day being 52°— on four of the 3,653 days. There is no fog, as in Santa Barbara and more northern latitudes, and very little moisture in the air. For consumptives and asthmatics, San Diego is probably as helpful a place of residence as any in Europe or America. The pleasantest months are November, December, January, and February. San Diego has been fixed by act of Congress as the western terminus of the Texas & Pacific R. R.; but its present connection with San Francisco is by steamer along the coast, or the Southern Pacific to Los Angeles, thence by the San Diego Division to Santa Ana, and thence by stage or by California Southern R. R. via Colton.

Los Angeles, the largest city in Southern California, is situated on the west bank of Los Angeles River, a small stream, 30 miles above its entrance into the Pacific, and 350 miles S. S. E. of San Francisco. A railroad twenty-two miles long connects it with Wilmington on the coast, whence it has connection with San Francisco by steamer; and it may also be reached from San Francisco via San Diego Division of the Southern Pacific R. R. (470 miles). From the east and south there is also direct access by the Southern Pacific R. R. The city was settled by the Spaniards in 1780, and was called Pueblo de los Angeles ("town of the angels"), from the excellence of its climate and the beauty of its surroundings. Its present population is about 16,000, and there are many large and imposing structures. It has a large and varied trade with the interior, and contains three banks, a Roman Catholic college, several public schools, a public library, churches of the various denominations, and good hotels (the *Pico House* and the *St. Charles*). In the northwest portion is a hill 60 feet high, commanding a fine view of the city, which lies in a sheltered valley, bounded on the west by low hills, that extend from the Santa Monica Mountains, 40 miles distant, and on the east by the San Gabriel plateau. The climate of Los Angeles is almost as mild as that of San Diego, and some invalids prefer it, because here they escape the winds, which blow all along the coast. The nights, however, are chilly, and it is not considered a desirable residence for persons affected with throat-diseases. Los Angeles is the centre of the orange-growing business of California, and lemons, olives, and other tropical fruits are cultivated in the vicinity.

San Bernardino.

San Bernardino, the most frequented of the inland resorts, lies about 60 miles east of Los Angeles, in a beautiful valley with picturesque mountains on three sides of it. It is reached from Colton on the Southern Pacific R. R. by a short stage-ride of two hours. The town contains about 4,000 inhabitants, two hotels, four churches, an excellent school, and private boarding-houses, where reasonable accommodation can be had. It is supplied with water by artesian wells, and all parts of the town, especially Old San Bernardino, are embowered in fruit and ornamental trees. Fruits of all kinds are grown here, and oranges and lemons are produced in great abundance. The view of Mount San Bernardino, the loftiest peak of the Coast Range, is exceedingly grand. The air of San Bernardino is drier than that of points nearer the coast, and for this reason is preferable for some consumptives. Little rain falls during the year, malaria is unknown, and the climate is a perpetual invitation to an open-air life. Many invalids find a residence in *Old San Bernardino* (which lies higher than the new town), or in *Riverside*, more beneficial than one in the town proper; but the entire valley is remarkably salubrious. About 4 miles distant, near Mount San Bernardino, are some *hot springs*, containing lime, soda, iron, and alumina; their medicinal properties have not been fully ascertained, and the waters should be taken with caution. Horses may be bought at from $20 to $50 each at San Bernardino; their keep costs very little, and many attractive excursions may be made in the vicinity—to the San Gorgonio Pass, the Great Yuma Desert, the San Jacinto tin-mines, or the placer gold-diggings.

The Paso-Robles Hot Springs.

The Paso-Robles mineral springs lie on the line of the old stage-route between Santa Ana and San Diego, and are reached by stage from the former point, which is on the Southern Pacific R. R. Another way of reaching them from San Francisco is *via* steamer to San Luis Obispo, and thence by a pleasant stage-ride of 28 miles. The springs are situated on the great Paso-Robles ranch, and contain sulphuretted hydrogen, carbonic acid, soda, magnesia, potassa, iron, bromine, iodine, alumina, and sulphuric acid. The waters are taken chiefly in the form of baths, at the natural temperature, and are considered among the most valuable in America for rheumatism, gout, and chronic diseases of the skin. There are good accommodations for visitors at the springs, and the climate has the salubrity common to all Southern California.

Sacramento.

Sacramento, the capital of California, and third city in the State in population and importance, lies northeast of San Francisco, 86 miles distant by the California Pacific R. R., and 139 miles by the Central Pacific R. R. It is also reached from San Francisco by the steamers of the California Steam Navigation Company up the

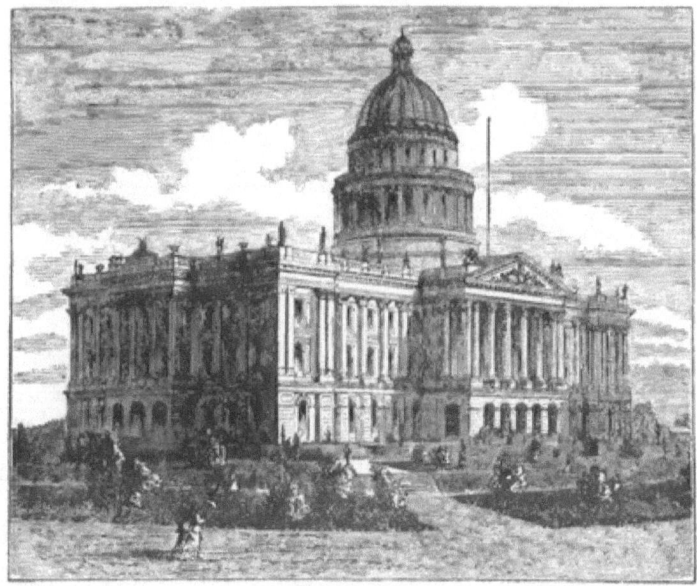

State Capitol.

Sacramento River (117 miles). The city is built in an extensive plain on the east bank of the Sacramento River, immediately south of the mouth of the American River. Its site is very low, having originally been only fifteen feet above low-water mark; and as the river often rises twenty feet, it has been subjected to frequent overflows. The business portion of the city has been artificially raised about eight feet above the original level, and the exposed portions surrounded by a great levee; but in seasons of floods the land for miles around is saturated with moisture, and the air is apt to be damp and penetrating. For these reasons, though the climate of Sacramento is delightfully mild and equable in winter, it is not considered so propitious for invalids as other portions of the State, and is not likely to secure it a reputation as a health-resort. Still, many prefer to remain here instead of going to more remote points, attracted by the social and other advantages of the place; for Sacramento is one of the handsomest cities west of the Rocky Mountains. The streets are straight and wide, and cross each other at right angles; those in the business portion are paved with Nicolson pavement and cobble-stones, and are lighted with gas. The shops and stores are mostly of brick, the dwellings mostly of wood, and surrounded by gardens. Shade-trees are abundant, and a luxuriant growth of flowers and shrubs may be seen in the open air at all seasons of the year. The only important public building is the *State Capitol*, but this is one of the finest structures of the kind in the United States. It is situated almost in the heart of the city, and the grounds cover eighteen blocks, beautifully laid out with trees, shrubs, and flowers. The State Library, in the Capitol, has upward of 35,000 volumes; and the Sacramento Library, in a fine building belonging to the association, about 7,000 volumes. The State Agricultural Society has ample accommodations for the exhibition of stock, and one of the finest race-courses in the world. It holds a fair annually, about the middle of September. There are a number of fine church edifices in the city, excellent hotels, many schools, public and private, charitable institutions, a convent, and vast manufactories and machine-shops. Sacramento is a great railroad and steamboat centre, and connects directly with all parts of the State. On this account it is a favorable temporary stopping-point and headquarters for either tourists or invalids. Leading hotels are the *Capitol House*, *Golden Eagle*, and *Western*.

Stockton and Visalia.

Stockton and Visalia are situated in the great San Joaquin Valley, east of the Coast Range, and are, like San Bernardino, peculiarly favorable to such invalids as are liable to be affected injuriously by even mild sea-air. **Stockton** has a climate very closely resembling that of Naples, but the atmosphere is drier and more bracing, with fewer variations of temperature. It is situated at the head of the San Joaquin Valley, 92 miles from San Francisco, *via* the Central Pacific R. R., and at the head of tide-navigation on the San Joaquin River. It occupies a level site, and is substantially and compactly built, with handsome, wide streets, and public buildings that indicate enterprise and taste. The population at present is about 15,000, and is rapidly increasing. The *Court-House* and *City Hall*, near the centre of the city, is surrounded with choice shade-trees and shrubbery, as are also many of the residences. The business-blocks are principally of brick. The city is lighted with gas, and is supplied with water through pipes from three artesian wells. The State lunatic asylum is located here, and there are twelve churches, several of which are costly structures, and excellent public schools. Of the hotels the *Yosemite House*, the *Mansion*, and the *Grand* are best. The city is surrounded by the most extensive and productive wheat-growing lands in the State, and its business consists chiefly in furnishing supplies to the farmers of the San Joaquin Valley and in the shipment of wheat, wool, and other produce. Stockton may be reached from San Francisco by steamer as well as by rail, and is an excellent starting-point for excursions to the Yosemite Valley, the Big Trees, and other popular resorts.

Visalia lies about 150 miles farther down the San Joaquin Valley than Stockton (a railway connecting the two is lately completed), and has a climate slightly warmer, but equally dry and healing. It is a thriving and well-built town of 3,000 inhabitants, and is situated in the midst of a forest of magnificent oaks, which shelter it from the winds that sometimes sweep over the broad San Joaquin plains. The *Palace Hotel* is of good repute, and there are many private boarding-houses where good board may be had at from $30 to $50 per month. The tropical fruits produce abundantly in the neighborhood, and the surrounding scenery is attractive. There is no better spot in California for persons who are troubled with a tender throat than Visalia.

San José and the Santa Clara Valley.

The Santa Clara Valley lies between the Coast and Santa Cruz Mountains, and is about 100 miles in length; it is watered by the Coyote and Guadalupe Rivers and by artesian wells, and is considered by many to be the most fertile in the world. Vineyards covering hundreds of acres, vast wheat-fields one and two miles in length, stately trees, forests of live-oak, and finely-cultivated farms, are to be seen on every hand; and the vegetation is of tropical luxuriance and beauty. Being protected north and south by mountain-ranges, its climate is wonderfully bland and genial in winter; while, being open to the ocean toward the west, it has all the advantages of the sea-breezes. In the heart of the valley, 40 miles southeast of San Francisco and 8 miles from the head of San Francisco Bay, is the city of **San José**, with a population in 1880 of 12,567. The main portion of the city occupies a gently-rising plateau between the Coyote and Guadalupe Rivers, here 1½ miles apart, with suburbs extending some distance beyond them. It is handsomely laid out, lighted with gas, and well supplied with water. Horse-cars run through the main streets. The principal public buildings are the *Court-House*, a massive Corinthian structure, costing $200,000, with a dome commanding a fine view; the *Jail*, adjoining it, the finest in the State, costing $80,000; the *City Hall;* two *markets*, costing more than $40,000 each; 8 public-school buildings; and 10 churches, of which the largest and most expensive is an unfinished edifice belonging to the Roman Catholics. The city is noted for its educational institutions. Besides the public schools, there are the *College of Notre Dame* (Roman Catholic), a day and boarding school for girls; the *San José Institute*, a day and boarding school for both sexes; the *University of the Pacific* (Methodist), connected with which is a young ladies' seminary; and the *State Normal School*, whose building, erected at a cost of $275,000, is the finest of the kind on the Pacific coast. The *San José Library Association* owns 4,000 volumes. There is an *Opera House*, seating 1,200 persons, and a commodious *Music Hall*. The city has three public parks, containing 2, 8, and 30 acres respectively, and owns a tract of 400 acres in Penitencia Cañon, 7 miles east, reserved for a public park. The surrounding country yields grain and fruits abundantly, and in the vicinity are some of the finest vineyards in California. San José is a favorite excursion-point for San Franciscans, and to the stranger the streets are highly interesting from the strongly-contrasted groups that pass through them. "Here," says a correspondent of the Springfield *Republican*, "we see an American, with his fine broadcloth and silk hat, his light wagon and well-groomed trotter; there, two or three rancheros, with their slouched hats, loose and shabby garments, on rough-coated horses, stained with the mud of a former day; here, a Mexican on a compactly-limbed mustang, with the high peak and broad stirrups of the Mexican saddle (which is the only one in use here), with his big, broad-brimmed hat, his loose, but jaunty jacket, with all the seams of his clothing trimmed with rows of small steel or silver buttons, and heavy spurs. Chinese and negroes abound among the passers-by on foot. There is a street in San José occupied entirely by the French. The houses are unpretending, but very cheerful and pretty, with small grounds a good deal decorated, abundance of flowers, and always a cluster of artichoke-plants in the garden." San José may be reached from San Francisco *via* Central Pacific R. R. (48 miles) or *via* Northern Division of Southern Pacific R. R. (50 miles).

The famous *Almaden Quicksilver Mines* are about 14 miles from San José, and may be reached by a pleasant two hours' ride in a stage-coach. They are well worth a visit. There are many fine drives in the vicinity of San José, notably one to the *Lick Observatory* (in course of erection) on the summit of Mt. Hamilton, 12 miles distant. This mountain is 4,443 feet high, and affords a magnificent view of the Santa Clara valley.

Three miles west of San José is the picturesque village of **Santa Clara**, with a population of about 5,000. Horse-cars connect the two, running along the *Alameda*, a beautiful avenue bordered by fine residences, and rows of superb trees planted by the Jesuit fathers in 1777. Santa Clara contains several fine churches, and is the site of the Santa Clara College (Jesuit), which occupies a number of elegant buildings in an inclosure of about 12 acres. Included in this institution is the Old Mission, founded by the Spanish missionaries in early times, and the orchards planted by them may still be seen. Stages run from the depot at Santa Clara to the Pacific Congress Springs (10 miles S. W.) These waters contain carbonate and sulphate of soda, chloride of sodium, lime, iron, silicate of alumina, and magnesia, and are regarded as a specific for rheumatism.

San Rafael and Monterey.

Near the western shore of San Pablo Bay, about 15 miles from San Francisco (reached by steamer to San Quentin and thence by rail), is the pretty little town of San Rafael. It is sheltered on the north and west by mountains, which protect it from the ocean-winds and fogs that prevail at San Francisco, and is much frequented both in winter and summer. The air is pure and bracing, and, though hardly warm enough for consumptives in advanced stages of the disease, is admirably adapted for such as are in the preliminary stages, and only need a dry and tonic climate inviting to an out-door life. The scenery about San Rafael and in the approaches to it is extremely fine, and horses may be had in the village for the ascent of *Mount Tamalpais* (12 miles distant). Of course, its proximity to San Francisco gives it important advantages for many.—**Monterey** is beautifully situated on the southern extremity of a bay of the same name, which lies 78 miles south of San Francisco by water. Until 1847 this town was the seat of government and principal port on the California coast; but since the rise of San Francisco its commerce and business have dwindled away, and it is now one of the least commercial places in the State. Within the past five or six years, however, it has begun to attract attention as a health-resort; its climate being warm in winter, cool in summer, and dry all the year round. The Southern Pacific R. R. Co. have erected a fine hotel here (the *Hotel del Monte*), and spent a million dollars in other improvements, with the design of making Monterey a great health and pleasure resort. The view of the town from the water is very fine. The green slopes upon which the hotel and houses are built contrast beautifully with the forest of pines which grows upon the ridges beyond. The Rocky Bluffs above the town also afford fine views. Monterey is reached by steamer from San Francisco, or *via* Southern Pacific R. R. to Salinas (118 miles), and thence by a branch road (20 miles). On the north side of Monterey Bay, opposite Monterey, is the town of **Santa Cruz**, which is the principal watering-place of California. Bathing, fishing, and hunting are among the attractions of Santa Cruz; and near by are *Aptos* and *Soquel,* popular seaside resorts.

Pescadero (reached by stage from San Mateo or Redwood City, on the Southern Pacific Railroad) is a thriving town, beautifully situated in a remarkably productive valley, on both sides of Pescadero Creek, near its confluence with the Butano, about a mile from the sea-shore. The new San Francisco Water Company takes its supply from the head of the creek. Near the town is the famous pebble-beach, where agates, opals, jaspers, carnelians, and other siliceous stones, of almost every conceivable variety of color, are found in great abundance, with a natural polish imparted by the action of the waves and the smooth sea-sand. The industrious little town of Pescadero annually makes and exports to San Francisco 175,000 pounds of cheese and 50,000 pounds of butter. The great "Sanitary Cheese," weighing 4,000 pounds, measuring five feet and six inches in diameter, and twenty-two inches thick, manufactured for the benefit of the "Sanitary Fund," 1863, was made in the Pescadero Valley. Pescadero is a favorite resort for San Francisco pleasure-seekers.

Napa City and Calistoga.

Steamers leave San Francisco twice daily for South Vallejo (26 miles), where connection is made with the California Pacific R. R. The route of this railway lies through Napa Valley, which is about 50 miles long, 1 to 6 miles wide, and, in point of cultivation and beauty, second to none on the Pacific coast. Napa City (46 miles from San Francisco) is a thrifty place of about 4,000 inhabitants, and is surrounded by a highly productive agricultural region, rich in fruits of all kinds, and in immense fields of grain that stretch away in every direction. The climate is less mild than that of Southern California, but is equable and salubrious, and is considered highly beneficial for those suffering from general nervous prostration. There are many beautiful drives in the environs of Napa, one of the most attractive of which is that to Santa Rosa, taking in the famous wine-cellars of Sonoma. The *Napa Soda Springs* are situated in the foot-hills, about 5 miles northeast of the town. The water is palatable, and is said to possess valuable medicinal properties, but their precise nature has not been sufficiently ascertained.—**Calistoga** (68 miles from San Francisco), the terminus of the Napa Valley branch of the California Pacific R. R., is a pretty little town, lying in a valley a mile in width, and encircled by hills and mountains covered with oak, pine, maple, ash, and madrona. It is supplied with pure water from a reservoir on the adjacent mountain-side, and there are several bath-houses. The public warm swimming-bath, 40 feet square, is one of the features of the place. The leading hotels are the *Magnolia* and *Cosmopolitan*. The scenery is exceedingly picturesque, the well-cultivated fields, green lawns, sunny slopes, and shaded villas, contrasting pleasantly with the wild grandeur of the rugged mountains. This region is not a desirable residence for consumptives; but those suffering from rheumatic or gouty affections, or skin-diseases, derive much benefit from the mineral springs, which are numerous in the vicinity. The most noted of the springs are *Harbin's* (20 miles north of Calistoga), and the *White Sulphur Springs*. The latter are situated in a deep and picturesque gorge of the mountains, which rise on either side to a height of about 1,000 feet. About 5 miles southeast of Calistoga is the *Petrified Forest*, which is justly regarded as one of the great natural wonders of California. Portions of nearly 100 distinct trees, of great size, prostrate and scattered over a tract 3 or 4 miles in extent, have been found, some on the surface and others projecting from the mountain-side. They are supposed to have been silicified by an eruption of the neighboring Mount St. Helena, which discharged hot alkaline waters containing silica in solution.

The Geyser Springs.

Steamers leave San Francisco twice daily for Donahue (34 miles), where connection is made with the North Pacific R. R. From *Cloverdale*, on this road (90 miles from San Francisco), stages run in 12 miles to the famous Geyser Springs, which are situated in Sonoma County, in a gorge of the Napa Valley, called the "Devil's Cañon," near the Pluton River. The approaches to the springs are very impressive, the scenery being finer, according to Bayard Taylor, than anything in the Lower Alps. The narrow Geyser ravine, which is always filled with vapor, is shut in by steep hills, the sides of which, marked with evidences of volcanic action, are smoking with heat and bare of vegetation. A multitude of springs gush out at the base of these rocks. Hot and cold springs, boiling springs, and quiet springs lie within a few feet of each other. They differ also in color, smell, and taste. Some are clear and transparent, others white, yellow, or red with ochre, while still others are of an inky blackness. The *Steampipe* is an orifice in the hillside, about 8 inches in diameter, from which a volume of steam rises with a continuous roar to a height varying from 50 to 200 feet. In a cavity called the *Witches' Caldron* a mass of black fetid mud is ever bubbling with heat, the vapor from it depositing black flowers of sulphur on the rocks around. Opposite is a boiling alum-spring, very strongly impregnated; and within 12 feet is an intermittent scalding spring, from which issue streams and jets of boiling water. The surface of the ground about the springs, which is too hot to walk upon with thin shoes, is covered with the minerals deposited by the waters, among which are sulphur, sulphate of magnesia, sulphate of aluminum, and various salts of iron. A properly-directed course of these waters is said to afford an almost certain cure for rheumatism, gout, and skin-diseases; but persons suffering from throat or pulmonary affections should not reside in the neighborhood. The Geysers are also reached by daily stages from Calistoga. A good plan is to go by one route and return by the other.

THE LOWER MISSISSIPPI.

There is, perhaps, not a spot in the entire Mississippi Valley, between St. Louis and New Orleans, which offers to the invalid any special attractions as a residence; but a winter-voyage down the river is one of the most delightful of experiences. The traveler who makes such a voyage feels as if he were indeed going "from lands of snows to lands of sun;" and, though he may miss the picturesque and beautiful scenery that distinguishes the Upper Mississippi from St. Paul to the mouth of the Missouri, his eye will be alternately charmed and amazed by the strange panorama that unfolds itself before him from day to day. The dreary solitude, and often the absence of all living objects save the huge alligators, which float past apparently asleep on the drift-wood, and an occasional vulture attracted by its impure prey on the surface of the waters; the trees, with a long and melancholy drapery of pendent moss fluttering in the wind; and the gigantic river, rolling onward the vast volume of its dark and turbid waters through the wilderness, form the leading features of one of the most dismal yet impressive landscapes on which the eye of man ever rested. "The prevailing character of the Lower Mississippi," says a recent

A Bayou of the Mississippi.

traveler, "is that of solemn gloom. I have trodden the passes of Alp and Apennine, yet never felt how awful a thing is Nature, till I was borne on its waters through regions desolate and uninhabitable. Day after day and night after night we continued driving right downward to the south; our vessel, like some huge demon of the wilderness, bearing fire in her bosom, and canopying the eternal forest with the smoke of her nostrils. The effect on my spirits was such as I have never experienced before or since. Conversation became odious, and I passed my time in a sort of dreamy contemplation. At night I ascended to the highest deck, and lay for hours gazing listlessly on the sky, the forests, and the waters, amid silence only broken by the clanging of the engine. The navigation of the Mississippi is not unaccompanied by danger, arising from what are called *planters* and *sawyers*. These are trees firmly fixed in the bottom of the river, by which vessels are in danger of being impaled. The distinction is, that the former stand upright in the water, the latter lie with their points directed down the stream. The bends or flexures of the Mississippi are regular in a degree unknown in any other river. The action of running water, in a vast alluvial plain like that of the basin of the Mississippi, without obstruction from rock or mountain, may be calculated with the utmost precision. Whenever the course of a river diverges in any degree from a right line, it is evident that the current can no longer act with equal force on both its banks. On one side the impulse is diminished, on the other increased. The tendency in these sinuosities, therefore, is manifestly to increase, and the stream which hollows out a portion of one bank, being rejected to the other, the process of curvature is still continued, till its channel presents an almost unvarying succession of salient and retiring angles. In the Mississippi the flexures are so extremely great, that it often happens that the isthmus which divides different portions of the river gives way. A few months before my visit to the South, a remarkable case of this kind had happened, by which forty miles of navigation had been saved. The opening thus formed was called the *new cut*. Even the annual changes which take place in the bed of the Mississippi are very remarkable. Islands spring up and disappear; shoals suddenly present themselves where pilots have been accustomed to deep water; in many places, whole acres are swept away from one bank and added to the other; and the pilot assured me that in every voyage he could perceive fresh changes. Many circumstances contribute to render these changes more rapid in the Mississippi than in any other river. Among these, perhaps the greatest is the vast volume of its waters, acting on alluvial matter peculiarly penetrable. The river, when in flood, spreads over the neighboring country, in which it has formed channels, called *bayous*. The banks thus become so saturated with water, that they can oppose little resistance to the action of the current, which frequently sweeps off large portions of the forest. The immense quantity of drift-wood is another cause of change. Floating logs encounter some obstacle in the river, and become stationary. The mass gradually accumulates; the water, saturated with mud, deposits a sediment, and thus an island is formed, which soon becomes covered with vegetation. Some years ago the Mississippi was surveyed by order of the Government, and its islands, from the confluence of the Missouri to the sea, were numbered. I remember asking the pilot the name of a very beautiful island, and the answer was, "573," the number assigned to it in the hydrographical survey, and the only name by which it was known."

The voyage down the Mississippi may be begun at either Cincinnati or St. Louis; but as we have already described the Upper Mississippi from St. Louis to St. Paul in APPLETONS' HAND-BOOK OF AMERICAN SUMMER RESORTS, we shall, for the purpose of linking on with that, begin our present description at St. Louis. The city of St. **Louis** is one of the oldest and most picturesque in the country, and before leaving it the traveler should, if possible, acquaint himself with its more salient and attractive features. The steamers which ply on the Mississippi between St. Louis and New Orleans are among the largest in American waters; and as about 8 days are consumed in the passage to New Orleans, their commodiousness will be found an important item in the sum of the traveler's enjoyment. Almost immediately after getting out of sight of the wharves and smoke of St. Louis, the steamer enters upon the vast solitudes which one finds so impressive on the Mississippi. Every now and then a stop is made at a small landing, or at the towns and villages that cluster along the banks; and the clamor of lading and unlading causes a momentary excitement that subsides at once as the steamer resumes her course. About 125 miles below St. Louis the mouth of the Ohio River is reached, and a somewhat prolonged stay is made at **Cairo**, a lively little city and railroad centre, built on a low point of land at the junction of the two rivers. There is a fine cut-stone custom-house here, and other handsome public buildings; and vast levees protect it from the inundations to which its position renders it peculiarly liable. Cairo is the southern terminus of the Illinois Central R. R., and is connected by ferry with **Columbus, Ky.**, which lies on the river 18 miles below. Columbus is situated on the southern slope of a high bluff commanding the river for about 5 miles, and at the outbreak of the Civil War was strongly fortified by the

Confederates, who regarded it as the northern key to the mouth of the Mississippi. They collected in the town and its vicinity an army of 30,000 men, but after the fall of Forts Henry and Donelson, in February, 1862, it was promptly evacuated. Just above the town are the *Iron Banks*, extending along the river on the same side for about 2 miles, and so called from their color resembling iron-rust. *Island No.* 10 (51 miles below Columbus) was the scene of a terrific bombardment by the Mississippi River fleet, extending from March 16 to April 17, 1862, in which the Federals were completely successful. The canal which was cut to assist in the investment of the island, and the remains of some of the earthworks, can still be seen in passing the island. Ten miles below, in Missouri, is *New Madrid*, which was captured at the same time as Island No. 10, both places having formed parts of one position, and mutually dependent upon each other. This was the first battle of the war in which the superiority of gunboats to stationary batteries was clearly demonstrated. New Madrid was settled in 1780, and was the scene of a great earthquake in 1811.

From Columbus to Memphis the river skirts the bluffs of the eastern or Kentucky shore, having on its west the broad, alluvial lands of Missouri and Arkansas. A number of small towns dot either bank, and at intervals spots are pointed out which events of the Civil War have rendered interesting. Conspicuous among these is *Fort Pillow* (148 miles below Columbus), situated on the first Chickasaw Bluff. It was evacuated by the Confederates on June 4, 1862; but on April 12, 1864, was the scene of the shameful butchery by the troops under General Forrest, known in history as the Fort Pillow massacre, concerning which the testimony is conflicting, and probably exaggerated, on both sides. Below Fort Pillow a journey of about 100 miles, along desolate and almost uninhabited shores, brings the voyager to **Memphis**, the chief city of Tennessee, and the largest on the Mississippi between St. Louis and New Orleans. It is situated on the fourth Chickasaw Bluff, 420 miles below St. Louis, and 780 above New Orleans, and has a population of 33,593.

Memphis.

The city presents a striking appearance as seen from the water, with its esplanade several hundred feet in width, sweeping along the bluff, and covered with large warehouses. The streets are broad and regular, and lined with handsome buildings; and many of the residences on the avenues leading from the river are surrounded with beautiful lawns. The city extends over 3 square miles. In the centre there is a handsome park, filled with trees, and containing a bust of Andrew Jackson. The principal of the six cemeteries is Elmwood, on the southeast border of the city. Memphis has an immense railroad and steamboat traffic, a vast cotton trade, and numerous manufactures. There are large hotels, two theatres, seating respectively 800 and 1,000 persons, fine churches and charitable institutions, excellent public and private schools, and a library with 9,000 volumes. Memphis was captured by the Federals early in the war (June 6, 1862), and was never after held by the Confederates. The best hotels are the *Peabody Hotel* and *Gastin's*.

A short distance below Memphis the Mississippi turns toward the west, and crosses its valley to meet the waters of the Arkansas and White Rivers. The latter enters the Mississippi 161 miles below Memphis, and the former about 15 miles farther down. The Arkansas River is a large stream 2,000 miles in length, for 800 of which it is navigable by steamers. It rises in the Rocky Mountains, and, next to the Missouri, is the largest tributary of the Mississippi. The town of *Napoleon* lies at its mouth. Near this point commences the great cotton-growing region, and the banks of the river are an almost continuous succession of plantations. Fifty miles below begins the growth of the Spanish moss, which, covering the trees with its dark and sombre drapery, forms one of the most notable features of the river scenery. Having received the waters of the two affluents above mentioned, the Mississippi again crosses its valley to meet the Yazoo near Vicksburg, creating the immense Yazoo reservoir on the east bank, extending from the vicinity of Memphis to Vicksburg, and the valleys and swamps of the Macon and Tensas on the west side. Vicksburg is situated on the Walnut Hills, which extend for about 2 miles along the river, rising to the height of 500 feet, and displaying the finest scenery of the Lower Mississippi. It is a well-built city of 11,814 inhabitants, the largest between New Orleans and Memphis, and about equidistant from both. As at Memphis, the view of the city from the water is in the highest degree picturesque and animated, and the pleasing impression is confirmed by a closer examination of the town. Vicksburg was founded in 1836 by a planter named Vick, members of whose family are still living there. As the chief commercial mart on this portion of the river, it has long been a place of some note, but it is more widely known as the scene of one of the most obstinate and decisive struggles of the Civil War. After the loss successively of Columbus, Memphis, and New Orleans, the Confederates made here their last and most desperate stand for the control of the great river. The place was surrounded by vast fortifications, the hills crowned with batteries, and a large army under General Pemberton placed in it as a garrison. Its capture by General Grant after a protracted siege (July 4, 1863) " broke the backbone of the Confederacy and cut it in twain." Above Vicksburg, at the point where Sherman made his entrance from the " Valley of Death," is the largest national cemetery in the country, containing the remains of 16,000 soldiers.

From Vicksburg to Baton Rouge the river hugs the eastern bluffs, with Mississippi on one side and Louisiana on the other. *Grand Gulf*, in Mississippi, is a pretty little town 60 miles below Vicksburg, lying upon some picturesque hills overhanging the river ; and Natchez, 60 miles nearer New Orleans, is built mostly upon a high bluff, 200 feet above the level of the stream. That portion of the city lying on the narrow strip of land between the foot of the hill and the river is called " Natchez-under-the-Hill," and, though containing some important business-houses, can make no claim to beauty. It communicates by broad and well-graded roads with the upper town, called " Natchez-on-the-Hill," which is beautifully shaded, and contains many handsome residences and other buildings. The streets are regular, lighted with gas, and generally graveled in the roadway. The houses are principally of brick, and the residences are adorned with gardens. The brow of the bluff along the whole front of the city is occupied by a park. The principal buildings are the Court-House, in a public square shaded with trees, the Masonic Temple, the Catholic cathedral, with a spire 128 feet high, the Episcopal church, and the Presbyterian church, with a spire containing a clock. The City Hall and the Market-House are immediately back of the Court-House. In the suburbs there were formerly numerous residences of wealthy planters, expensively furnished, and surrounded with beautiful lawns and gardens; but many of these were destroyed in the Civil War.

Natchez.

On the bluff adjoining the city there is a national cemetery, handsomely laid out and decorated. The climate of Natchez is pleasant and very salubrious; the winters are temperate, though variable, and the summers long and equable. Natchez was founded by D'Iberville, a Frenchman, in 1700, and is replete with historic associations. Here once lived and flourished the noblest tribe of Indians on the continent, and from that tribe it takes its name. Their pathetic story is festooned with the flowers of poetry and romance. Their ceremonies and creed were not unlike those of the Fire-worshipers of Persia. Their priests kept the fire continually burning upon the altar in their Temple of the Sun, and the tradition is, that they got the fire from heaven. Just before the advent of the white man, it is said, the fire accidentally went out, and that was one reason why they became disheartened in their struggles with the pale-faces. The last remnant of the race were still existing a few years ago in Texas, and they still gloried in their paternity. It is probable that the first explorer of the Lower Mississippi River, the unfortunate La Salle, landed at this spot on his downward trip to the sea. It is a disputed point as to where was the location of the first fort. Some say it lay back of the town, while others say it was established at Ellis's Cliffs. In 1713, Bienville established a fort and trading-post at this spot. The second, Fort Rosalie, or rather the broken profile of it, is still visible. It is gradually sinking, by the earth being undermined by subterranean springs, and in a few years not a vestige of it will be left. Any one now standing at the landing can see the different strata of earth distinctly marked, showing the depth of the artificial earthworks.

The present capital of Louisiana, **Baton Rouge**, is pleasantly situated on the last bluff that is seen in descending the Mississippi. The site is 30 to 40 feet above the highest overflow of the river. The bluff rises by a gentle and gradual swell, and the town, as seen from the water, rising regularly and beautifully from the banks, with its singularly-shaped French and Spanish houses, and its queer squares, looks like a finely-painted landscape. From Baton Rouge to New Orleans "the coast," as it is called, is lined with plantations. Every spot susceptible of cultivation is transformed into a beautiful garden, containing specimens of all those choice fruits and flowers which flourish only in tropical climes. From the deck of the steamer the traveler overlooks a kaleidoscopic succession of the most exquisite land and water views; and when, at last, the steamer rounds the great bend of the river, and he sees the "Crescent City" spread out before him, and knows that his long journey is ended, he will probably experience a feeling of regret.

New Orleans.

How to reach.—In the preceding paragraphs is described the method of reaching New Orleans from St. Louis or Cincinnati by steamer down the Mississippi River. From New York direct New Orleans is reached by rail *via* "Great Southern Mail Route" through Washington, Lynchburg, Knoxville, Montgomery, and Mobile (time, 73 hours); or through Washington, Lynchburg, Atlanta, and Mobile (time, 70 hours); also through Cincinnati, Louisville, and Mobile; or through Chattanooga, Meridian, and Mobile. Fare, $32. By steamer from New York every Saturday ("Cromwell's Line" from Pier 9, North River; "Morgan's Line" from Pier 36, North River). Time, 7 days; fare (cabin), $40. From Philadelphia *via* semi-monthly steamers, touching at Havana. Time, 11 days; fare, $60. From Baltimore *via* semi-monthly steamers, touching at Havana and Key West. Time, 8 days; fare, $40. From Louisville by rail, *via* "Louisville & Great Southern R. R.," and from Chicago and St. Louis *via* the southern division of the Illinois Central R. R.

Hotels, Restaurants, and Clubs.—The *St. Charles Hotel*, bounded by St. Charles, Gravier, and Common Streets, is the largest and finest in the city. *Underbanck's Hotel*, in Magazine Street, between Gravier and Natchez, is a large, comfortable, and well-kept house. The *City Hotel*, at the corner of Camp and Common Streets, is much frequented by merchants and planters. The *Hotel Royal*, in St. Louis Street, formerly the St. Louis Hotel, has been reopened. Other hotels are every way good (*Cassidy's*, the *Waverly*, and the *Hôtel des Étrangers*). Good board may be obtained in all parts of the city at rates ranging from $6 to $20 a week, by consulting advertising columns of the morning papers.

Of restaurants, New Orleans is said to have some of the best in America, where is still practised the famous creole *cuisine* of ante-war times. The most noted are *Moreau's*, in Canal Street; *Victor's*, 38 and 40 Bourbon Street; *Pizzini's*, 182 Canal Street; *Antoine's*, 65 St. Louis Street; and *Denechaud's*, 8 Carondelet Street. In the French quarter, *cafés* are to be found in nearly every block.

There are about twenty clubs in the city, prominent among which are the Boston, the Pickwick, the Louisiana, the Harmony, and the Commercial. The *Jockey Club* has a fine house and beautifully decorated and cultivated grounds near the fair-ground. The *Shakespeare Club* gives occasional dramatic entertainments which are always largely and fashionably attended. The privileges of these as well as of the *Social Club* are obtained by introduction by a member.

Location, Climate, and History.—New Orleans, the most important city and commercial metropolis of Louisiana, is situated on both banks (but chiefly on the left) of the Mississippi River, 100 miles above its mouth, in latitude 29° 57′ north and longitude 90° west. The older portion of the city is built within a great bend of the river, from which circumstance it derives its familiar *sobriquet* of the "Crescent City." In the progress of its growth up-stream, it has now so extended itself as to follow long curves in opposite directions, so that the river-front on the left bank presents an outline somewhat resembling the letter S. The statutory limits of the city embrace an area of nearly 150 square miles, but the actual city covers an area of about 41 square miles. It is built on land gently descending from the river toward a marshy tract in the rear, and from 2 to 4 feet below the level of the river at high-water mark, which is prevented from overflowing by a vast embankment of earth, called the Levee. This Levee is 15 feet wide and 14 feet high, is constructed for a great distance along the river-bank, and forms a delightful promenade during the fall and winter months.

The *climate* of New Orleans is more severe in winter than that of corresponding latitudes on the Atlantic coast, owing to the cold north winds; and the variations of temperature are too great and too sudden to entitle it to be considered as propitious for invalids. According to observations taken in 1873, the mean temperature of the year at New Orleans is 67.55°. The mean temperature of the hottest month was 82.40°, and of the coldest month (January), 49.5°. The mercury often falls below the freezing-point, and variations of fifteen degrees in a day are not unusual.

The rainfall is heavy, amounting to 50.+ inches per year, and the low-lying situation of the city—lower than the surface of the river—adds the aggravation of exceptional dampness to its other climatic drawbacks. For these reasons, New Orleans cannot be recommended as a winter residence for those suffering from pulmonary or throat diseases; and consumptives, especially those in advanced stages of the disease, should avoid even a brief stay. In other respects New Orleans is a healthy city, and its winters, in spite of occasional inclemency, are so much more genial than those of our Northern States, that many resort there during the three coldest months, and not a few who are in the "weak lungs" and "general debility" stages of disease are benefited by the change. Numerous visitors from the North are attracted thither by the social and other attractions of the place; for, with the possible exception of New York and San Francisco, New Orleans is the most varied interesting city in the United States.

The site of New Orleans was surveyed in 1717 by De la Tour; it was settled in 1718, but abandoned in consequence of overflows, storms, and sickness; was resettled in 1723, held by the French till 1729, then by the Spanish till 1801, and by the French again till 1803, when, with the province of Louisiana, it was ceded to the United States. It was incorporated as a city in 1804, and in 1868 was made the capital of the State. The most memorable events in the history of New Orleans are the battle of January 8, 1815, in which the British were defeated by Andrew Jackson, and the capture of the city by Admiral Farragut on April 24, 1862. In 1810, seven years after its cession to the United States, the population of New Orleans was 17,243. In 1850 it had increased to 116,375; in 1860, to 168,675; and in 1870, to 191,418. According to the census of 1880 it amounted to 216,140.—In the value of its exports and its entire foreign commerce New Orleans ranks next to New York, though several ports surpass it in the value of imports. Not unfrequently from 1,000 to 1,500 steamers and other vessels may be seen lying at the Levee; and, except in the summer months, its wharves are thronged with hundreds of ships and sailing-craft from all quarters of the globe. New Orleans is the chief cotton-

New Orleans.

mart of the world; and, besides cotton, it sends abroad sugar, rice, tobacco, flour, pork, etc., to the total value in 1883 of $143,812,709. Its imports of coffee, sugar, salt, iron, dry-goods, liquors, etc., amounted in 1882 to $64,607,422. The manufactures of the city are not extensive.

Modes of Conveyance.—The *horse-car* system of New Orleans is perhaps the most complete in the country. Starting from the central avenue—Canal Street—tracks radiate to all parts of the city and suburbs, and passengers are carried to any point within the city limits for 5 cents. *Omnibuses* attend the arrival of trains and steamers, and convey passengers to the hotels, etc. (fare 25 cents). *Carriages* can be found at the stands in front of the St. Charles and other leading hotels (fare $2 an hour; $5 for the forenoon or afternoon.) The best plan for strangers is to hire a suitable conveyance by the hour and discharge at the end of each trip. *Ferries* connect the city with Algiers, Macdonough, and Gretna, on the opposite side of the river.

Streets and Drives.—The streets of New Orleans, in width and general appearance, are second to those of no city of its size. As far back as Claiborne Street those running parallel to the river and to each other present an unbroken line from the lower to the upper limits of the city, a distance of about 12 miles. Those at right angles to them run from the Mississippi toward the lake with more regularity than might be expected from the very sinuous course of the river. Many of the streets are well paved and some are shelled; but many are unpaved and consequently scarcely usable in wet weather, while in dry weather they are intolerably dusty. Some of the finest streets of the city are in this condition. **Canal Street** is the main business thoroughfare and promenade, and contains many fine stores and private residences. It is nearly 200 feet wide, and has a grass-plot, 25 feet wide and bordered with two rows of trees, extending in the centre through its whole length. Claiborne, Rampart, St. Charles, and Esplanade Streets, are similarly embellished. *Royal, Rampart,* and *Esplanade Streets,* are the principal promenades of the French quarter. —The favorite drive is out the *Shell Road* to Lake Pontchartrain, or over a similar road to Carrollton. Either route presents a highly-animated spectacle on Sunday afternoons.

Canal Street.

Public and Prominent Buildings.—New Orleans is not rich in architecture, but there are a few imposing buildings. Chief among these is the **Custom-House**, which, next to the Capitol at Washington, is the largest building in the United States. This noble structure is built of Quincy granite brought from the Massachusetts quarries. Its main front on Canal Street is 334 feet; that on Custom-House Street, 252 feet; on Peters Street, 310 feet; and on Decatur Street, 297 feet. Its height is 82 feet. The Long Room, or chief business apartment, is 116 by 90 feet, and is lighted by 50 windows. The building was begun in 1848, and is not yet entirely finished. The *Post-Office* occupies the basement of the Custom-House, and is one of the most elegant and commodious in the country. The **State-House** has been lately removed to Baton Rouge, 110 miles above. Prior to 1874 the building recently used for the State-House was the St. Louis Hotel, and has been reopened as the *Hotel Royal.* The old dining-hall is one of the most beautiful rooms in the country, and the great circle of the dome is frescoed with allegorical scenes and busts of eminent Americans. The *United States Branch Mint* stands at the corner of Esplanade and Decatur Streets. It is built of brick, stuccoed in imitation of brown-stone, in the Ionic style, and, being 282 feet long, 180 feet deep, and three stories high, presents an imposing appearance. Coining was resumed about two years ago by virtue of act of Congress, and is now extensively carried on. The window, under the front portico of the main building, from which Mumford was hung by order of General Butler, June 7, 1862, is still pointed out. The *City Hall*, at the intersection of St. Charles and Lafayette Streets, is the most artistic of the public buildings of the city. It is of white marble, in the Ionic style, with a wide and high flight of granite steps leading to an elegant portico supported by eight columns. The City Library occupies suitable rooms in this building. The *Court-Houses* are on the right and left of the Cathedral, in Jackson Square. They were constructed toward the close of the last century, through the liberality of the founder of the Cathedral, Don Andre Almonaster, and are conspicuous for their quaint style

United States Mint.

of architecture, which is Tusco-Doric. The *City Prisons*, which comprise a parish jail and a police jail, are in Orleans and Ann Streets, opposite the Tremé Market. They are of brick, plastered to imitate granite, and three stories high. The *Merchants' Exchange*, a handsome marble structure in Royal Street near Canal, was formerly a place of great resort, but since the removal of the Post-Office to the Custom-House its glory has departed, and it exists now in little more than name. *Masonic Hall*, corner St. Charles and Perdido Streets, is an imposing edifice, 103 by 100 feet. *Odd-Fellows' Hall* is a massive square structure in Camp Street, opposite Lafayette Square. It is of brick, stuccoed and painted white, four stories high, and cost $210,000. *St. Patrick's Hall*, on the site of the old Odd-Fellows' Hall, is one of the most elegant buildings in the city. Its concert-room seats 3,500 people. *Exposition Hall* is a spacious building in St. Charles Street, between Julia and Girod, in which are given floral displays and other exhibitions. The St. Charles Hotel and the State-House, which are among the largest and finest edifices in the city, have already been mentioned. The *Mechanics' Institute*, in Dryades Street, near Canal, is one of the finest buildings in the city. The *Pontalba Buildings* are immense brick structures on Jackson Square.

Theatres and Places of Amusement.—The French *Opera-House*, corner Bourbon and Toulouse Streets, is a well-arranged building of modern construction. It has seats for 2,000, and is fitted up in the style of the Théâtre Français, Paris. The *Academy of Music*, in St. Charles Street, between Poydras and Commercial Streets, is the usual place for variety performances. The *St. Charles Theatre*, in St. Charles Street, between Perdido and Poydras, is handsomely appointed, and has a good company. The *National* (or *Globe*) *Theatre* is at the corner of Perdido and Baronne Streets, and the *Varieties Theatre* in Canal Street. Besides the theatres, there are a score or more of halls in which entertainments of various kinds are given. The principal of these are the *Masonic Hall, Odd-Fellows' Hall, St. Patrick's Hall*, and *Exposition Hall*, previously mentioned; and *Grünewald Hall*, in Baronne Street, near Canal. *Horse-races* occur at the Fair-Grounds race-track (reached by Shell Road and 3 lines of horse-cars).

Besides the regular sources of amusement which it enjoys in common with other cities, New Orleans is noted for its great displays during the holiday and carnival season. Among the many societies which contribute to these displays, the most famous are the *Twelfth-Night Revellers*, who appear on the night of January 6th, and the *Mystick Krewe of Comus*, who appear on the night of "Mardi Gras," or Shrove-Tuesday. On the same day (Shrove-Tuesday), Rex, King of the Carnival, arrives with a large retinue, takes formal possession of the city for the nonce, and makes a grand display, followed by his staff, courtiers, and attendants, all mounted and dressed in the most gorgeous Oriental costumes. The processions are followed by receptions, tableaux, and balls, which are largely attended by the *élite* of the city, and by strangers sojourning there, who in some mysterious manner are always the recipients of unique cards of invitation.

Churches.—The most famous church edifice in New Orleans is the old **Cathedral of St. Louis** (Roman Catholic), which stands in Chartres Street, on the east side of Jackson Square. It has an imposing façade surmounted by a lofty steeple and flanked by two towers, each surmounted by a smaller steeple. The foundation was laid in 1792, and the building completed in 1794 by Don Andre Almonaster, perpetual *regidor* of the province. It was altered and enlarged in 1850, from designs by De Louilly. The paintings on the roof of the building are by Canova and Rossi. The *Church of the Immaculate Conception* (Jesuit), corner Baronne and Common Streets, is a striking edifice in the Moorish style of architecture. High-mass, both here and at the Cathedral, at 10 o'clock every Sunday. *St. Patrick's* (Roman Catholic) is a fine Gothic structure in Camp Street, north of Lafayette Square. Its tower, 190 feet high, was modeled after that of the famous minster at York, England. The church of St. John the Baptist, in Dryades Street, between Clio and Calliope, which was opened in 1872, is a very elegant building. The most fashionable Episcopal churches are *Trinity*, corner Jackson and Coliseum Streets, and **St. Paul's**, corner Camp and Gaiennie Streets. The latter is a handsome specimen of the Gothic style, and has a rich interior. The oldest of the Episcopal organizations, dating back to 1806, is *Christ Church*, corner Canal and Dauphin Streets. The **First Presbyterian**, fronting on Lafayette Square, is a fine structure in the Greco-Doric style, much admired for its elegant steeple. The *McGhee Church*, in Carondelet Street, near Lafayette, is the principal of the Methodist Episcopal churches South. The *Unitarian Church*, corner St. Charles and Julia Streets, is a handsome building. The Temple Sinai (Jewish synagogue), in Carondelet Street, near Calliope, is one of the finest places of worship in the city. Party-colored bricks and pointing give its walls a light, airy appearance, and it has a handsome portico, flanked by two towers capped with tinted cupolas. The Gothic windows are filled with beautifully-stained glass. *St. Antoine's Chapel*, corner Rampart and Conti Streets, is generally known as the "Mortuary Chapel," all funeral ceremonies of resident Catholics being performed here. One of the most interesting relics of the early church history of New Orleans is the old Ursuline Convent in Condé Street. This quaint and venerable building was erected in 1787, during the reign of Carlos III., by Don Andre Almonaster. It is now occupied by the bishop, and is known as the "Bishop's Palace."

Educational and Charitable Institutions.—The **University of Louisiana** is in Common Street, near Baronne, and occupies the entire front of the block. Only two departments, law and medicine, have been organized, but these are of a very high order, and are largely attended. The Medical College, which stands in the centre of the block, has a façade of 100 feet. It contains a large anatomical museum, and extensive and valuable collections of many kinds. *Straight University* is exclusively for colored students, and gives instruction of good grammar-school grade. There are 80 public schools, and numerous private ones, mostly Roman Catholic.

The **Charity Hospital**, in Common Street, is one of the noblest buildings in the city, and one of the most famous institutions of the kind in the country. It was founded in 1784, has stood on its present site since 1832, and has accommodations for 500 patients. The *Hôtel Dieu*, ½ mile farther back from the river, is a very fine hospital established by the Sisters of Charity, and supported entirely by receipts from patients, some of whom are, nevertheless, beneficiary. It occupies a full square, and is surrounded by a well-kept garden of shrubbery and flowers. The *Maison de Santé*, corner of Canal and Claiborne Streets, being one of the most noted infirmaries of New Orleans, is now deserted, and, like the *United States Marine Hospital* (corner of Common and Broad Streets), which has not been used since 1860, is rapidly falling into decay. Other prominent charitable institutions are the *Poydras Female Orphan Asylum*, in Magazine Street, the *St. Anna's Widows' Asylum*, the *St. Vincent Orphan Asylum*, the *Indigent Colored Orphan Asylum*, and the *German Protestant Asylum*. The *Howard Association* is one of the greatest charitable bodies in the world, its special mission being to labor for the relief of sufferers in epidemics, particularly the yellow fever and cholera.

Public Squares and Cemeteries.—There are 10 public squares in the city, most of them inclosed with iron railings, but some barely more than in embryo. The largest of these inclosures is the *City Park*, near the northeast boundary (reached by Canal Street and Ridge Road cars. It embraces 150 acres, tastefully laid out, and was the location of the WORLD'S FAIR AND COTTON EXHIBITION BUILDINGS of 1884–'85. Jackson Square (formerly known as the *Place d'Armes*), on the river-front, is the favorite resort. It is adorned with beautiful trees and shrubbery, and shell-strewed paths, and in the centre stands Mill's equestrian statue of General Jackson. The imposing fronts of the cathedral and courts of justice are seen to great advantage from the river-entrance to the square. *Lafayette Square*, in the First District, bounded by St. Charles and Camp Streets, is another handsome inclosure. The fine marble front of the City Hall, the tapering spire of the Presbyterian Church, and the massive façade of Odd-Fellows' Hall, present a striking appearance. In the square is a fine white-marble statue of Franklin, by Hiram Powers. In Canal Street, between St. Charles and Royal, is a colossal bronze statue of Henry Clay, by Hart. *Douglas Square* is beautifully laid out and well kept. *Annunciation Square* and *Tivoli Circle*, at the head of St. Charles Street, are worth a visit. There are some handsome private residences in the neighborhood of the former.

The *Cemeteries* of New Orleans are noteworthy for their unique arrangement and peculiar modes of interment. From the nature of the soil, which is semi-fluid at a depth of 2 or 3 feet below the surface, all the tombs are above-ground. Some of these are very costly and beautiful structures, of marble, iron, etc.; but the great majority consist of cells, placed one above another, generally to the height of 7 or 8 feet. Each cell is only large enough to receive the coffin, and is hermetically bricked up at its narrow entrance as soon as the funeral rites are over. In most instances a marble tablet, appropriately inscribed, is placed over the brickwork by which the vault (or "oven," as it is called here) is closed. There are 33 cemeteries in and near the city; of these the *Cypress Grove* and *Greenwood*, on the Metairie Ridge, at the north end of Canal Street, are best worth visiting. *St. Louis Cemetery No. 1*, at the corner of Basin and St. Louis Streets, contains some fine monuments, of which the more noteworthy are the vaults of the "Société Française de Bienfaisance," "Orleans Battalion of Artillery," and "Italian Benevolent Society." The last is of white marble, and is one of the most beautiful structures of its kind in the country.

The Markets and the Levee.—The great "sight" of New Orleans, and perhaps the most picturesque to be seen in America, is the *French Market*, which comprises several buildings on the Levee, near Jackson Square. The best time to visit it is between 8 and 9 o'clock on Sunday morning, or at 6 A. M. on other days. At break of day the gathering commences, and it would seem as if all nations and tongues were represented in the motley crowd which surges in and out until near 10 o'clock. The noise, far from being unpleasant, however, is musical to the stranger's ears; and nowhere else will he find such an infinite variety of articles exposed for sale. Fruits are especially abundant and various, embracing all the products of both temperate and tropical regions, and the flowers are wonderful to behold. French is the prevailing language, and it will be heard in every variety, from the silvery elegance of the polished creole to the childish jargon of the negroes. The *Levee* affords the visitor one of the most striking and characteristic sights of the Crescent City. For extent and activity it has no equal on the continent. The best points from which to obtain a view of the city and its environs are the roof of the St. Charles Hotel and the tower of St. Patrick's Church. The public markets transact their business at the *Abattoir*, constructed by a corporate company styled "The Crescent City Live-Stock Landing and Slaughter-House Company." It is situated on the left river-bank, adjacent to the lower line of the city. The establishment comprises 2 cattle-landing wharves; 12 covered cattle-pens, each having an area of over 1,000 square feet; 28 open pens, each with an area of about 1,125 square feet; 18 other pens for sheep, hogs, etc.; 2 receiving-pens, each of an area of 600 square feet, for cattle to be immediately slaughtered; a slaughter-house for cattle, in 22 divisions, each of an area of 800 square feet; a slaughter-house for smaller animals, well supplied with hot as well as cold water, and covering an area of 21,200 square feet; and 22 stables. These buildings are separated from each other by wide and well-constructed causeways, and are lofty and airy. Attached to them are two steam-engines by which a plentiful supply of water is commanded, and the fluid offal is pumped off; also covered hide-vats, an apparatus for the rapid curing of hides, and a Barbarin patent gas-apparatus for lighting the whole establishment. Several dwellings and other buildings are also comprised within the property of the Slaughter-House Company. The average number of cattle slaughtered is about 400 a day in winter and about 300 a day in summer. The slaughtering of any of these animals elsewhere within the city limits is prohibited by law. An inspector, appointed by the Governor, examines all cattle killed, and certifies to their fitness for food.

Suburbs.—The *Battle-field*, the scene of General Jackson's great victory over the British, January 8, 1815, is the most interesting spot in the vicinity of New Orleans. It lies 4½ miles south of Canal Street, and may be reached either by carriage along the Levee or by horse-cars. It is washed by the waters of the Mississippi, and extends back about a mile to the cypress-swamps. A marble monument, 70 feet high and yet unfinished, occupies a suitable site overlooking the ground, and serves to commemorate the victory. A National Cemetery occupies the southwest corner of the field. Between the Battle-field and the city the *Ursuline Convent*, an imposing building, 200 feet long, overlooks the river. *Lake Pontchartrain*, 5 miles north of the city, is famous for its fish and game. It is 40 miles long and 24 miles wide. It is reached by 3 lines of railway with cars drawn by steam, and by drive in carriages on a fine shell road. The swamps which lie between the city and the lake are covered with a thick growth of cypress and other trees peculiar to this locality. *Carrollton*, in the northern suburbs, has many fine public gardens and private residences. *Algiers*, opposite New Orleans, has extensive dry-docks and ship-yards. Communication by ferries. *Gretna*, on the same side, is a pretty rural spot, abounding in pleasant, shady walks.

The River below New Orleans.

Those who, taking an ocean steamer, pursue the journey below New Orleans, traverse a portion of the river not less interesting if less attractive than that left behind. Very soon after leaving the city the phenomena of a "delta-country" become conspicuous, and one can fairly witness the eternal and ever-varying conflict between land and sea. The thick forest vegetation disappears, giving place to isolated and stunted trees; the river-banks grow less and less defined, and finally lose themselves in what appears to be an interminable marsh; and through this marsh the "passes" furnish channels to the Gulf, which are discernible only by the practised eyes of the pilots. The "delta" protrudes into the Gulf of Mexico far beyond the general coast-line, and is slowly but imperceptibly advancing into the Gulf by the shoaling caused by the deposition of the sediment brought down by the river. It is impossible, however, for the inexperienced traveler to say where land ends and sea begins; and before he is aware of having reached the "mouth" of the river, he is far out on the Gulf of Mexico, where a muddy surface-current is the only relic of the mighty Father of Waters.

THE WEST INDIES.

Just off the southern coast of Florida, and stretching across the entrance to the Gulf of Mexico, lies a very extensive group of islands, which, though their sovereignty is distributed among nearly all the leading European powers, are known collectively as "The West Indies," and are so laid down upon the maps. The total length of this group is upward of 3,000 miles, and it embraces more than 1,000 islands and islets, with a total area of about 150,000 square miles. They lie between lat. 10° and 28° north and lon. 59° and 85° west, and are divided into four groups: 1. The Bahamas, about 600 in number, low, flat islands of coral formation, southeast of Florida, and extending toward Hayti; 2. The Greater Antilles, between the Bahamas and Central America, comprising the four great islands of Cuba, Hayti or San Domingo, Jamaica, and Porto Rico, with a few neighboring small ones; 3. The Lesser Antilles or Caribbean Islands, extending in a semi-circular line from Porto Rico to the mouth of the Orinoco, and by some geographers also called collectively Windward Islands; 4. The group off the coast of Venezuela (the Leeward Islands of the Spanish explorers), embracing Margarita, Tortuga, Buen Ayre, Curaçoa, and several smaller islands. The West Indies are generally considered to be the remains of a mountain-range which at some remote period united the continents of North and South America. The Bahamas are low, level, and of coralline formation. Some of the Lesser Antilles are flat, but the general character of the entire group is bold, with a single mountain or cluster of mountains in the centre, which slope to the sea all around—more precipitously on the east side, which is exposed to the force of the Atlantic current. Volcanic action in the archipelago is confined to the smaller islands; others possess craters recently extinct, that have vomited ashes and lava within historical periods. The latest violent eruption was in St. Vincent, in 1812; but, more remotely, Hayti and Jamaica have been the scene of some of the most tremendous earthquakes on record. Hurricanes occur nearly every year, and are sometimes very destructive, especially in the Lesser Antilles. The characteristic feature of the vegetation of the West Indies is the predominance of ferns and orchidaceous plants. The forests furnish mahogany, lignum-vitæ, granadilla, rosewood, and other valuable woods. Tropical fruits abound; and maize, sugar, coffee, tobacco, and cotton, are extensively cultivated. Of the formerly-existing wild animals—the agouti, peccary, raccoon, and wild-boar—the last only remains. Birds are numerous, and their characteristics are, beautiful and varied plumage and lack of song. Fish are very abundant, as are also reptiles, including turtles, lizards, and snakes. Insects and reptiles are the pests of the islands.

San Salvador, one of the Bahamas, was the first land discovered in America, Columbus having landed on it in October, 1492; and it was not until the next voyage of the great navigator that the American continent was discovered. When first visited, all these islands teemed with a dense native population; but the natives were speedily exterminated by the early Spanish colonists, and for many generations have been wholly extinct. Some of the smaller islands are barren and uninhabited, but for the most part they are covered with a vegetation of tropical luxuriance and beauty. Owing to their generally delightful climate, the West Indies have for many years been the resort, especially in winter, of consumptives and other invalids from the United States. In the following pages we shall describe those places which are most frequented and most easily accessible to travelers.

Cuba.

Cuba, "The Queen of the Antilles," the largest and most important of the West India Islands, lies between the Caribbean Sea and the Gulf of Mexico, about 130 miles south of Florida, from which it is separated by the Strait of Florida. The greatest length of the island from east to west is 760 miles, and its width varies from 20 to 135 miles, the total area being 47,278 square miles. In shape it is long, narrow, and slightly curved, the convex side being on the north. The entire coast-line is about 2,200 miles in extent, but, owing to the almost continuous reefs, and the low level of the land skirting the sea-shore, it is in general very difficult of approach, and there are but few really good harbors. A range of mountains, more or less broken, traverses the island from end to end, dividing it into two unequal sections, that on the north side being for the most part the narrower of the two. This range gives great diversity to the surface, and from the bases of the highlands the country opens into extensive meadows or beautiful plains and savannas, with occasionally some low, swampy tracts. There are very few rivers of any magnitude in Cuba, and a large portion of the territory is subject to severe droughts; yet the gently undulating surface, the continually renewed verdure, and the wonderful distribution of vegetable forms, give rise to the most varied and beautiful landscapes. Everywhere the eye falls only upon a mass of luxuriant vegetation, and nowhere is the structure of the country to be seen except on the scarred and treeless mountain-slopes. Coming in winter from the North Atlantic seaboard, where half the United States are buried in snow, and the forests are stripped naked, the traveler finds in Cuba a more wooing climate, and a more bountiful profusion and luxuriance of vegetable growth, than even in imagination he ever pictured to himself. The climate is warm and dry during the greater part of the year, but it is more temperate than in other islands of the same latitude, and more equable than in many more northern countries. The thermometer never rises so high as it sometimes does in New York in the hot months, and sunstrokes are unknown. From May to October the heat seldom reaches 100° Fahrenheit in any part of the island. The highest recorded temperature, in observations extending over many years since 1801, was 104°. In December and January the air is cooled by the north winds, and the thermometer has occasionally fallen to the freezing-point. The average temperature of Havana is 77°; maximum 89°; minimum, 50°. The average temperature of the hottest month is 82°, and of the coldest 72°. In Santiago de Cuba the average of the year is 80°; of the hottest month, 84°; of the coldest, 73°. The topographical position of Cuba reduces the four seasons of the year to two, the *wet* and the *dry*. In the former, extending from May or June to November, the rain pours down in torrents almost every day. The rainfall in the island in one year has been known to reach 133 inches, and the average annual number of rainy days is 102. The most rain falls in September and October. In the dry season the dews are very abundant, both at night and in the early morning. There is no record of snow having fallen in Cuba, excepting on December 24, 25, 1856, when the coldest term ever known on the island was experienced, and snow fell near Villa Clara, in the central part of the island; but hailstorms are frequent in the eastern department, and hoar-frosts are not uncommon. Violent thunder-storms occur from June to September. Earthquakes are seldom felt in the western districts, but are frequent in the eastern, especially in the vicinity of Santiago de Cuba. The climate is considered to be, in general, remarkably healthy. In the lowlands, summer fevers sometimes prevail, and to these strangers are said to be especially liable; but the higher parts of the island are salubrious all the year round. The yellow fever is justly feared by those coming from more temperate climates, but the Cuban physicians believe that this disease is not indigenous, and was not known in the island until 1762. It is not yet known in the interior, and its appearance at many places is recent. The best time to visit Cuba is between the first of December and the last of March, and during this period those suffering from lung and throat diseases usually find a residence there highly beneficial and agreeable.

Havana, the largest city and chief commercial port of the West Indies, is situated on the northwest coast of Cuba, on a beautiful bay of the Gulf of Mexico. Its harbor, formed by this bay, which nowhere exceeds a mile and a half in width, is one of the best in the world, being deep enough for vessels of the largest size, capacious enough to accommodate at least 1,000 ships-of-war, and so sheltered that vessels ride securely without cable or anchor. The approach from the sea is very impressive, the entrance to the harbor being half a mile in length, so narrow that only a single vessel can pass at a time, and with massive fortifications on either side throughout the whole distance. At the mouth of the channel, which is less than a quarter of a mile wide, are two strong castles, the *Punta* on the west side, connected with another castle in the city, and on the east the famous *Morro Castle*, beetling with artillery, and surmounted by a fixed light 144 feet high. *La Cabaña*, situated a little southeast of Morro Castle, is the strongest fortress of Havana, and half a dozen others are passed before the inner harbor is reached. The city, as viewed from the harbor,

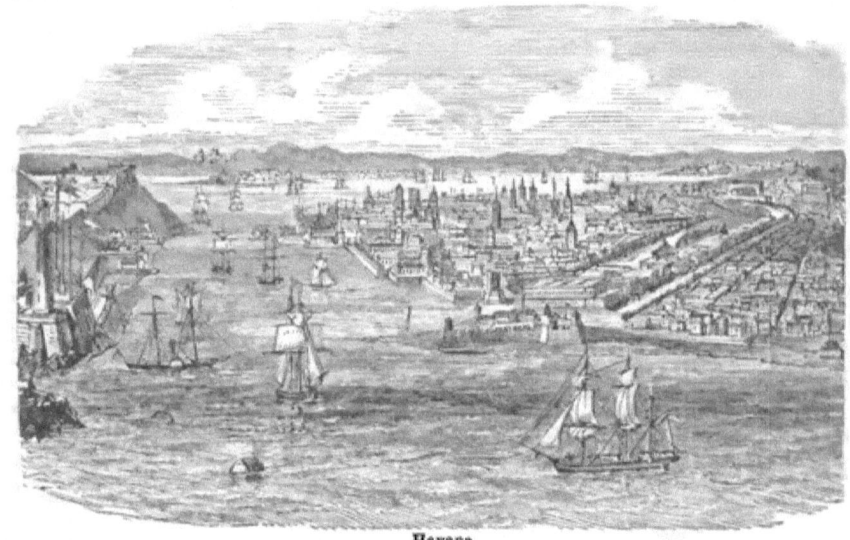

Havana.

has a very picturesque and beautiful appearance, with its numerous spires, its massive edifices, its wide-spreading suburbs, and its background of hills; but this impression is hardly confirmed by closer acquaintance. The city stands on a sort of peninsula, formed on one side by the bay and on the other by the waters of the Gulf, and is commonly distinguished into two portions, the intramural or old town, and the extramural or new town, beyond the walls. In the former, the streets, though for the most part regular and well paved, are extremely narrow, and, being lowest in the middle, favor the accumulation of great pools of water in the rainy season; and the sidewalks are barely wide enough for one pedestrian. The macadamized thoroughfares of the other portion, rather resembling roads than streets, are broad and ample, and fringed on either side with rows of graceful palm-trees. The prevailing style of architecture is identical with that of the south of Spain. The houses are solidly built of stone, with very thick walls, often painted within and without in showy colors, especially blue, green, or yellow, and occasionally a mingling of all three; they are either of one story and roofed with tiles, or of two stories with a flat roof of substantial masonry, at times surmounted by a *mirador* (lookout), affording at once a fine view and a cool and agreeable retreat after sunset. The windows, which are extremely high, are never glazed, but defended on the outside by strong iron bars, and within by wooden shutters secured, like the doors, with massive bars or bolts. The doors, almost always double, are very ponderous, and open either directly into the *sala* or parlor, or into a large gateway guarded by a janitor, and leading into an open *patio* (court-yard) whence a spacious staircase leads to the apartments above. All the rooms open upon a covered veranda, which surrounds the patio. In the dwellings of the rich the floors and stairs are usually of marble, the decorations and furniture luxurious and tasteful, and the patio is generally embellished with a parterre of exotic flowers and an elegant fountain in the centre. Many of the residences in the new portion of the city are constructed in a more modern style, particularly in *El Cerro* (the Hill), a handsome street three miles long leading to a village of the same name, and chiefly inhabited by the wealthy and fashionable. There is, however, no quarter of the town exclusively occupied by the higher classes, and in any street a miserable hovel may be seen side by side with a stately mansion.

The handsomest portion of Havana is in the vicinity of the great central square, or *Plaza de Armas*, which comprises four gardens, with a statue of Ferdinand VII. in the centre, and spacious walks bordered by magnificent palms and other trees. On the west side of the plaza is the *Governor's Palace*, a yellow two-story edifice, with a handsome colonnade in front, and containing the offices of the captain-general, his staff, and of the other Government departments. Opposite the palace is a beautiful chapel (*El Templete*), erected on the spot where the first mass was celebrated in Havana after the removal of the city to its present site, in 1519. Foremost among the public edifices is the *Cathedral*, erected in 1724, and used as a college by the Jesuits till 1789; but it is less remarkable for the beauty of its architecture than as containing the ashes of Christopher Columbus, transferred thither from Santo Domingo, January 15, 1796. On one of the walls is a stone slab with the bust of Columbus in relief, and an inscription beneath. There are fifteen other churches, nine of which are attached to certain monastic orders. Two—*Santa Catalina* and *San Juan de Dias*—date from the sixteenth century; one—*San Agustin*—from the beginning of the seventeenth; and all are noteworthy for the richness and splendor of their decorations. The *Custom-House*, fronting on the bay, is a spacious building, devoid of architectural interest; but the *Customs Warehouse*, formerly the church of San Francisco, has the loftiest tower in the city. Other buildings or public establishments worthy of notice are the *Admiralty*, the *Exchange*, the *Royal University*, the *Prison* (a vast quadrangular structure, erected in 1771, near the mouth of the bay), and the *Real Casa de Beneficencia*, a large building, with beautiful grounds, and comprising an orphan asylum and an asylum for vagrants. There is also a hospital for those afflicted with a species of leprosy peculiar to the West Indies, and reputed incurable; a lying-in, a charity, and a military hospital, and an insane asylum. Monasteries and nunneries are numerous. Havana has three theatres, one of which, the *Tacon Theatre*, is said to be equal in size to La Scala, of Milan; an arena for bull-fights, this amusement being still popular in Havana; a gymnasium, a circus, and a number of well-arranged and commodious public baths. Of the eight hotels, we may mention the *Hotel de Inglaterra*, in the Calle del Prado, beside the Tacon Theatre, and affording an excellent view of the harbor; *El Telegrafo*, in the newer part of the city, in Amistad Street; and *San Carlos*, overlooking the harbor. *Madame Almy's* is a very popular boarding-house. Restaurants and *cafés* are numerous; the best of the former is at 72 Cuba Street.

Few cities in the world have a larger number of *paseos*, or public promenades, and public parks, than Havana. Besides the Plaza de Armas, already mentioned, there is the *Alameda de Paula*, bordering the bay, and having an elegant fountain, surmounted by a marble column, with military trophies and national symbols. A favorite evening resort is the *Parque de Isabel*, tastefully laid out, and having in the centre a statue of Isabella II. The *Campo de Marte*, used as a drill-ground for the military, is a large inclosure resembling a trapezium in shape, the longest side of which is 375 feet; it has four handsome gates, distinguished respectively by the names Colon, Cortes, Pizarro, and Tacon. The *Paseo de Tacon* is a magnificent wide drive, with double rows of trees, a promenade for pedestrians, and profusely embellished with columns and statues, some of the latter, especially one of Charles III., ranking among the finest specimens of art in America. Adjoining this promenade is a beautiful gate opening into the *Botanic Garden*, in which are specimens of countless tropical plants; and beside these gardens are the magnificent grounds attached to the *quinta*, or country residence, of the captain-general. Other paseos, such as those of La Reina, El Prado, La Cortina de Valdés, and El Salon de O'Donnel, vie in beauty of scenery with those enumerated. In the vicinity of the city are numerous places of fashionable resort, such as *Marianao*, *Puentes Grandes*, and *Guanabacoa*. In consequence of the heat of the climate, the inhabitants of Havana, save the business community, remain in-doors during the day; but in the evening the delightful promenades of the city and its environs present a most animated spectacle, being thronged with the gay and fashionable of both sexes. The elegant dress, grace, and beauty of the Havanese ladies (who always ride when abroad) displayed on these occasions, and at the theatres, seldom fail to elicit the admiration of visitors. There are also many beautiful drives around Havana, and driving is one of the favorite recreations of the wealthier classes. A popular drive is to Marianao. On Sunday afternoons all Havana may be seen driving on the Paseo.

From New York Havana may be reached by "New York and Cuba S. S. Line" (Ward's), sailing every Thursday from Pier 16 East River; also by "Alexandre's Line," sailing every Thursday from Pier 3 North River (fare, cabin, $50 gold). From Philadelphia, Baltimore, or New Orleans, by weekly steamers. From Tampa, Florida, by steamers sailing twice weekly.

Havana is the terminal point of nearly all the railway-lines in Cuba, and connects by steamer with Matanzas, Cardenas, Jucaro, Santiago de Cuba, and other chief ports.

Matanzas, which ranks next to Havana in commercial importance, is also situated on the northwest coast of Cuba, 53 miles east of Havana. It may be reached in two hours from Havana three times a day by one railway, and in four hours twice a day by another; also by a daily line of steamers which make the trip in five hours. Travelers remaining even a few days in Havana will find a visit to Matanzas very interesting; they should go by regular route and return *via* Güines to Villanueva. The bay which forms the port of Matanzas is spacious, easy of access, and completely sheltered from all winds except those from the northeast, which bring in a heavy swell. The city, strongly fortified, is situated on an extensive flat on both sides of the San Juan River, here crossed by a bridge, and contains about 40,000 inhabitants. The streets are wide, regular, well kept, and lighted with gas; and the houses, chiefly of stone, are solidly built in the same style as those of Havana. The handsomest of the public squares is the *Plaza de Armas*, where military bands perform every evening, and the walks are crowded with fashionable promenaders. There are two churches, a palace, a massive castle (*San Severino*), fine barracks, a hospital, a good theatre, and a cock-pit. The climate of Matanzas is more salubrious than that of Havana, and the winters are extremely mild and equable. For consumptives this is in many respects the most desirable resort in Cuba; but a residence on the adjacent hills is preferable to one in the town itself. The country around Matanzas is covered with magnificent sugar-estates. The leading hotels are the *Leon de Oro* and the *Hotel Frances*. While at Matanzas, the tourist should visit

Matanzas.

the celebrated Yumuri Valley, and the Caves of Bellamar. The latter are only 2 miles from the city. (Matanzas may be reached from New York *via* Nassau by steamers of the Mallory Line, sailing every other Wednesday from Pier 20 East River.)

Santiago de Cuba (locally called Cuba), situated almost at the other end of the island and on its south side, was formerly the capital of Cuba, and is still the second city in rank and population, containing in 1875 about 45,000 inhabitants. It lies on the river Santiago, 6 miles from its mouth, and has a port 4 miles long, which is deep enough for ships-of-war, and strongly fortified. The city is regularly laid out on a steep acclivity, with wide streets, some very precipitous, and handsome houses which are chiefly of stone. The *Cathedral*, completed in 1819, is the largest on the island, and there are several other churches, a theatre, a custom-house, barracks, a college, and three hospitals. Santiago is an archbishop's see and the residence of the Governor of the Eastern Department, who is independent of the Captain-General of Cuba; it is, consequently, next to Havana the liveliest city in Cuba. The city is supplied with bad water through an aqueduct, and, as it is shut in from the northern breezes, the suffocating heat and the miasmatic effluvia from the adjacent marshes render it the most unhealthful abode in the Antilles. Still, some consumptives have derived great benefit from its remarkably warm winter climate. Santiago may be reached by taking the railway from Havana to Batabano, and a steamer from the latter point, which touches at Cienfuegos, Trinidad, Santa Cruz, and Manzanillo, reaching Santiago in five days.

Puerto Principe is the chief city of the interior, and in population nearly equals Matanzas. It is the capital of the Central Department, and lies about midway between the north and south coasts, 305 miles E. S. E. of Havana. The city is irregularly built between two small streams, the Tinima and the Jatibonico, in a rich agricultural district, the chief products of which are sugar and tobacco. Its trade is insignificant compared with its population. The principal buildings are several churches and monasteries, a hospital, and two theatres. The town was threatened several times during the recent war by the Cuban patriots, and two or three battles were fought in its vicinity. The climate is hot and moist, but the winters are remarkably mild, and the town is at that time somewhat resorted to by invalids who wish to get away from the coast. Puerto Principe is connected by a railway 56 miles long with the port of Nuevitas, through which it communicates with the outside world.

Isle of Pines.

This island lies in the Caribbean Sea, 33 miles off the coast of Cuba, and is under the jurisdiction of the political governor of Havana. It is 43 miles long and 35 miles wide in the widest part, with an area of 1,200 square miles and a population of about 2,000. The coasts are deeply indented by bays and inlets, some of which afford commodious anchorage, though surrounded by innumerable rocky islets or keys. A mountain-chain over 1,600 feet high, the Sierra de la Cañada, traverses the island, and the country is well watered by several rivers. The centre is somewhat marshy, but the soil is elsewhere very fertile and productive. Timber and precious woods are very abundant; and among the mineral productions are silver, quicksilver, iron, sulphur, and rock crystal, while marble of various beautiful colors occurs in large quantities. The climate is exceedingly mild and salubrious, and there is no place in the West Indies better adapted for invalids. Being sheltered on the north by Cuba, the thermometrical range is very small, and the winters are strangely bland and equable. The towns on the island are *Nueva Gerona* (which in 1870 had a population of 100), *Santa Fé*, and *Jorobado*. The island was discovered by Columbus in 1494, and was long the favorite haunt of pirates, among whom was Gibbs. It is reached from Havana by steamer at irregular intervals.

The Bahamas—Nassau.

The Bahamas are the most northern section of the West India group, and stretch from the north side of San Domingo to the coast of Florida, between lat. 21° and 27° 30′ north and lon. 70° 30′ and 79° 5′ west. They are about 600 in number, of which only about 15 are inhabited, a great many of them being mere rocky islets. The most important of them are Grand Bahama, Great and Little Abaco, Andros, New Providence, Eleuthera, San Salvador, Rum Bay, Great Exuma, Watling Island, Long

Island, Crooked Island, Atwood's Key, and Great and Little Inagua. The group is about 600 miles long, and has an estimated area of 3,000 square miles, with a population of about 40,000. Most of the islands are situated on those remarkable flats called the Bahama Banks, of which the Great Bank (lying at the western extremity of the archipelago) occupies a space 300 miles in length and 80 miles in breadth. The deepest water on this bank is 30 feet. These banks rise almost perpendicularly from an unfathomable depth of water, and are formed of coral, with an accumulation of shells and calcareous sand. The character of the islands is generally long and narrow, low, and covered with a light sandy soil. Fruit, including oranges, lemons, limes, bananas, tamarinds, mango, guava, custard-apples, and pine-apples, is produced in abundance; and maize, yams, and sweet-potatoes are extensively cultivated. The climate is salubrious, and very beneficial to consumptives. The more northern islands, during the winter months, are rendered cool and agreeable by the northwest breeze that blows off the continent of America; the more southern are hot throughout the year, and are low, barren, and rocky.

Nassau, which is pretty much the only place in the Bahamas frequented by travelers, is the capital of the island of New Providence and the seat of government for all the islands. It is situated on the northern side of the island, extending along the water-front for about three miles and back to the crest of a slope, on which stand the Government-House and many of the finest private residences at an elevation of 90 feet above the harbor. The streets are laid out at right angles with each other, and are uniformly macadamized, as are also the numerous excellent drives around the island; and the houses are generally built of stone, with the surrounding grounds ornamented with a tropical profusion of flowers and trees. The city has a public library of 6,000 volumes, a museum, numerous churches, some barracks, a prison, and a hospital. During the late civil war it developed a great business as rendezvous for vessels engaged in running the blockade of the Southern ports. This temporary prosperity has now departed, but Nassau has excellent hotel accommodations, and is still probably the pleasantest and most frequented invalid resort in the West Indies. Its climate is remarkably healthy, and the winters are delightfully mild and equable, without being depressing. The temperature never falls below 64° Fahrenheit, nor rises above 82°, and the variation rarely exceeds 5° in the 24 hours. Little rain falls in the winter months, which are almost uniformly dry and clear. Not the least attractive feature of Nassau is the *Royal Victoria Hotel*, which was erected by the British Government in 1860, especially to meet the requirements of invalids. It is of stone, four stories high; and each of the first three stories is surrounded by a broad piazza, forming a continuous promenade over 1,000 feet long, and affording to those unable to endure the fatigues of out-door exercise ample facilities for enjoying the fine scenery and refreshing breezes. The rooms are large and carefully ventilated, and the house has all the modern improvements. Convenient arrangements for sea-bathing exist, and, for such as prefer it, salt-water baths, both hot and cold, are provided in the hotel. The hotel is open from the 1st of November to the 15th of May; terms, $3 a day in gold. Nassau may be reached from New York direct by C. H. Mallory & Co.'s Line of Mail-steamers, from Pier 20 East River, or New York and Cuba S. S. Co., Pier 16 East River; fare, $50. Also from Fernandina, Fla., by steamers of the same line every two weeks; fare, New York to Nassau *via* Fernandina, $50; Fernandina to Nassau, $25; excursion tickets at reduced rates.

Harbor Island, a few miles distant from Nassau, is preferred by some invalids to New Providence, though the climate is the same and the conveniences fewer. *Dunmore Town*, on Harbor Island, is the largest in the Bahamas, next to Nassau, and is a very pretty place, encircled by cocoanut-groves. *Turk's Island*, at the southeastern extremity of the Bahama group, 90 miles north of Hayti, is also well spoken of. Its climate is slightly warmer than that of Nassau.

Jamaica.

Jamaica, one of the Greater Antilles, lies in the Caribbean Sea, about 90 miles south of Cuba and 118 southwest of Hayti, from which it is separated by the Wind-

JAMAICA.

ward Channel. It is the largest of the British West India islands, and forms the chief possession of Great Britain in this portion of the world. It is 145 miles long by 53 miles wide, and has an area of 4,473 square miles, with a population in 1871 of 506,154. The general appearance of the island is extremely beautiful. On the north it rises into hills of gentle ascent, covered with groves of pimento and a brilliant verdure, and intersected by vales which exhibit the most romantic scenery; while on the south it presents abrupt precipices and inaccessible cliffs, the general effect being heightened by the profusion of streams which pour from every valley, and frequently precipitate themselves from the overhanging rocks into the ocean. The Blue Mountains traverse the island in all directions, reaching an altitude in some localities of 7,200 feet. The declivities are covered with stately forests, and between the mountain-ranges and the foot of the central plain are spacious savannas and extensive plains. The coast-line is 500 miles long, and is indented with a great number of excellent harbors, of which Port Royal, the harbor of Kingston, is the most considerable. Jamaica was discovered by Columbus during his second

Kingston, Jamaica.

voyage, in 1494, and was taken possession of by the Spaniards in 1509. So great was the inhumanity of the conquerors that, fifty years after the Spanish invasion of the island, the native population had entirely disappeared. On May 3, 1655, a British expedition, sent out by Oliver Cromwell, under Admirals Penn and Venables, captured the island, which was formally ceded to England by the Treaty of Madrid, in 1670. During the 150 years of Spanish domination, the inhabitants, including Africans and Europeans, had not attained the number of 3,000. Within about the same period of English rule the estimated census showed 340,000. In 1861 the total population was 441,264, of whom 13,816 were whites and the rest half-breeds or blacks. In 1865 there was an insurrection of the blacks, which was put down by the notorious Governor Eyre with relentless rigor. These blacks had been liberated in 1832. The *climate* in the low regions is essentially tropical, the average temperature being 72° Fahr., and the maximum 100°; but the sea-breeze (called "the doctor") during the day, and the land-breeze at night, temper to a considerable degree the excessive heat. In the elevated districts the thermometer ranges from 45° to 70°, and the atmosphere is mild and agreeable. In few parts of the world does so slight an elevation produce so great a modifying effect upon the heat as in Jamaica; at about 2,500 feet above the sea, the fevers, dysenteries, and other maladies which usually prevail along the coast, are unknown. The rainy seasons, comprising the months of April, May, September, October, and November, are usually preceded by a cessation of the day and night breezes, when the atmosphere becomes most oppressive, and almost insupportable for Europeans. Heavy rain falls every day during these seasons, and is often accompanied by terrific thunder and lightning, and violent gusts of wind from the north. Earthquakes are frequent and sometimes violent; in 1692 the town of Port Royal was submerged several fathoms beneath the ocean. Hurricanes in the summer months, between the rainy seasons, are of frequent occurrence and occasionally of great violence. One of the most appalling occurred on the 3d of October, 1780. The little seaport town of Savana la Mar, on the southwest coast of the island, was completely destroyed. During the conflict of the elements, the sea burst furiously over it, and in an instant swept inhabitants and houses into the abyss, leaving no vestige of either.

Kingston, the capital and chief commercial city of Jamaica, is situated on the north coast of the island, in lat. 18° north and lon. 76° 50′ west. It stands on the gentle slope of a branch of the Blue Mountains, on the north shore of a magnificent bay defended by two forts. It is built in the form of an amphitheatre, with wide and regular streets; the houses, mostly two stories in height, are solidly constructed of brick or wood and painted green and white. The houses in the centre of the city form blocks, or squares, and in the principal streets are furnished with verandas below, and covered galleries above; while those in the outskirts are detached, and surrounded by delightful gardens. Besides the English church, which is the handsomest in the city, there are a Scottish, some Methodist, and several Roman Catholic churches, and two synagogues; but neither these, nor the other public edifices, such as the theatre, hospital, court-house, new penitentiary, work-house, barracks, and jail, possess any architectural beauty. The environs are covered with fine sugar-plantations, interspersed with picturesque villas. The region to the west is extremely marshy, and to the east rises Long Mountain. In December, January, February, and March the weather is delightful, and the climate peculiarly favorable for invalids suffering from bronchitis and pulmonary affections. At other seasons of the year the climate is hot and exceedingly unhealthy for strangers; the thermometer ranges from 70° to 95°; but alternate sea and land breezes in the morning and evening temper the almost suffocating heat. Kingston may be reached from New York by the Atlas Mail Line, sailing fortnightly from Pier 55 (old No. 51) North River (fare, $50). It is also in steam communication with all the West India Islands as far as Trinidad. Spanish Town, or Santiago de la Vega, the former capital of Jamaica, is situated on the bank of the river Cobre, 12 miles west of Kingston, with which it is connected by rail. It is ill-built and unhealthy. The most desirable places in Jamaica for invalids lie back in the elevated districts, but there are few localities that have made any special reputation as health-resorts.

Hayti and Santo Domingo.

The island of Hayti, or Santo Domingo, is also one of the Greater Antilles, and, after Cuba, is the largest and most beautiful of the West India islands. It lies 48 miles E. S. E. of Cuba and 118 E. N. E. of Jamaica, between lat. 17° 36′ and 19° 59′ north, and lon. 68° 20′ and 74° 38′ west. It is about 400 miles long and 165 miles wide, with an area, including the islands off the coast, of 28,030 square miles, and a population of 708,500, three-fourths of whom are negroes or mulattoes. The island is very irregular in form, being so deeply indented by bays and inlets as to constitute a coast-line of about 1,500 miles, presenting numerous excellent harbors. It is intersected east and west by three chains of mountains, connected by transverse ridges, and intervening are extensive plains and savannas. The central chain, the principal part of which is the Sierra del Cibao, runs E. S. E. from Cape San Nicolas to Cape Engano; its culminating point, near the centre of the island, attains an elevation variously estimated at from 7,200 to 9,000 feet. Nearly parallel with this chain is the Sierra de Monte Cristo, stretching from near the town of Monte Cristo to Escocesa Bay, where it terminates abruptly. Between these two ranges lies the Vega Real or Royal Valley, 130 miles long, watered by the Yuna and Gran Yaque Rivers, and comprising extensive pasture-lands. The third or southern mountain-range begins at Cape Tiburon, extends eastwardly through the southwest peninsula, and terminates at the Rio Neiva, about midway between the cities of Port-au-Prince and Santo Domingo. The secondary chains, running from the main ones toward the sea, divide the country into plains of various figures and extent, which are intersected by still other ridges, reaching sometimes to the beach. Besides the Vega Real there are other extensive plains and valleys, one of the most important of which is the plain of Les Cayes, at the western end of the island. This plain has been greatly extended by the formation of a kind of rock, consisting of comminuted shells and coral, incrusted with calcareous cement, resembling travertine, a species of rock which is in process of formation throughout the whole of the West India islands. There are numerous rivers, the navigation of which, however, is obstructed by sand-bars, and many lakes, both fresh and salt. The vegetation of the island is of a tropical character, and for beauty and luxuriance is unsurpassed by any in the world. The mountains are clothed with majestic forests of pine, mahogany, ebony, fustic, satinwood, oak, lignum-vitæ, and various other cabinet woods; while the graceful *palma real*, or royal palm, flourishes everywhere in the lowlands. The richest of flowering plants abound; and the usual tropical esculents, grains, and fruits, including plantains, bananas, yams, batatas, maize, millet, oranges, pineapples, sapodillas, with melons, grapes, and tamarinds, grow in all parts of the island. There is a species of agave (*Fourcroya Cubense*) extremely abundant, from the fibres of which is made almost all the rope used in the country. The articles chiefly raised for export are coffee, cotton, cacao, sugar-cane, indigo, and tobacco. The native animals are small, the largest being the agouti; but those introduced from Europe, and now in a wild state, have thriven prodigiously, large numbers of cattle, swine, and dogs, roaming freely in the savannas. The cattle of hundreds of owners graze in herds, and are annually collected and counted, and the young branded. Birds are not numerous, though large numbers of pigeons are annually taken and used as food, while ducks and other water-fowl frequent the marshy places. Insects abound, and many of them are venomous—such as scorpions, tarantulas, and centipedes. There are many species of snakes and lizards; the iguana sometimes attains a length of five feet, and is then much feared; its flesh is considered a delicacy by the natives. The lakes and rivers contain caymans and alligators; in the surrounding sea whales are frequently taken; manatees or sea-cows are numerous; and turtles, lobsters of enormous size, and crabs, abound on the coast.

Hayti was discovered by Columbus in December, 1492, and was the seat of the first Spanish colony founded in the New World. For three hundred years it was the arena of fierce struggles between the French, Spaniards, and English; passed alternately under the domination of each of these powers; was torn for many years by insurrections and civil wars; and in 1804 achieved its independence. At the present time the island is occupied by two independent states, the Republic of Hayti to the west, and the Dominican Republic to the east. The latter, commonly called Santo Domingo (or San Domingo), comprises nearly two-thirds of the area of the island, but is much less populous than Hayti proper and far inferior in productiveness and wealth. Its physical characteristics have already been summarized in the general description of the island. The climate of this eastern portion is said to be much more salubrious than that of any of the other West India islands; and statistics show the average health and longevity to be about equal to that of the United States. In the highlands the temperature is equable and agreeable all the year round; in the lowlands the thermometer ranges from 84° to 91° Fahr. The intensity of the summer heat is tempered by the sea-breeze which blows nearly all day long, and by the land-breeze which begins two or three hours after sunset and continues until sunrise. The winters are wonderfully mild and soothing, and favored localities are wholly free from those sharp variations which are so trying to invalids elsewhere. At Santo Domingo City the extremes of temperature are 60° and 95°, with an annual mean of 78.5°; and at Port-au-Prince the extremes are 63° and 104°, with an annual mean of 81°. From May to October heavy rains fall, frequently accompanied by thunder and lightning. November, December, and January, have a moderate rainfall, and from February to April it is uniformly dry. It is only on the southern coasts that hurricanes are common. The island has on several occasions suffered from earthquakes; the most disastrous on record being those of 1564, 1684, 1691, 1751, 1770, and 1842. By that of 1751 Port-au-Prince was destroyed, and the coast for 60 miles submerged; and by that of 1842 many towns were overturned and thousands of lives lost.

The city of **Santo Domingo**, capital of the republic, is situated on the right bank of the mouth of the Ozama River, in lat. 18° 28' north. It is the oldest existing settlement by white men in the New World, having been founded by Bartholomew Columbus in 1494; in 1871 it had a population of about 6,000. The town is built on a solid limestone formation, with a perceptible incline toward the river, and is surrounded by a wall 8 feet thick and 10 feet high. The streets are straight, wide, and at right angles to each other. Many of the ancient houses and public buildings are still standing, but are only remarkable for their solidity. Few of the many churches that once graced the city now remain. The most noteworthy is the *Cathedral*, in which the remains of Columbus and of his brother Bartholomew reposed

Cathedral of Santo Domingo.

for two and a half centuries. It was begun in 1512 and finished in 1540, and was modeled after a church in Rome. On the bank of the river are the ruins of the so-called *Castle of Columbus*, a fortified stone-house built by Diego Columbus. There are in the city a seminary, a college, and a primary school, all under the care of the Church, with about 300 pupils. The government buildings are spacious but of no architectural pretensions. The climate, as of all this portion of the island, is delightful, and the city could easily be made an attractive winter resort for invalids, were proper accommodations provided. At present there is no hotel worthy of the name; but the traveler will be well taken care of by inquiring for "Monsieur Auguste." In the vicinity of Santo Domingo are the curious natural caves of Santanna, reputed to have been one of the places of resort of the aborigines of the island who came here to worship their *zemes* or gods. From New York Santo Domingo is reached by the steamers of W. P. Clyde & Co., 35 Broadway.

Samana Bay, rendered famous by the attempt of President Grant to secure it for the United States, is formed by the peninsula of Samana on the northeast end of the island. It is about 35 miles long and 10 to 13 miles wide, but its entrance is narrow and easily defended. There are several small towns on the shores of the bay, of which the principal is *Santa Barbara*, which has a population of about 1,000 souls. Its site is locally considered unhealthy, but there are delightful situations in the immediate vicinity. *Savana la Mar*, on the opposite shore of the bay, is a little village of about 300 inhabitants, situated at the end of a vast plain 80 miles long by 12 miles wide. **Puerto Plata** (or Porto Plata) is situated on the northern coast of the island, about 100 miles northwest of Santo Domingo City. It lies on the slope of a mountain at the foot of a crescent-shaped bay, and contains about 3,000 inhabitants. The harbor has good anchorage, but shallows so rapidly near the shore that ships have to be loaded and unloaded by lighters. The city is a very old one, having been projected, it is said, by Columbus himself, but it has been completely destroyed several times, and is now a mere collection of small wooden houses, irregularly built on narrow and ill-paved streets. The location is very healthy, being fully open to both the sea and land breezes, and its winter climate is highly spoken of by residents and visitors. The leading element in the population are Germans, who have a monopoly of the tobacco-trade, which furnishes the chief business of the port. There are two small hotels, one kept by a Frenchman and the other by a German. For invalids probably the most favorable spots in Santo Domingo are the high inland valleys, but these must be selected by personal inspection.

The Haytian portion of the island has always been the best cultivated and most populous; but owing to its physical configuration the *climate* is less favorable to strangers than that of Santo Domingo proper. Except in the north, the air is both hot and moist, and malarious and febrile diseases are apt to prevail. The coast-regions generally are unhealthy; but doubtless in the more elevated localities of the interior there are many favored spots where the ordinary climatic drawbacks may be avoided, though none have achieved as yet more than a local reputation. Port-au-Prince, the capital of Hayti, is situated on the west coast of the island, at the head of the beautiful bay of Gonaives, and has a population of about 21,000. The town itself stands on somewhat elevated ground, but the surrounding country is for the most part marshy. The streets, though generally wide, are ill paved and very filthy, and the houses, mostly built of wood, are apt to present a dilapidated appearance. Among the public edifices are the President's House, the Senate House, a church, the Custom-House, a mint, and a hospital. There are also a lyceum, a college, and a few schools. The climate is hot, moist, and unhealthy for foreigners; the mean annual temperature is 81° and the extremes 63° and 104°. Hotel accommodations are very meagre. There is a bimonthly steam service to and from New York, by the Atlas S. S. Co., Pier 55 North River. Cape Haytien, on the north coast, formerly had the reputation of being "the Paris of the West Indies," but its magnificence has now greatly dwindled. In 1789 it had a population of nearly 20,000, and was the commercial capital of the rich French planters who controlled the eastern half of the island; in 1851 the population had sunk to 6,000, and is now about 15,000, the great majority of whom are negroes. It lies at the foot of some noble mountains that stretch boldly out into the sea, and presents a fine view from the harbor. On the street next the wharf are some fine stone warehouses, and a few handsome stone buildings are still found in various portions of the city, but ruins and flimsy wooden structures line most of the streets. The climate of Cape Haytien is much more salubrious than that of Port-au-Prince, and but for the lack of good hotel accommodations this would doubtless prove a beneficial winter residence for invalids. The country about the town is extremely picturesque; and about half a day's journey away, in a charming valley near the village of Milot, are the famous "Sans-Souci" palace and "Citadel" of the Emperor Christophe. Other towns in Hayti are *Port de la Paix, Gonaives, Saint-Marc, Miragoane, Jérémie*, and *Jacmel*, all of them open ports. Gonaives, Saint-Marc, and Port-au-Prince are reached from New York *via* Atlas S. S. Co., sailing bimonthly direct from Pier 55 (old No. 51) North River. On the south side, Aux Cayes and Jacmel are reached by the same line fortnightly.

Porto Rico.

Porto Rico, the smallest and most easterly of the Greater Antilles, lies 76 miles southeast of Santo Domingo, from which it is separated by the Mona Passage, and is after Cuba the most important of the Spanish dependencies in the West Indies. It is nearly rectangular in shape, about 100 miles long by 40 miles wide, and has an area, including the adjacent small islands, of 3,530 square miles, with a population of 731,650, rather more than half of whom are white. The coasts are generally regular, but there are many bays and inlets, and the northern shore is lined with navigable lagoons. A range of mountains extends through the island from east to west, having a general height of about 1,500 feet above the sea, with one peak (Luquillo) in the northeast which attains a height of 3,678 feet. From these mountains descend many small streams, some of which are navigable a few miles inland for small vessels. In the interior are extensive plains, and there are level tracts from five to ten miles wide on the coast. The soil is exceedingly fertile, and agriculture, which is mostly in the hands of the natives, is prosecuted with great success. The chief productions are sugar-cane, coffee, tobacco, cotton, rice, and maize; and many varieties of cabinet and dye woods, including mahogany, ebony, lignum-vitæ, cedar, and logwood, and many plants valuable in the arts and pharmacy, abound. All the tropical fruits grow in perfection; but the poverty of the fauna and flora is remarkable, there being scarcely any wild animals, birds, or flowers. The *climate* of Porto Rico, though very warm, is in general more healthy than that of the other Antilles; and owing to the diversified surface of the island almost any desired degree of temperature can be secured. The prevailing winds are easterly and northeasterly, but from November to March north winds are frequent. The land-wind, so constant at night in the other islands of the Antilles, is felt but seldom. The island has suffered much from hurricanes, of which those in 1742 and 1825 were particularly destructive. The winters are mild and equable, comparatively free from rain, and healthy for strangers. The capital and principal town is **San Juan de Puerto Rico**, situated on a small island off the north coast, in lat. 18° 29' north and long. 66° 7' west. It is strongly fortified, contains a population of about 23,000, and is well though not handsomely built. The streets are regularly laid out, well kept, and lighted with gas. The public buildings are the old Government-House, the Royal Military Hospital, the Bishop's Palace and Seminary, a large Cathedral, a Citadel, Custom-House, and City Hall, and several fine castles now used as barracks. There are a House of Refuge, an Insane Asylum, and other benevolent institutions; also a college and a fine library. The port is difficult of access, but is considered one of the most important in the Antilles, and a direct trade has been established with Europe and the United States. Other important towns of Porto Rico are *San German, Ponce, Mayaguez, Arecibo, Guayama, Aguadilla,* and *Bayamon*, most of which are seaports. (Porto Rico is reached from New York by the steamers of the "Atlas S. S. Co.," leaving Pier 55 North River every month.)

St. Thomas.

St. Thomas is one of the principal islands of the Virgin Group, lying south of the Bahamas, 30 miles east of Porto Rico, and belongs to Denmark. It is formed by a mountain-ridge extending the whole length and attaining an elevation of 1,480 feet, has an area of 35 square miles, and a population of 15,000. The shores are deeply indented, and the adjacent waters are studded with islands and rocks. There is no running stream on the island, and only one small spring; rain-water is the sole reliance, and droughts are frequent. The soil is not fertile, and the products are not sufficient for one-twentieth of its inhabitants; but nearly all the steamers visiting the West Indies make this a stopping-place, and give it considerable commercial importance and prosperity. The *climate* is warm, the thermometer ranging from 70° to 90°, and those suffering from consumption or from Bright's disease of the kidneys usually derive benefit from a winter residence here. Hurricanes pass over the island about once in twenty years, and do great damage. Earthquakes are very frequent, but serious shocks do not occur oftener than once in fifty years. St. Thomas is reached from New York by the steamers of the United States and Brazil Mail S. S. Co. (calling at Newport News for passengers and mail) every three weeks, and from Havana by French steamers leaving Havre on the 22d of each month. **Charlotte Amalie,** the only town, contains about 12,000 inhabitants, and is built along the shore of an excellent bay on the south side of the island, in lat. 18° 20' north, and lon. 64° 56' west.

Santa Cruz, or St. Croix.

This island, the largest and southernmost of the Virgin Group, lies about 35 miles east of St. Thomas, forming with the latter and St. John the Danish Government of the West Indies. It is 25 miles long by 5 miles broad, with an area of 84 square miles and a population in 1870 of 22,760. The surface is generally level, but a range of low heights follows the line of its northern shore and throws out numerous spurs. There are numerous streams, the soil is fertile, and nearly the whole island is in a high state of cultivation, about half being planted with sugar-cane. Sugar and rum are the principal products; the others being cotton, coffee, and indigo. All varieties of tropical fruits are produced in abundance, and flowers are perpetually in bloom. The roads throughout the island are admirable, and the scenery is remarkably picturesque and pleasing. English is the language generally spoken. The *climate* is warm and strikingly equable. During the winter the thermometer ranges from 76° to 82°, and in summer the heat is but slightly increased. Little rain falls at any time of the year, so that the air is dry, and there is no malaria. Many invalids who have made trial of it consider Santa Cruz the best health-resort in the West Indies, especially for those in advanced stages of consumption. The west side of the island is somewhat more sheltered than the eastern side. **Christiansted** is the capital of the island, and here and at the little town of **Frederickstadt** are good hotels and boarding-houses. Santa Cruz is reached by sailing-vessel from St. Thomas in a few hours.

St. Vincent.

St. Vincent is an island of the British West Indies, belonging to the Windward Group, in lat. 13° 13' north and lon. 61° west. It is 17 miles long and 10 broad, with an area of 131 square miles, and a population in 1871 of 35,688. The surface is divided in the middle by a mountain-ridge, culminating in the volcano of Morne Garou (Souffrière), about 5,000 feet high, which contains a crater $\frac{1}{2}$ mile in diameter, and 500 feet deep; the most recent eruption was on April 30, 1812. The soil is fertile; the mountains are clothed with valuable forests; the valleys are well watered and cultivated, yielding sugar-cane, arrow-root, cotton, and cacao. The *climate* is warm and very humid, but not unhealthy, and exactly suits those consumptives who thrive best in a warm, moist atmosphere. The thermometrical range in winter is between 72° and 84°; in summer between 78° and 87°. The mountainous districts are cooler, and there is considerable field for choice. **Kingston**, the chief town of the island, is built on the shore of a fine bay on the southwest coast. It is a pleasant place, and has considerable reputation as a health-resort.

Barbadoes.

This also is an island of the British West Indies, the most easterly of the Caribbean Group, in lat. 13° 10' north and lon. 59° 32' west. It is of an oval form, 22 miles long and 14 broad, with an area of 166 square miles, and a population of 162,000. The population of Barbadoes is denser than that of any other country in the world except Malta, averaging nearly 1,000 to the square mile. The island is divided by a deep valley into two parts. Near the centre of the northern and larger part Mt. Hillaby rises to the height of 1,147 feet. From the west coast the ground rises in successive terraces, broken by ravines, to the central ridge, from which hills of a conical form radiate in a northeast direction to the sea-shore. The soil in parts is sandy and porous, in others rich and extremely productive; and the whole island is under cultivation. There are several chalybeate springs, containing chiefly iron, carbonic acid, and fixed alkali in different proportions. The coast is encircled by coral-reefs, which in some parts extend seaward for 3 miles, and are dangerous to navigation. Carlisle Bay, the port and harbor of Barbadoes, is a spacious open roadstead, capable of containing 500 vessels; but it is exposed to south and southwest winds. The *climate* of the island is warm, but equable and salubrious, and residence here seldom fails to benefit those suffering from consumption or from Bright's disease of the kidneys. In December the thermometer ranges from 73° to

Barbadoes.

85°; in February from 71° to 84°. **Bridgetown**, the capital of Barbadoes, contains 25,000 inhabitants, and is the seat of government. There are only three other towns. The most prominent resorts are Hastings (2 miles from Bridgetown) and Bathsheba (16 miles). Barbadoes is reached from New York by steamers of the Quebec S. S. Co., leaving every 14 days, or by the United States and Brazilian Mail S. S. Co.

Curaçoa.

This is one of the Dutch West Indies, and lies in the Caribbean Sea, 46 miles north of the coast of Venezuela, in lat. 12° 20′ north, an' long. 60° west. Its extreme length from northwest to southeast is 36 miles, its breadth is about 8 miles, and its area 164 square miles. The population in 1870 was 21,319. It has a hilly surface, with rugged coasts, and is exceedingly barren. Fresh water is scarce, and is obtained either from rain or from deep wells. Severe droughts frequently occur; the soil is so poor that provisions are imported, and some of the products once cultivated, as indigo, cotton, and cacao, are now entirely neglected. Sugar, tobacco, maize, cochineal, cattle, horses, asses, sheep, and goats are raised; and from the lime is made the celebrated Curaçoa liqueur. The *climate* is dry and hot, but the island is not unhealthy, and it has long been a favorite resort for sufferers from Bright's disease of the kidneys. Some consumptives have also derived great benefit from a residence here, and except for its remoteness it would probably be one of the most frequented of the West India health-resorts. The capital and principal town of the island is *Willemsted*, situated at the entrance of Santa Anna harbor, on the southwest coast. There is irregular connection by steamers with New York.

"Down the Islands."

It is of course impossible for us to even enumerate the countless islands which make up the West Indian archipelago, but some of the attractions, which are common to nearly all of them, are admirably pointed out by Charles Kingsley, in his book on "The West Indies," and from his second chapter we condense the following account of a sail "down the islands" (from St. Thomas):

"I had heard and read much from boyhood," he writes, "about these 'Lesser Antilles.' I had pictured them to myself a thousand times, but I was altogether unprepared for their beauty and grandeur. For hundreds of miles, day after day, the steamer carried us past a shifting diorama of scenery, which may be likened to Vesuvius and the Bay of Naples, repeated again and again, with every possible variation of the same type of delicate loveliness. Under a cloudless sky, upon a sea lively, yet not unpleasantly rough, we thrashed and leaped along. Ahead of us, one after another, rose high on the southern horizon banks of gray clouds, from under each of which, as we neared it, descended the shoulder of a mighty mountain, dim and gray. Nearer still, the gray changed to purple; lowlands rose out of the sea, sloping upward with those grand and simple concave curves which almost always betoken volcanic land. Nearer still, the purple changed to green. Tall palm trees and engine-houses stood out against the sky; the surf gleamed white around the base of isolated rocks. A little nearer, and we were under the lee or western side of the island. The sea grew smooth as glass; we entered the shade of the island-cloud, and slid along in still, unfathomable blue water, close under the shore of what should have been one of the Islands of the Blessed.

"It was easy, in presence of such scenery, to conceive the exaltation which possessed the souls of the first discoverers of the West Indies. What wonder if they seemed to themselves to have burst into Fairy-land—to be at the gates of the earthly paradise? With such a climate, such a soil, such vegetation, such fruits, what luxury must not have seemed possible to the dwellers along those shores? What riches, too, of gold and jewels might not be hidden among those forest-shrouded glens and peaks? And, beyond, and beyond again, ever-new islands, new continents, perhaps, an inexhaustible wealth of yet undiscovered worlds.

"I said that these islands resembled Vesuvius and the Bay of Naples. Like causes have produced like effects, and each island is little but the peak of a volcano, down whose shoulders lava and ashes have slidden toward the sea. Some carry several crater-cones, complicating at once the structure and scenery of the island; but the majority carry but a single cone, like that little island, or rather rock, of *Saba*, which is the first of the Antilles under the lee of which the steamer passes. *Santa Cruz*, which is left to leeward, is a long, low, ragged island, of the same form as St. Thomas and the Virgins, and belongs, I should suppose, to the same formation. But Saba rises sheer out of the sea some 1,500 feet or more, without flat ground or even harbor. From a little landing-place to leeward a stair runs up 800 feet into the bosom of the old volcano, and in that hollow live some 1,200 honest Dutch, and some 800 negroes, who were, till of late years, their slaves, at least in law. But in Saba, it is said, the whites were really the slaves, and the negroes the masters; for they went off whither and when they liked; earned money about the islands, and brought it home; expected their masters to keep them when out of work, and not in vain. The island was, happily for it, too poor for sugar-growing and the 'grande culture;' the Dutch were never tempted to increase the number of their slaves; looked upon the few they had as friends and children, and, when emancipation came, no change whatsoever ensued, it is said, in the semi-feudal relation between the black men and the white. So these good Dutch live peacefully aloft in their volcano, which, it is to be hoped, will not explode again. They grow garden-crops, among which, I understand, are several products of the temperate zone, the air being, at that height, pleasantly cool. They sell their produce about the islands. They build boats up in the crater—the best boats in all the West Indies—and lower them down the cliff to the sea. They hire themselves out, too—not having lost their forefathers' sea-going instincts—as sailors about all those seas, and are, like their boats, the best in those parts. They all speak English, and, though they are nominally Lutherans, are glad of the services of the excellent Bishop of Antigua, who pays them periodical visits. He described them as virtuous, shrewd, simple, healthy folk, retaining, in spite of the tropical sun, the same clear, white-and-red complexions which their ancestors brought from Holland two hundred years ago—a proof, among many, that the white man need not degenerate in these isles.

"Much more recent—in appearance at least—is the little *Isle of St. Eustatius*, or, at least, the crater-cone, with its lip broken down at one spot, which makes up five-sixths of the island. St. Eustatius may have been in eruption, though there is no record of it, during historic times, and looks more unrepentant and capable of misbehaving itself again than does any other crater-cone in the Antilles; far more so than the *soufrière* in St. Vincent, which exploded in 1812.

"But these two are mere rocks. It is not till the traveler arrives at *St. Kitts* that he sees what a West Indian island is.

"The 'Mother of the Antilles,' as she is called, is worthy of her name. Everywhere from the shore the land sweeps up, slowly at first, then rapidly, toward the central mass, the rugged peak whereof goes by the name of Mount Misery. Only once, and then but for a moment, did we succeed in getting a sight of the actual summit, so pertinaciously did the clouds crawl around it. Thirty-seven hundred feet aloft a pyramid of black lava rises above the broken walls of an older crater, and is, to judge from its knife-edge, flat top, and concave eastern side, the last remnant of an inner cone, which has been washed, or, more probably, blasted away. Beneath it, according to the report of an islander to Dr. Davy (and what I heard was to the same effect), is a deep hollow, longer than it is wide, without an outlet, walled in by precipices and steep declivities, from fissures in which steam and the fumes of sulphur are emitted. Sulphur in crystals abounds, incrusting the rocks and loose stones, and a stagnant pool of rain-water occupies the bottom of the *soufrière*.

"The steamer passes each island only once a fortnight, so that to land in an island is equivalent to staying there at least that time, unless one chooses to take the chances of a coasting-schooner, and bad food, bugs, cockroaches, and a bunk, which —but I will not describe them. 'Non ragionam di lor, ma guarde' (down the companion) 'e passa.'

"I must therefore content myself with describing, as honestly as I can, what little we saw from the sea of islands, at each of which we would gladly have staid several days. As the traveler nears each of them—*Guadaloupe, Dominica, Martinique* (of which last two we had only one passing glance), *St. Vincent, St. Lucia,* and *Grenada*—he will be impressed not only by the peculiarity of their form, but by the richness of their color. All of them do not, like St. Kitts, Guadaloupe, and St. Vincent, slope up to one central peak. In Martinique, for instance, there are three separate peaks, or groups of peaks, the Mont Pelée, the Pitons du Carbet, and the Pitons du Vauclain. But all have that peculiar jagged outline which is noticed first at the Virgin Islands.

"Flat 'vans' or hog-backed hills, and broad sweeps of moorland, so common in Scotland, are as rare as are steep walls of cliff, so common in the Alps. Pyramid is piled on pyramid, the sides of each at a slope of about 45°, till the whole range is a congeries of multitudinous peaks and peaklets, round the base of which spreads out, with a sudden sweep, the smooth lowland of volcanic ash and lava. This extreme raggedness of outline is easily explained. The mountains have never been, as in Scotland, planed smooth by ice. They have been gouged out, in every direction, by the furious tropic rains and tropic rain-torrents. Had the rocks been stratified and tolerably horizontal, these rains would have cut them out into table-lands, divided by deep gullies, such as may be seen in Abyssinia and in certain parts of the Western United States. But these rocks are altogether amorphous and unstratified, and have been poured or spouted out as lumps, dikes, and sheets of lava, of every degree of hardness; so that the rain, in degrading them, has worn them, not into tables and ranges, but into innumerable cones. And the process of degradation is still going on rapidly. Though a cliff, or sheet of bare rocks, is hardly visible among the glens, yet here and there a bright, brown patch tells of a recent landslip; and the masses of *débris* and banks of shingle, backed by a pestilential little swamp at the mouth of each torrent, show how furious must be the downfall and down-roll before the force of a sudden flood, along so headlong an incline.

"But, in strange contrast with the ragged outline, and with the wild devastation of the rainy season, is the richness of the verdure which clothes the islands, up to their highest peaks, in what seems a coat of green fur, but, when looked at through the glasses, proves to be, in most cases, gigantic timber. Not a rock is seen. If there be a cliff here and there, it is as green as an English lawn. Steep slopes are gray with *groogroo* palms, or yellow with unknown flowering trees. High against the sky-line tiny knots and lumps are found to be gigantic trees. Each glen has buried its streamlet a hundred feet in vegetation, above which, here and there, the gray stem and dark crown of some *palmiste* tower up like the mast of some great admiral. The eye and the fancy strain vainly into the green abysses, and wander up and down over the wealth of depths and heights, compared with which European parks and woodlands are but paltry scrub and shaugh. No books are needed to tell that. The eye discovers it for itself, even before it has learned to judge of the great size of the vegetation from the endless variety of form and color; for the islands, though green intensely, are not of one, but of every conceivable green, or rather of hues ranging from pale yellow through all greens into cobalt blue; and as the wind stirs the leaves, and sweeps the lights and shadows over hill and glen, all is ever-changing, iridescent, like a peacock's neck, till the whole island, from peak to shore, seems some glorious jewel—an emerald with tints of sapphire and topaz, hanging between blue sea and white surf below, and blue sky and cloud above. If the reader fancies that I exaggerate, let him go and see. Let him lie for one hour off the Rousseau at Dominica. Let him sail down the leeward side of Guadaloupe, down the leeward side of what island he will, and judge for himself how poor, and yet how tawdry, my words are, compared with the luscious yet magnificent coloring of the Antilles.

"The traveler, at least, so I think, would remark also, with some surprise, the seeming smallness of these islands. The Basse Terre of Guadaloupe, for instance, is forty miles in length. As you lie off it, it does not look half or even quarter of that length, and that not merely because the distances north and south are foreshortened, or shut in by nearer headlands. The causes, I believe, are more subtile and more complex. First, the novel clearness of the air, which makes the traveler, fresh from misty England, fancy every object far nearer, and therefore far smaller, than it actually is. Next, the simplicity of form. Each outer line tends upward so surely toward a single focus—each whole is so sharply defined between its base-line of sea and its background of sky, that, like a statue, each island is compact and complete in itself, an isolated and self-dependent organism, and therefore, like every beautiful statue, it looks much smaller than it is. So perfect this isolation seems, that one fancies, at moments, that the island does not rise out of the sea, but floats upon it; that it is held in place, not by the root of the mountains, and deep miles of lava-wall below, but by the cloud which has caught it by the top, and will not let it go. Let that cloud but rise, and vanish, and the whole beautiful thing will be cast adrift, ready to fetch away before the wind, and (as it will seem often enough to do when viewed through a cabin-port) to slide silently past you, while you are sliding past it."

THE BERMUDAS.

THE Bermudas—the "still vext Bermoothes" of Shakespeare's "Tempest"—are a group of small islands belonging to Great Britain, lying in the Atlantic Ocean, about 580 miles S. S. E. of Cape Hatteras, between lat. 32° 14′ and 32° 25′ north and lon. 64° 38′ and 64° 52′ west. They are formed upon a coral-reef, and, though only 18 miles long by 6 in greatest breadth, they are no less than 365 in number. They are separated from each other by very narrow channels, and are mostly mere rocky islets, only 5 being of any considerable size, and only 12 or 15 being inhabited. Bermuda or Long Island is the principal member of the group; it is 16 miles long and about 1½ mile wide. The other principal islands are St. George's, Ireland, Somerset, and St. David's. Dangerous coral-reefs surround the islands on the north, west, and south, and as these are nearly all under water and extend in some places 10 miles from land, access is difficult and navigation of the waters should not be attempted except with the aid of experienced native pilots. There are some excellent harbors, however, that of St. George's, the easternmost island, having been formed at great cost by blasting away the reefs and constructing a breakwater on the point of the adjacent island of Ireland. St. George is now an important naval station, and is strongly fortified. When viewed from the sea the Bermudas are of slight elevation, the highest point of land scarcely attaining the height of 200 feet. In their general aspect they closely resemble their neighbors the West Indies. Vegetation is green throughout the year, and the soil, though overworked, still yields abundance of garden vegetables, potatoes, fruit, and arrow-root. Pomegranates, figs, and bananas, are produced in profusion, and oranges, strawberries, and pineapples, are raised to some extent. The cocoanut, the India-rubber tree, the cabbage-palm, the tamarind, and the Pride of India, give a tropical character to the vegetation, which, however, lacks the tropical richness and luxuriance. The *climate* of the Bermudas is damp, but mild. The mean temperature in winter is 60° Fahr. and the thermometer rarely records 40°; but rain falls copiously during the winter months and violent storms are frequent. At such times the variations of temperature are sudden and marked, and the air becomes surcharged with a penetrating moisture. Asthma, rheumatism, and bronchitis, are nearly always benefited by residence in the Bermudas; but consumptives in advanced stages of the disease are apt to find the climate very trying, and even those in the earlier stages should seek sheltered locations, and be extremely careful about exposure to the night air. Hamilton is recommended with this view.

Hamilton, the capital of the Bermudas, is situated on Bermuda or Long Island, the largest of the group, and is a pretty little town of 1,500 inhabitants, built on the slope of a gentle elevation, and containing about 500 houses, constructed for the most part of freestone. The government buildings are located here, the hotel ac-

Bermuda.

commodations are good. The new *Princess Hotel* is managed by an American, and the *Hamilton Hotel* ($2.50 to $3 a day) is a comfortable house. Several churches add to the attractions of the place, and there are good schools. Pleasant excursions from Hamilton may be made to *Harrington Sound* and *Fairy-Land*. The former is a salt-water lake, with a narrow outlet to the sea, and shores honey-combed with caves, in some of which are beautiful stalactite formations. In the neighborhood are Moore's cottage and the calabash tree under which he composed his poems. Fairy-Land is a delightful bit of sea-coast scenery, in perfecting which Nature and Art have joined hands. The waters around Hamilton invite to bathing and boating, and yachting is a favorite amusement. From New York Hamilton is reached in

3 days by steamers of the Quebec Steamship Co., leaving Pier 47 North River on alternate Thursdays, and more frequently during the winter season. Fare, $30.

St. George, situated on the east side of the island of the same name, is the largest town and chief port of the Bermudas. It has a magnificent harbor, made, as we have said, by blasting away the coral-reef, and is an important military and naval station, a regiment of the line and one or more vessels being always stationed here. The town is pleasantly located on a gentle acclivity fronting the harbor, but it is built in a very straggling and irregular manner, and possesses neither the external nor the social attractions of Hamilton. Hotel accommodations, though limited, are fairly good.

A lively article in a recent number of *Harper's Magazine* contains an animated description of the Bermudas, from which we cull such items as are likely to prove interesting to the tourist or invalid: "Not more than 16 or 20 of the numerous islands are inhabited, and of these the five largest are St. David's, St. George's, Bermuda proper, sometimes styled the Continent, Somerset, and Ireland. They are about 15 miles in length, and the greatest breadth is about 5 miles. There are no mountains, no rivers, and so, while they are without magnificence in scenery, in a quiet sort of beauty they are unique. There are about 150 miles of good hard roads, which are generally free from dust. In many places deep cuttings have been made, and the rock towers above the carriage even. The scenery is exceedingly picturesque, and changes continually. Now you drive through wide stretches of country, and the landscape bears a striking resemblance to that of New England; then through a narrow road, with high walls of rock on either hand, on the sides of which the maiden-hair fern grows in profusion, and the road is so winding that every new view which bursts suddenly upon you is a surprise; and then there are delightful glimpses of the sea, with its many islands. Walls of stone extend along the road-side, and over them clamber the morning-glory, the prickly-pear, and the night-blooming cereus. Great beds of geraniums, which mock our hot-houses in their profusion, grow wild. Hedges of oleander line the roads or border cultivated patches of land, protecting them from the high winds which at times sweep over the islands. Thirteen varieties of it are found here, and wherever you go it is one mass of pink-and-white blossoms. The lantana also grows wild along all the hedges. The passion-flower peeps out from its covert of green leaves, creeping up the branches of tall trees. The profusion of flowers is wonderful, and one can always have a bouquet for the gathering. The winter is the regal time for them. About Christmas the roses, magnificent in size and of great variety, are in all their glory. One gentleman assured me that he had upward of 150 varieties. No great care seems to be taken to cultivate them. Here and there one sees a fine garden, but nothing that even approaches what might be accomplished with such a soil and climate. The beauty and variety of flowers are fully equaled by the excellence and diversity of fruits. Oranges of superior quality are raised, though their culture is not general. The lemon grows wild. The mango, guava, papaw, pomegranate, fig, arocado pear—whose lovers (for they can be called nothing else) become eloquent in its praise—the custard-apple, the banana—the lazy man's delight, bearing its wealth of fruit, and dying as it yields its single bunch, while the new plants springing up about its dead stalk maintain the supply the year round—all these fruits grow readily, and with due effort would grow abundantly. Apples and pears are raised, but lack the flavor they possess with us. Peaches, heretofore excellent, have been destroyed for two years past by an insect. Strawberries ripen from November till July. Grapes grow luxuriantly. The most common tree is the Bermudian cedar, with which nearly all the hill-sides are wooded. Occasionally one sees the mountain-palm, while tamarind, tamarisk, palmetto, cocoanut, India-rubber, mahogany, and calabash trees are quite common. In gardens many West Indian trees are found.

"Although three crops of vegetables can be raised annually, still agriculture is in a very backward state, and most of the fruits enumerated are specially rather than generally cultivated. In the early colonial days it was the chief occupation of the people, but was afterward abandoned for other pursuits, and after the introduction of slavery the land was mostly tilled by slaves, and a certain disgrace attached to this kind of labor. Ignorance reigned in the fields, and it is only recently that an attempt has been made to wrest them from its sway. The most progressive men are now deeply interested in the subject, and strong efforts are being made to induce the people to cultivate something besides the stereotyped onion, potato, tomato, and arrow-root, the last said to be the best in the world, though the quantity raised is constantly diminishing, as it exhausts the soil, and does not prove as remunerative as some other crops. Small patches of land are selected here and there, are carefully spaded—the plough not being in common use—and from them the surprisingly large crops are realized. The land is quite generally inclosed by the oleander, and to prevent inroads upon it all creatures that feed out-of-doors, from a hen to a cow, are usually tied. The poor things have that resigned look peculiar to individuals linked to any thing from which they are too weak or too stupid to escape.

"In traveling through Bermuda one's thoughts continually revert to Spain. The name of old Juan Bermudez, its discoverer, has been bestowed upon the islands, and it would seem as if his spirit still floats over them, so thoroughly Spanish are the outward characteristics; and in no place is this more marked than in the quaint old town of St. George's. The harbor is beautiful, and much more accessible than that of Hamilton. The streets are narrow—mere lanes, in fact—across which you can shake hands with your neighbor if so disposed, and they are, moreover, sandy and disagreeable for pedestrians. Houses are huddled together in the most miscellaneous manner, and from one perfumed with the onion, with its unkempt and uninteresting-looking occupants bursting out at doors and windows, you come pat upon a beautiful garden, with its pretty Bermudian cottage, only to find repetitions of the experience throughout the town. On its most commanding height are fortifications, and the work now in progress is said to be particularly fine. There are barracks all over the hill, and soldiers sitting or loafing about wherever you go. During the war St. George's was a busy town, being a great resort for blockade-runners, which were hospitably welcomed by our English friends. Goods purchased abroad were brought here, and then transferred to the craft waiting to receive them. It was risky business, but one well followed, and many men here who flattered themselves at the beginning of the war that they were amassing large fortunes were bankrupt or nearly so at its close. Some few, however, realized large amounts. The town was crowded, and at night every available space out of doors or in was occupied. Men lay on verandas, walls, docks, and floors. Money was plenty, and sailors sometimes landed with $1,500 in specie. The price of labor advanced; wages were doubled. Liquor flowed freely, and the common laborer had his champagne and rich cake to offer. Here, too, was concocted the fiendish plot by Dr. Blackburn and others for introducing the yellow-fever into Northern cities by sending thither boxes of infected clothing; but it was fortunately discovered in season to prevent injury to any save the plotters. During the entire war it was one of the hot-beds of secession, and with its close there came a sudden collapse. If a door-nail is deader than anything else in Nature, then St. George's is as dead as that nail.

"From St. George's to Hamilton there is a fine ocean-drive of 8 or 9 miles. Going by Harrington Sound, you will pass the Devil's Hole, or Neptune's Grotto, between which and the sound there is a subterranean communication—the sound, by-the-way, being an arm of the sea. Fish caught at the most favorable seasons of the year are kept here until wanted for use. The usual number is 1,000, though it will hold twice as many. There are many varieties of fish, and the spectacle is as pleasing as it is novel. These ponds, on a small scale, are quite numerous throughout Bermuda.

"Like most limestone countries, Bermuda abounds in caves, and nowhere are they more beautiful than in Walsingham, not far from Neptune's Grotto, on the road leading around Harrington Sound, one of the loveliest sheets of water imaginable. The whole region is singularly attractive. Mimic lakes, reflecting the varied hues of the rocks which inclose them, with trees overhanging their banks, teem with fish wonderful in variety and color, whose motions are the very ideal of grace. By-paths through the tangled wildwood lead one through a wilderness of beauty.

Nature has been lavish of her gifts all through this locality, and as it is geologically one of the oldest sections of Bermuda, all the rocks seem to have the weather-stain which the vines love so well. Over the whole is thrown the charm of poetry, from the fact that it was one of Tom Moore's favorite haunts while living in Bermuda. It is fitting that Nature should have her temples in such a place. Humility is one of the conditions of entrance to them, and so, bending low, making a slight descent, we are soon standing in a room from whose arched roof hang large stalactites. Artificial lights bring out each in its full proportions, and one contemplates with wonder this strange architecture, regardless of the ages it has endured. In a second one near by, and which is much more spacious, is a beautiful sheet of water, clear as crystal, and of an emerald tint. The finest cave is the Admiral's, which guides may fail to mention from the fact that it is more difficult of access than any of the others; but to one at all accustomed to climbing there is little danger and no great difficulty in visiting any of them.

"Back to the enchanted ground we lunch under 'Moore's calabash-tree,' hacked by specimen-hunters, but beautiful still. Here he sat and wrote, and so acquired the divine right to all this place. Of course there is a love-story, and the characters in it are this same poet and the handsomest lady in all the Bermudas at that time, Miss Fanny Tucker, sometimes prettily called the 'Rose of the Isles,' whom Moore in his poems addresses as 'Nea.' Well, he wrote verses to her, and about her, and went on in true lover-like style; but she seems not to have been moved by his strains, and liked her own name so well that she did not change it on her marriage. Moore lived to love again, as we all know. In fact, all the people in this little story are said to have lived happily ever after.

"One of the most delightful places in Bermuda to visit is Clarence Hill, the residence of the admiral, who is supposed to live here three months each year. The road from Hamilton is a wild one, and full of variety, with most charming combinations of the woods, country, and sea. We pass Undercliff Cottage, designed for happy lovers, who can here spend the honey-moon in a retreat so secure that there will be no demand for the farce of 'Old Married People,' always a failure when enacted by amateurs. There are flowers in abundance, which with the air and views will sustain life for a month or so. A pretty veranda overlooks the water, with its

"Summer Isles of Eden lying in dark purple spheres of sea."

Steps lead almost from the door down to the boat, which will bear them out into all the loveliness, which is ever beckoning to them. For absolute beauty I know of but one other view in Bermuda comparable with this—that from the summit of St. David's Island. The atmospheric effects are marvelous, and lead one to consider matrimony very favorably, so closely are the place and the condition connected. The grounds at Clarence Hill are quite extensive and well kept. The house is plain, but the attractiveness of the place is in its marine views, and in the fact that Nature has been left in. On a hill-side overlooking the sea, in a most sequestered spot, is an exquisite bit of gardening. Mosses, ferns, and many tropical plants, grow in such profusion and grace, peeping from under rocks, climbing over them, that it is only by critical inspection that you perceive that their presence is due to cultivation. Near by is a cave, against whose outer wall the sea is ever dashing. It was tunneled by a former admiral, and is so large that on its completion a ball was given in it by way of celebration.

"Some pleasant morning a visit must be made to Ireland Island, the site of the dock-yard and naval establishment, and one of the four telegraphic signal-stations. We land, and encounter at once the British sentinel, who is very courteous, and splutters in the most unintelligible English, using words on general principles, more as a relief to himself than as an assistance to any one else. Not being in any sense dangerous to Great Britain, we are allowed to proceed. There are marines everywhere, and with few exceptions they seem to be a most disagreeable set of fellows. The most remarkable object of interest is undoubtedly the floating-dock, one of the largest structures of its kind in the world, which was built in England, and was towed across the Atlantic to its present position by 5 ships. Its length is 381 feet, and its breadth 124 feet. The largest and heaviest man-of-war can be docked. It is divided into 48 water-tight compartments, which are fitted with valves worked from the upper deck. By placing some 4,000 tons of water in the upper chambers its keel can be brought five feet out of water and cleaned—a process which it has once undergone. You ascend a ladder or steps on the outside, and get a fine view, having your head nearly blown off while doing it. People whose heads are of no consequence invariably ascend, while the more severely intellectual remain at the foot of the ladder. There is the usual number of machine-shops, officers, and magazines, with vast quantities of powder—much more than a quiet little place like Bermuda would seem to require. Places have been tunneled out here and there, and filled with munitions of war. Everything is arranged in the most deliberate and scientific manner to injure the feelings of other people. There is no suggestion of peace or its congresses, unless the maiden-hair fern which grows on the rocks wherever there is sufficient moisture may be considered one. Among so many suggestions of disaster and death the hospital and cemetery are harmonious accompaniments. The former is commodious and well managed. The latter has more inmates, and is a pleasant place to go to when one cannot go elsewhere, and is rendered attractive by flowers and trees—a fact deserving mention, since most cemeteries here are the lonesomest kind of places, though they are not particularly gay in any country.

"If the moon, tide, and party, are just right, Fairy-Land presents as great a contrast to Ireland Island as can well be imagined. Five or six hours are needed for the expedition. You row into little coves, then into what seem to be lakes, so perfectly inclosed is the water; hard by the shore, looking up through dells in which you can almost see the fairies dancing under the trees; under great rocks which threaten to send you down among the fishes; around islands, into inlets, where the mangroves, every leaf glistening in the moonlight, throw out their branches in the most welcoming way. All this, and much more, is in store for him who goes to Fairy-Land, the enchanted spot of Bermuda.

"Bermuda having suffered several times from yellow fever, grave errors have arisen in regard to the healthfulness of the climate. The fever seems to have been due rather to imperfect drainage and defective quarantine regulations than to any predisposing causes in the climate. Several years since there was a convict establishment here, which was the means of introducing a very low class physically—men predisposed to disease, and who succumbed at once to attacks of fever. All this has subjected Bermuda to unfavorable criticisms respecting the healthiness of its climate; but any country might suffer under like sanitary conditions. The convict establishment has recently been broken up, thereby removing a fruitful source of disease; and the enactment of strict quarantine laws, which are rigidly enforced upon all vessels, goes far toward preventing the introduction of epidemics from other places. So admirably are the islands situated that there is no excuse for defective drainage or quarantine. Strangers usually resort here in the winter, and generally speak highly of the agreeability of the climate. Rains are quite prevalent at this season, and most houses are not sufficiently protected from dampness, as the native Burmudian thinks fires unhealthy, and sits on his veranda throughout the year. But grates and stoves are gaining in favor, and are being used more and more. A few people have learned that Bermuda is a pleasant summer resort, and act accordingly. There is almost invariably a good breeze from some quarter, and the nights and mornings are cool and delightful. Sunstroke is unknown. August and September are the hottest and most disagreeable months, owing to the enervating southerly winds. The mercury seldom rises above 85° or falls below 40°, while the average is about 70°. There seem to be no diseases peculiar to the climate, but there are ailments enough to keep several excellent physicians actively employed. Consumptives often resort here, but seldom derive that benefit which they experience in a dry climate, though they often improve, and in some cases are nearly cured. The climate seems to be especially beneficial to those afflicted with rheumatism and certain nervous diseases. Bronchial affections are generally relieved, and not unfrequently cured.

"'What shall we wear?' may be answered by saying that in summer ladies find muslins and thin wash materials most desirable, and they are worn quite late in the fall. White dresses are very much worn. At other seasons what is suitable for autumn in New York is worn here. The dress is usually very simple in material as well as style."

THE SANDWICH ISLANDS.

How to reach.—The elegant steamships of the Oceanic S. S. Company make the trip twice a month from San Francisco to Honolulu. Fare $75. "The voyage down to the islands," says Mr. Nordhoff, "lasts from 8 to 9 days, and even to persons subject to sea-sickness is likely to be an enjoyable sea-journey, because after the second day the weather is charmingly warm, the breezes usually mild, and the skies sunny and clear. In 48 hours after you leave the Golden Gate, shawls, overcoats, and wraps, are discarded. You put on thinner clothing. After breakfast you will like to spread rugs on the deck and lie in the sun, fanned by deliciously soft winds; and before you see Honolulu you will, even in winter, like to have an awning spread over you to keep off the sun. On the way you see flying-fish, and, if you are lucky, an occasional whale or a school of porpoises, but no ships. It is one of the loneliest of ocean-tracks, for sailing-vessels usually steer farther north to catch stronger gales. But you sail over the lovely blue of the Pacific Ocean, which has not only softer gales but even a different shade of color than the fierce Atlantic."

Strictly speaking the Sandwich Islands cannot be called an *American* resort, yet as they are chiefly under American influence and as American invalids are almost the only ones that are found there, our little book would be incomplete without some mention of them. The Hawaiian or Sandwich Islands are the most northerly cluster of the Polynesian Archipelago, and lie in the North Pacific between Mexico and China, extending in a curve about 360 miles from N.W. to S. E., between lat. 18° 55' and 22° 20' N. and long. 154° 55' and 160° 15' W. There are 12 islands in the group, and their names and areas, in order from S. E., are: Hawaii, 4,040 square miles; Maui, 603 square miles; Molokini, islet; Kahoolawe, 60 square miles; Lanai, 150 square miles; Molokai, 169 square miles; Oahu, 522 square miles; Kauai, 527 square miles; Lehua, islet; Niihau, 70 square miles; Kaula and Bird, islets: total about 6,100 square miles, of which two thirds are included in the principal island which gives its name to the group. The islands are of volcanic formation and mountainous, the fertile lands being mostly confined to the valleys and to a belt of alluvial soil at the shore. The uplands are better adapted to grazing than to tillage. The mountains, covered with dense forests, are not cultivable. The windward coasts, which receive the northeast trade-winds, intercept the rains and are fertile, while the leeward side of the same island may be almost rainless. On the windward side the mountains are densely wooded. Here are the largest active and also the largest extinct craters in the world, and in no part of the islands can one journey far without seeing extinct craters, which are generally overgrown with a luxuriant vegetation. Many hundred square miles are covered with recent and barren lavas. Near the shore the natives cultivate sweet potatoes upon lavas that are hardly cooled, pulverizing the scoria and mixing with it a little vegetable mould. The chief productions of the islands are sugar, rice, coffee, cotton, sandal-wood, tobacco, wheat, maize, arrow-root, oranges, lemons, bananas, tamarinds, bread-fruit, guavas, potatoes, yams, kalo, and ornamental woods. Neat-cattle, sheep, goats, and hogs, are raised; and hides, tallow, and wool, figure largely in the exportations. The *climate* of the islands is healthful and remarkably equable, so much so that the Hawaiian language has no word to express the general idea of weather. Extreme heat is never known; the mean temperature of the year at Honolulu is 75° Fahr., and the daily variation seldom exceeds 15°. On the windward side the variation is greater and the weather rougher, but even there it is seldom either so cold or so hot as to cause discomfort. The islands being mountainous, almost any kind of climate can be found, the temperature becoming more bracing as the elevation increases. June is the hottest month of the year, January the coolest and most rainy. There is no special rainy season, though rain is more abundant in winter than during the summer months. The trade-wind, which is also the rain-wind, greatly controls the rainfall; and visitors should bear in mind that on the windward side of every one of the islands rains are frequent, while on the lee side the rainfall is much less, and in some places there is scarcely any. At Hilo, for example, on the weather-side of Hawaii, the rainfall is about 17 *feet* in the year, while at Kowa, on the other side of the island, it is only 45 *inches*, and water has to be carried in barrels for the ordinary uses of the inhabitants. Thus an invalid may secure at will either a dry or a moist climate, and this often by moving but a few miles. The climate in the more favored localities has the reputation of being an excellent one for consumptives, and many remarkable cures have been effected; but Mr. Nordhoff thinks it cannot be recommended for all cases. He says: " If a patient has the disease fully developed, and if it has been caused by lack of nutrition, the island air is likely to be insufficiently bracing. For persons who have 'weak lungs' merely, but no actual disease, it is probably a good and perfectly safe climate; and if sea-bathing is part of your physician's prescription, it can be enjoyed in perfection here by the tenderest body all the year round."

Honolulu.

Honolulu, the capital of the Hawaiian kingdom, is situated on the south side of the island of Oahu, in lat. 21° 18' 12" north and long. 157° 55' west. It covers the lower portion of Nuuanu Valley, and extends over the raised coral-reef at the base of the lofty mountains for several miles, having a population of about 15,000, consisting largely of foreigners. The houses are usually of wood, seldom more than two stories high, with spacious verandas, and mostly surrounded by trees; but on the commercial streets are large brick and stone warehouses. The aspect of the place is surprisingly like that of a thriving New England town, and Americans in particular soon feel quite at home. American gold and silver coins are the standard currency; there are two American churches; and the American colony is numerous and influential. The *Hawaiian Hotel* is a large stone building, erected and owned by the Government, and affording all the conveniences of a first-class hotel in any part of the world. It has roomy, shaded court-yards, broad piazzas, wide halls, and large rooms, baths and gas, and a billiard-room. "You might imagine yourself in San Francisco were it not that you drive in under the shade of cocoanut, tamarind, guava, and algeroba trees, and find all the doors and windows open in mid-winter, and ladies and children in white sitting on the piazzas." Honolulu, being the seat of government and residence of the king,

Parliament-House.

contains, of course, a number of public buildings. The *Parliament-House* is a substantial edifice, built of a concrete stone made on the spot, and contains most of the public offices. The royal or *Iolani Palace* is a spacious one-story edifice, built of coral from the reef in the harbor, and standing in the midst of ample grounds. It is unpretentious-looking from the outside; but is richly furnished, and contains a number of rare curiosities. Other important public buildings are the *Supreme Court*, the *Treasury*, and the general *Post-Office*, and there are a theatre and a bank. The charitable and penal institutions are admirably administered, and the *Queen's Hospital* and the *Reform School* are well worth the attention of the stranger. The *Prison* not only deserves a visit for itself, but from its roof is obtained one of the finest views of Honolulu and the adjacent country and ocean. Besides the American churches, there are a Catholic cathedral, an Anglican church, and two native churches; numerous schools for native and foreign children; an academy called Oahu College, attended mainly by foreign youths; and three weekly and two monthly publications. There is a pleasant foreign society in Honolulu, principally American and English. The people are extremely hospitable and kind, and do their utmost to make the stranger feel at home. There is a certain old-fashioned formality, but no striving after effect, no petty cliques or coteries, and no effort at exclusiveness. The average of intelligence is very high; both men and women are well-read; and the ladies are lively and well-dressed. An excellent band plays in public places several times a week; and the monotony of life is agreeably broken by parties, dinners, and social entertainments.

The *climate* of Honolulu is remarkably mild and uniform; the extreme range of the thermometer is between 60° and 87°. In the winter months the range is between 68° and 81°, and during the summer between 75° and 87°. The hottest part of the day is shortly before noon. The mornings are often a little overcast until about half-past nine, when it clears away bright; the nights are cool enough for sound rest, but never cold; blankets are seldom or never required. The rainfall is irregular, but averages about 41 inches. The porous soil absorbs the water quickly, and miasmatic complaints are rare. Many invalids find it pleasant to reside in Honolulu all the year round; but for consumptives it is better to go higher up the mountains from the middle of May till the end of September.

The scenery around Honolulu is of the most charming tropical character, and a number of pleasant excursions can be made from the town. The usual way of making these excursions is on horseback; but carriages are easily procured, and several of the roads are good. A horse, with saddle and bridle, may be hired for $1 a day; but for a prolonged stay it is better to buy one, as it can be had for from $12 to $25, and costs only 50 cents a day to keep. The valley of Nuuanu, at the end of which Honolulu lies, offers some delightful rides and drives. It is the most fertile spot on the island, and contains many lovely gardens and villas, including that of Queen Emma. About 6 miles from the town is the Pali, or precipice of Nuuanu, 1,100 feet above the plain, with cliffs on each side rising nearly 1,600 feet higher still. The view from the precipice is grand and beautiful beyond description. Another favorite excursion is to Waikiki, the Long Branch of the Hawaiians, beautifully situated amid groves of cocoanut-trees. "When you have seen Honolulu and the Nuuanu Valley," says Mr. Nordhoff, "and bathed and drunk cocoanut-milk at Waikiki, you will be ready for a charming excursion—the ride around the island of Oahu. For this, you should take several days. It is most pleasantly made by a party of three or four persons, and ladies, if they can sit in the saddle at all, can very well do it. You should provide yourself with a pack-mule, which will carry not only spare clothing, but some provisions; and your guide ought to take care of your horses, and be able, if necessary, to cook you a lunch. The ride is easily done in four days, and you will sleep every night at a plantation or farm. The roads are excellent for riding, and carriages have made the journey. It is best to set out by way of Pearl River and return by the Pali, as thus you have the trade-wind in your face all the way. If you are accustomed to ride, and can do 30 miles a day, you should sleep the first night at or near Waialua, the next at or near what is called the Mormon Settlement, and on the third day ride into Honolulu. If ladies are of your party, and the stages must be shorter, you can ride the first day to Ewa, which is but 10 miles; the next to Waialua, 18 miles farther; the third to the neighborhood of Kahuku, 12 miles; thence to Kahana, 15 miles; thence to Kaalea, 12 miles; and the next day carries you, by an easy ride of 13 miles, into Honolulu. Any one who can sit on a horse at all will enjoy this excursion, and derive benefit from it; the different stages of it are so short that each day's work is only a pleasure. On the way you will see, near Ewa, the Pearl Lochs, which it has recently been proposed to cede as a naval station to the United States; and near Waialua an interesting boarding-school for Hawaiian girls, in which they are taught not only in the usual studies but in sewing and the various arts of the housewife. If you are curious to see the high valley in which the famous Waialua oranges are grown, you must take a day for that purpose. Between Kahuku and Kahana it is worth while to make a *détour* into the mountains to see the Kaliawa Falls, which are a very picturesque sight. The rock, at a height of several hundred feet, has been curiously worn by the water into the shape of a canoe. Here also the precipitous walls are covered with masses of fine ferns. At Kahana, and also at Koloa, you will see rice-fields, which are cultivated by Chinese. You pass also on your road several sugar-plantations; and if it is the season of sugar-boiling you will be interested in this process. For miles you ride along the sea-shore, and your guide will lead you to proper places for a mid-day bath, preliminary to your lunch. After leaving the Mormon Settlement, the scenery becomes very grand—it is, indeed, as fine as any on the islands, and compares well with any scenery in the world. That it can be seen without severe toil gives it, for such people as myself, no slight advantage over some other scenery in these islands and elsewhere, access to which can be gained only by toilsome and disagreeable journeys. There is a blending of sea and mountain which will dwell in your memory as not oppressively grand, and yet fine enough to make you thankful that Providence has made the world so lovely and fair.

"As you approach the Pali the mountain becomes a sheer precipice for some miles, broken only by the gorge of the Pali, up which, if you are prudent, you will walk, letting your horses follow with the guide—though Hawaiian horsemen ride both up and down, and have been known to gallop down the stone-paved and slippery steep. As you look up at these tall, gloomy precipices, you see one of the peculiarities of a Sandwich Island landscape. The rocks are not bare, but covered from base to crown with moss and ferns; and these cling so closely to the surface that to your eye they seem to be but a short, close-textured green fuzz. In fact, these great rocks, thus adorned, reminded me constantly of the rock-scenery in such operas as 'Fra Diavolo,' the dark green being of a shade which I do not remember to have seen before in Nature, though it is not uncommon in theatrical scenery.... You will sleep each night in a native house, unless, as is very likely to be the case, you have invitations to stop at plantation-houses on your way. At the native houses they will kill a chicken for you, and cook taro; but they have no other supplies. You can usually get cocoanuts, whose milk is very wholesome and refreshing. The journey is like a somewhat prolonged picnic; the air is mild and pure; and you need no heavy clothing, for you are sure of bright, sunny weather." A guide for such a journey costs $1 a day, which includes his horse; for a night's accommodation at a native house, 50 cents for each person is considered abundant.

Maui and Lahaina.

Maui, the second island of the group in size, contains 603 square miles and consists of two mountainous peninsulas connected by a low isthmus. It is the seat of the largest sugar-plantations, and yields more of this product than any of the other islands. It is notable also for possessing Mauna-Haleakala, an extinct volcano 10,200 feet high, which has the largest crater in the world—a monstrous pit 27 miles in circumference and 2,000 feet deep. **Lahaina,** the capital of Maui, lies on the southwest side of the island, and is reached from Honolulu by steamer or schooner once a week and sometimes oftener. It is a pretty little town, nestling along the shore at the foot of rugged mountains, and like Honolulu is sheltered from the violent trade-winds and rain-storms. The climate is rather milder than that of Honolulu, the range being between 54° and 86°. Above Lahaina, at an elevation of 3,000 feet, the thermometer ranges between 40° and 75°. The rainfall is about 39 inches, and the soil quickly absorbs it. There are fewer visitors to Lahaina than to Honolulu, and consequently the accommodations are much inferior, but private board may be obtained with certain resident families.

An excursion often made from Lahaina is to the summit of Mauna-Haleakala. It is neither dangerous nor difficult, but it is tedious, involving as it does a ride of about 12 miles mostly over lava and up-hill. It is advisable to go up during the day, and sleep in one of the lava-caves, so as to get the view of the crater at sunrise. For this a guide is necessary, with provisions and blankets, and water-proof clothing is likely to prove useful. Almost all the islands are visible from the summit of the crater, but the crater itself is the most impressive spectacle. It is 10 miles in diameter, and the vast irregular floor lies 2,000 feet below its crest. From this floor rise more than a dozen subsidiary craters or cones, some of them 750 feet high. From the summit the eye readily takes in the whole crater; not a tree, shrub, or even tuft of grass, obstructs the view. It is possible to ride down into the crater, and the natives have a trail, not much used, by which they pass; but it is very difficult to follow and must not be attempted without an experienced guide.

Hilo and the Volcanoes.

Hilo lies on the eastern or windward side of the great island of Hawaii, and after Honolulu is the largest town in the kingdom, having a population of about 5,000. It is reached from Honolulu by a little inland steamer which makes a weekly tour of nearly all the islands of the group. The time required for the journey from Honolulu to Hilo is three days, and the fare is $15, or $25 for the round trip. The town and district of Hilo are among the most beautiful regions of the tropics; the town consisting of shops and stores along the beach, and white houses hidden in umbrageous groves of cocoanut, bread-fruit, pandanus, and other southern trees, many of them bearing brilliant flowers. There are four churches in the town, but no hotel, though good accommodations may be had at the large house of Mr. Severance, Sheriff of Hawaii, or, if that is full, at other houses. There is a considerable population of Americans in the place, who are always ready to extend a welcome to anybody from "home." The climate of Hilo is warm and extraordinarily wet, the rainfall amounting, as we have already said, to 17 *feet* per annum. As much as 10 inches has been known to fall in a single day, and it rains nearly every day. Nevertheless the town is quite healthy, and some invalids seem to derive especial benefit from its moist atmosphere. The district of Hilo is cut up by the deep channels of no less than 50 large streams, which fall into the sea within a length of coast about 25 miles in extent, discharging the rains that are poured by the trade-winds upon the northeast flanks of Mauna-Kea. The freshets in these streams often come on so suddenly as to resemble the deluge produced by the sudden breaking of a mill-dam. The cocoanut and the banana are found in perfection at Hilo, and other characteristic tropical products are abundant.

Hilo is the most convenient point of departure for a visit to the great volcano of Kilauea, the largest active crater in the world. The distance to the crater is about 40 miles over a rough trail through forests and over immense fields of lava, and the entire journey can be made on horseback with no difficulty except what comes from the inevitable fatigue. Mr. Nordhoff made the ascent with a party of ladies and children in 1873, and gives some details which the traveler will find useful. The charge at Hilo for horses for the journey is $10 each, with $1 a day for the guide. At the Volcano House (at the crater) the charge for horse and man is $5 a day, with half-price for the guide. For a special guide into the crater there is an additional charge of $1. It is useless to wait for a fine day, as it will probably rain at any rate before the Volcano House is reached, and if you have started in a heavy rain the sun is likely to be out within two or three hours. Each traveler should take water-proof clothing upon his own saddle, and the pack-mule should carry some spare clothing, well covered with India-rubber blankets, and a lunch to be eaten at the Half-way House. The ascent is made in from 6 to 10 hours; the night may be comfortably spent at the Volcano House, and the next day should be given to the crater. Kilauea is situated on the eastern side of Mauna-Loa, at an elevation of 3,970 feet, and is a stupendous pit 8 miles in circumference and 1,000 feet in depth. It is of irregular shape, with almost perpendicular walls of a kind of limestone. The inside is rimmed with cooled lava, called the "black ledge," from 300 to 2,000 feet wide and about 800 feet deep. The descent into the crater is effected by a series of steps and a scramble over lava and rock *débris*. The greater part of the floor is a mass of dead though not cold lava, and at the farthest extremity of the pit, 3 miles from the Volcano House, are (or were in 1873, for the features of the place are constantly changing) two large caldrons or lakes about ½ mile long and 500 feet wide, filled with "a red, molten, fiery, sulphurous, raging, roaring, restless mass of matter," incessantly agitated, heaving to and fro in long, heavy waves, and occasionally shooting up a fiery tongue 30 feet or more into the air. The surface of this boiling lava is about 80 feet below the margin of the lakes, but the heat is so great that it will sometimes blister the feet through thick shoes, and it is impossible to approach save on the windward side. On the bank of the lake are several cones or orifices opening down into the fiery gulf below. "Into these holes we looked, and saw a very wonderful and terrible sight. Below us was a stream of lava, rolling and surging and beating against huge, precipitous, red hot cliffs; and higher up, suspended from other also red or white hot cliffs, depended huge stalactites, like masses of fiercely glowing fern-leaves waving about in the subterraneous wind; and here we saw how thin was in some such places the crust over which we walked, and how near the melting-point must be its under-surface. For, as far as we could judge, these little craters or cones rested upon a crust not thicker than 12 or 14 inches, and one fierce blast from below seemed sufficient to melt away the whole place. Fortunately, one cannot stay very long near these openings, for they exhale a very poisonous breath; and so we were drawn back to the more fascinating but less perilous spectacle of the lakes; and then back over the rough lava, our minds filled with memories of a spectacle which is certainly one of the most remarkable our planet affords." At the Volcano House (which is kept by an American) guides, provisions, and animals may be procured for the ascent of Mauna-Loa (14,000 feet high), but the ride is not easy, and one who undertakes it must be well prepared in the way of clothing. The crater is a pit about 3 miles in circumference, with precipitous walls, 2,000 feet deep. At the bottom is a burning lake which throws up a jet, more or less constant, to the height of 400 or 500 feet from the surface of the lake.

The return to Hilo should be by way of the Puna coast. This involves a ride of nearly 70 miles over a very desolate country, but it will afford some very wonderful and novel sights, and give one such a conception as can be obtained in no other way of the prodigious activity of the forces which have found periodical vents in the eruptions from Kilauea and Mauna-Loa. Another journey which Mr. Nordhoff recommends is a ride from Hilo along the northeastern coast, through the Hamakua and Kohala districts, to Kealakeakua Bay, where Captain Cook was killed. There a schooner may be taken for Honolulu, or the ride may be prolonged through Kau and Puna back to Hilo.

In the Hamakua district, in the interior of the island, is the little town of **Waimea**, which is noted for its even and comparatively low temperature. Observations extending over many years show the average to be 65° Fahr., and the place may be fairly called the sanitarium of Hawaii, for to it yearly flock those whose constitutions have become enervated by too long a residence near the coast.

Kauai.

Kauai is the most uniformly tropical in character of the entire group of islands, is fertile and abundantly watered, and contains much beautiful scenery. It lies farthest to seaward of the main islands, and as the steamer usually visits it but once a month, it is comparatively little visited by strangers. Nevertheless an excursion thither from Honolulu will prove a very enjoyable episode. The best method of making it without unnecessary waste of time is to take passage in a schooner, so timing your visit as to secure a week or ten days on the island before the steamer arrives to carry you back. Mr. Nordhoff made such an excursion, and thus describes it: "We took passage on a little sugar-schooner, the Fairy Queen, of about 75 tons, commanded by a smart native captain, and sailing one afternoon about two o'clock, and sleeping comfortably on deck wrapped in rugs, were landed at *Waimea* [not the Waimea already mentioned as being on Hawaii] the following morning at daybreak. When you travel on one of these little native schooners you must provide food for yourself, for poi and a little beef or fish make up the sea-ration as well as the land-food of the Hawaiians. In all other respects you may expect to be treated with the most distinguished consideration, and the most ready and thoughtful kindness, by captain and crew; and the picturesque mountain-scenery of Oahu, which you have in sight so long as daylight lasts, and the lovely starlit night, with its soft gales and warm air, combine to make the voyage a delightful adventure.

"As usual in these islands, a church was the first and most conspicuous landmark that greeted our eyes in the morning. Abundant groves of cocoanuts, for which the place is famous, assured us of a refreshing morning draught. The little vessel was anchored off the shore, and our party, jumping into a whale-boat, were quickly and skillfully steered through the slight surf which pours upon the beach. The boat was pulled upon the black sand; and the lady who was of my party found herself carried to the land in the stout arms of the captain; while the rest of us watched our chance, and, as the waves receded, leaped ashore, and managed to escape with dry feet. The sun had not yet risen; the early morning was a little overcast. A few natives, living on the beach, gathered around and watched curiously the landing of our saddles and saddle-bags from the boat; presently that pushed off, and our little company sat down upon an old spar, and watched the schooner as she hoisted sails and bore away for her proper port, while we waited for the appearance of a native person of some authority to whom a letter had been directed, requesting him to provide us with horses and a guide to the house of a friend with whom we intended to breakfast. Presently three or four men came galloping along the beach, one of whom, a burly Hawaiian, a silver shield on whose breast announced him a local officer of police, reported that he was at our service with as many horses as we needed. It is one of the embarrassing incidents of travel on these islands that there are no hotels or inns outside of Honolulu and Hilo. Whether he will or not, the traveler must accept the hospitality of the residents, and this is so general and so boundless that it would impose a burdensome obligation were it not offered in such a kindly and graceful way as to beguile you into the belief that you are conferring as well as receiving a favor. Nor is the foreigner alone generous; for a native, too, if you come with a letter from his friend at a distance, places himself and all he has at your service. When we had reached our friend's house, I asked my conductor, the policeman, what I should pay him for the use of three horses and his own services. He replied that he was but too happy to have been of use to me, as I was the friend of his friend. I managed to force upon him a proper reward for his attention, but I am persuaded that he would have been content without.

"Kauai is probably the oldest of the Hawaiian group; according to the geologists, it was first thrown up; the bottom of the ocean began to crack up there to the northwest, and the rent gradually extended in the southeasterly direction necessary to produce the other islands. It would seem that Kauai must be a good deal older than Hawaii; for, whereas the latter is covered with undecayed lava, and has two active volcanoes, the former has a rich and deep covering of soil, and, except in a few places, there are no very plain or conspicuous cones or craters. Of course, the whole island bears the clearest traces of its volcanic origin; and near Koloa there are three small craters in a very good state of preservation. Having thus more soil than the other islands, Kauai has also more grass; being older, not only are its valleys somewhat richer, but its mountains are also more picturesque than those of Maui and Hawaii, as also they are much lower. The roads are excellent for horsemen, and for the most part practicable for carriages, of which, however, there are none to be hired.

"The best way to see the island is to land, as we did, at Waimea; ride to a singular spot called the 'barking sands'—a huge sand-hill, sliding down which you hear a dull rumble like distant thunder, probably the result of electricity. On the way you meet with a mirage, remarkable for this that it is a constant phenomenon—that is to say, it is to be seen daily at certain hours, and is the apparition of a great lake, having sometimes high waves which seem to submerge the cattle which stand about, apparently, in the water. From the sands you return to Waimea, and can ride thence next day to *Koloa* in the forenoon, and to *Na-Wiliwili* in the afternoon. The following day's ride will bring you to *Hanalei*, a highly-picturesque valley which lies on the rainy side of the island, Waimea being on the dry side. At Hanalei you should take the steamer, and sail in her around the Palis of Kauai, a stretch of precipitous cliff 25 miles long, the whole of which is inaccessible from the sea, except by the native people in canoes; and many parts of which are very lovely and grand. Thus voyaging, you will circumnavigate the island, returning to Na-Wiliwili, and thence in a night to Honolulu.

"It is easy and pleasant to see Kauai, taking a store of provisions with you, and lodging in native houses. But if you have some acquaintances in Honolulu, you will be provided with letters of introduction to some of the hospitable foreign families on this island; and thus the pleasure of your visit will be greatly increased. Kauai has many German residents, mostly persons of education and culture, who have brought their libraries with them, and on whose tables and shelves you may see the best of the recent literature as well as the best of the old. A New-Yorker who imagines, cockney-like, that civilization does not reach beyond the sound of Trinity-chimes, is startled out of this foolish fancy when he finds among the planters and missionaries here, as in other parts of these islands, men and women of genuine culture, maintaining all the essential forms as well as the realities of civilization; yet living so free and untrammeled a life that he who comes from the high-pressure social atmosphere of New York cannot help but envy these happy mortals, who seem to have the good without the worry of civilization, and who have caught the secret of how to live simply and yet gently."

The raising of cattle is the chief industry of Kauai, and a large part of the island is given up to them. In the mountains they have gone wild, and parties are often made up to hunt and shoot them. Rice is also an important product, and is raised in increasing quantities on Kauai as on all the islands. There are four or five large sugar-plantations; and coffee grows wild in many of the valleys and on the hills. All the tropical fruits produce abundantly, and the cocoanuts of Kauai are particularly fine.[1]

MEXICO.

MEXICO, the land of mystery and romance, will in future be the resort of the valetudinarian, the pleasure-seeker, the tourist, the student, the artist, and the speculator. No portion of the Western Hemisphere offers so many attractions for a short tour, or presents so wide a field for the acquisition of curious and scientific information. In her colossal pyramids and in the sculptured ruins of massive temples and palaces, ante-dating the dawn of veritable history, the archæologist will find ample material for investigation. Comprising, as Mexico does, every variety of climate, and consequently producing every plant which is found between the equator and the north pole, the botanist no less than the general observer will delight in her matchless and gorgeous flora. Nowhere else, on the face of the globe, can the

[1] The visitor to the Sandwich Islands who desires more particulars than we could find space for should provide himself with Mr. Charles Nordhoff's "Northern California, Oregon, and the Sandwich Islands," and with Brigham's "Memoir on the Hawaiian Volcanoes." In Mrs. Brassey's "Around the World in the Yacht Sunbeam" there will also be found several highly interesting and instructive chapters on the Sandwich Islands.

ornithologist or the entomologist find, within a given space, so much to engage his attention. The beauty of her plains, gilded by an eternal summer; the grandeur of her volcanoes, lifting their heads for thousands of feet into the region of eternal snow and ice; the endless variety of her stupendous mountain-ranges, her lovely lakes, and fertile valleys, all seen through an atmosphere of wonderful transparency—all these, while they will furnish incomparable subjects for the easel of the painter, will forever live in the memory of every lover of Nature who may behold them. The memorials of an extinct religious worship can not fail deeply to interest the theologian, while the national archives in the capital are full of instruction for the historian and the ecclesiastical student.

With the completion of her gigantic system of railways now in course of construction, the practical will be mingled, as never before, with the ideal. Whatever concerns her vast mining interests, her agriculture, and her commerce, is destined to receive a new and unprecedented impulse. Manufactures of various descriptions will, for the first time, be naturalized within her borders.

Thus the capitalist and the enterprising man of business will be attracted to her soil. Heretofore nine tenths if not ninety-nine hundredths of all the foreigners who have visited the country have entered it by way of Vera Cruz. Every invader, from Cortez down, who has planted his standard in her capital, has landed his army at that port.

Scene in Mexico.

Topography.—The Republic extends from the 15th to the 32d parallel of north latitude, and from the 87th to the 117th meridian of longitude west of Greenwich (approximately).

The country is bounded on the north by Texas, New Mexico, Arizona, and California; on the east by the Gulf of Mexico and the Atlantic Ocean; on the south by the Republic of Guatemala and the British colony of Balize; and on the west by the Pacific Ocean.

The superficial area of Mexico is 756,336 square miles. The country is traversed by a lofty chain of mountains which is known as the *Sierra Madre*. Beginning at the Isthmus of Tehuantepec, it trends northwesterly.

This range has a moderate elevation in the southern States; but in latitude 19° the mean height amounts to about 9,000 feet above the sea-level, and two peaks, Popocatepetl and Orizaba, rise to the great altitudes of 17,720 feet and 17,200 feet respectively. The former mountain is the culminating point of North America. On the 21st parallel the Cordillera becomes very wide and divides itself into three parts. The eastern branch runs through the States of San Luis Potosi, Nuevo Leon, and Coahuila. The western branch traverses the States of Jalisco, Sinaloa, and Sonora; while the central ridge extends through Durango and Chihuahua, forming the watershed of the northern table-land. The country is divided into three zones, viz.: the *tierra caliente*, or hot region; the *tierra templada*, or temperate region; and the *tierra fria*, or cold region. About one half of the surface of Mexico lies in the last-named zone, the remainder being almost equally divided between the *tierra templada* and the *tierra caliente*. The coasts of the Republic are low, but the land rises gradually upon going toward the interior. Mexico consists for the most part of an elevated plateau, having a mean height of about 6,000 feet above the sea. Owing to the narrow form of the continent, which prevents the collection of a great mass of water, there are very few navigable streams in the country. The Goatzacoalcos and the

Pánuco are the principal navigable rivers. The *Rio de Santiago* is the longest, being 542 miles in length. The Republic contains many lakes, most of which are extensive lagoons, as in the valleys of Mexico and Parras.

How to reach Mexico.—The steamships of the Alexandre Line leave New York every week, calling at Havana, and at the Mexican ports of Progreso, Campeche, Frontera, and Vera Cruz. Fare to Vera Cruz: First class, $85; second class, $60; excursion tickets, $150. Time, about 10 days.

The tourist may land at Progreso, and proceed to Merida, the capital of Yucatan, 22 miles distant, by rail. The celebrated ruins of Uxmal, Mayapan, Chichen-Itza, and Kabah, lie within from two to four days' journey from Merida. There are, however, no hotel accommodations at these ancient cities.

Mexico may be reached from New Orleans by the steamers of the Morgan Line, or by those of the Alexandre Line. Fare: First class, $50; second class, $40; excursion tickets, $90.

The steamships of the Pacific Mail Company leave San Francisco on the 1st and 15th of every month. They touch at all Mexican ports, beginning with Mazatlan.

Tourists wishing to visit the republic by rail, may enter at *Laredo* and proceed southward *via* the Mexican National R. R.; or at *Paso del Norte*, and travel into the interior by the Mexican Central R. R. The latter road was completed to the city of Mexico in March, 1884, and the former will reach the same point early in 1888, as is now expected.

The plan of constructing these two trunk-lines has been to begin at both ends and build toward an intermediate point. Diligences connect the temporary termini of the M. N. R. R., and the tourist will find it easy to reach the capital by land.

The Mexican National R. R. is a narrow-gauge road, but on all the other leading railways the standard gauge has been adopted.

The Cost of Travel.—Should the traveler move about a great deal, his expenses in the country will be at least $40 a week. If, however, he intends to linger in the cities and stay at the best hotels, $20 a week will cover the cost of living outside of the capital. One month's trip from New York to Mexico City and return will cost about $225. The same tour *via* New Orleans by rail—steamer to Vera Cruz and return to New York by sea—will cost about $300. As yet, there are no professional couriers in Mexico. A *mozo*, or man-servant, may be hired at $30 a month. The *mozos* rarely speak any other language than Spanish.

Vera Cruz.

The steamships anchor in the harbor, and row-boats approach the vessel to take the traveler ashore. A bargain should be made with the boatman to convey the tourist's baggage to the custom-house on reaching the wharf, and *also to the hotel*. The fare for each passenger with ordinary baggage should not exceed $1.

During a *norte*, or norther, it is impossible to disembark at Vera Cruz. Accordingly, if the norther is severe, the traveler may be detained a few days on board the steamer.

There is little to be seen at this port, except the famous castle of San Juan de Uloa and the old parochial church. The stranger may obtain a fine view of the city from the tower of the latter. The mean annual temperature is 77° Fahr. The *vomito*, or yellow fever, rarely prevails at Vera Cruz during the winter months. The city is, however, hot and unhealthy. Mosquitoes abound, and the hotels are inferior. The tourist is advised to leave for the interior as soon as possible.

The leading hotels are the *Diligencias* and *de Méjico*. Vera Cruz lies in latitude 19° 11' N. It is built on a sandy plain.

The main street is the *Calle de la Independencia*. A horse-car track runs through the entire length of this thoroughfare. A walk may be taken to the *Alameda* in the evening. There is really no drive.

The post-office is in the *Calle de Cinco de Mayo*. The postage to the United States is six cents.

From Vera Cruz to the City of Mexico.

Distance, 263 miles. Time, 14¼ hours. Fares: First class, $16; second class, $12.50.

The new-comer is advised not to proceed directly to the table-land, but to spend a few days at *Cordoba* or *Orizaba*, and accustom his lungs gradually to the rarefied atmosphere of the *tierra fria*. The stations on the Mexican Railway are as follows: *Vera Cruz: Tejeria*, 9½ miles; *Soledad*, 26 miles; *Camaron*, 39¼ miles; *Paso del Macho*, 47¼ miles; *Atoyac*, 53½ miles; *Cordoba*, 65¾ miles; *Fortin*, 70¾ miles; *Orizaba*, 82 miles; *Enurial*, 88½ miles; *Maltrata*, 94½ miles; *Bota*, 97½ miles; *Alta Luz*, 103 miles; *Boca del Monte*, 107¼ miles; *Esperanza*, 111¼ miles; *San Andres*, 126¼ miles; *Rinconada*, 139 miles; *San Marcos*, 150¼ miles; *Huamantla*, 161 miles; *Apizaco*, 176¾ miles; *Guadalupe*, 186¼ miles; *Soltepec*, 192¾ miles; *Apam*, 205¾ miles; *Irolo*, 215½ miles; *Ometusco*, 221½ miles; *La Palma*, 225¼ miles; *Otumba*, 229 miles; *San Juan Teotihuacan*, 236 miles; *Tepexpam*, 243 miles; *Mexico*, 263¼ miles.

At **Tejeria** a branch road (tramway) extends to *Jalapa*, 70 miles from Vera Cruz. Hotels, *Nacional* and *Vera Cruzano*.

The climate of Jalapa is very damp.

Population, 12,400.

At **Cordoba** there are extensive plantations of coffee and tropical fruits. The town contains a small hotel. It is 1 mile distant from the railway-track.

At **Orizaba** the best hotels are *A la Borda* and *Cuatro Naciones*. There are many churches and a beautiful *paseo* in the city. Population, about 17,000.

At *Apizaco* there is a branch to *Puebla*, 30 miles distant.

Puebla.

Hotels.—The best hotels are the *Español* and *Diligencias*. Horse-cars run from the railway station past the doors of both of them. There are a few *cafés* on the *Plaza*; that adjoining the *Teatro de Guerrero* is the best.

Location, Climate, and History.—Puebla, the capital of the State of the same name, lies in latitude 19° 2′ 45″ N. It was formerly christened *Puebla de los Angeles*, or town of the angels, the name given to it by the Spanish conquerors. Since the 5th of May, 1862, it has been called *Puebla de Zaragoza*, after General Zaragoza, who defeated the French, under the command of Marquez, at Fort Guadalupe, near the city.

Puebla is situated on a fertile plain, upon which extensive fields of wheat are cultivated. On the eastern side of the valley lies the picturesque mountain of *Malinche*, the name given to Cortez by the Aztecs. To the west rises the lofty range which includes the majestic volcanoes of Popocatepetl and Iztaccihuatl.

The climate of the city is similar to that of the capital. Its elevation above the sea-level is 7,201 feet, or about 150 feet lower than that of the City of Mexico.

During the Spanish invasion (in 1519) this place, then a small village in the territory of Cholula, was occupied by Cortez for a brief period. He set out from the neighboring city of Cholula, and, crossing the *Sierra*, entered the valley of Mexico. The city of Puebla was founded on the 28th of September, 1531.

In the summer of 1847 it was assaulted and captured by the American army, commanded by General Winfield Scott. In 1803 Puebla was the second city in New Spain, the population being 67,800; in 1879 it became third in rank (Guadalajara being second), the population having decreased to 64,588. The city is noted for its manufactures of cotton, wool, thread, crockery, glass, and soap.

Streets and Drives.—The main street is the *Calle de Mercaderes*. The streets are clean and well paved. The *Plaza* is bounded on the south by the Cathedral, and on the other three sides are buildings with arcades. There are many stalls or stands in these arcades where small wares are sold. Public letter-writers are found here, each of whom has a small bench on the sidewalk.

There are two parks, the *Paseo Viejo* and the *Paseo Nuevo*. They lie on opposite sides of the city. The best drive is to the former, which adjoins the *Alameda*. A bathing establishment is situated on the edge of the *Alameda*. (Baths, one *real*.)

Prominent Buildings.—The stranger should not fail to visit the *Cathedral* and the church of *La Compañia*. Each contains paintings by Murillo. The Cathedral was built in 1664. Both the exterior and interior will compare favorably with those of any cathedral in Europe. The wood-carvings of the choir (*coro*) and of the altar are very artistic, and the beautiful *tecali*, or Mexican onyx, is used in the pulpit and in some of the altars. The tourist should ascend one of the towers of the Cathedral, from which a fine view of the city and environs may be obtained.

San Francisco and *San Cristobal* are the only other churches worthy of a visit. The Museum and State College are the remaining objects of interest.

Suburbs.—Fort Guadalupe lies on a small eminence about a mile north of the city. The town of Cholula is situated 7 miles west of Puebla. During the Spanish Conquest, Cortez described this place as containing 20,000 houses within the walls, and as many more in the environs. It was the capital of the republic of the same name. At present the population does not exceed 10,000 souls. Cholula is remarkable chiefly for its pyramid, which is the largest, oldest, and most important in Mexico. The original dimensions were as follows: height, 177 feet; horizontal width of the base, 1,423 feet; and area, 45 acres. It is built of alternate strata of brick and clay, and the sides correspond to the direction of the meridians and parallels. At present three terraces are distinctly visible, and the outlines of two others may be traced. A winding road, which is paved with stone, leads up to the summit. The latter is about 200 feet square. It affords a fine view of the plain of Puebla. A chapel has been erected by the Mexicans on the platform of this great mound. It is built of brick and stone, with a dome and two towers; and the interior is adorned with frescoes and decorations. It is called *San Tuariol de los Remedios*. Some vegetation is seen on the pyramid. It consists of the cactus, *pito*, and a few *pirú* trees. Several writers have suggested that the founders of the mound at Cholula may have had some design in building it near the lofty volcano of Popocatepetl, or "the smoking mountain." This primitive race may have been fire as well as serpent worshipers. Unfortunately, the great temple of Cholula has been partly destroyed. A few years since a cut was made in the western side of it for a railroad-track!

There are several churches in the town of Cholula, but only one of them is worthy of a visit. This one is inclosed by a high wall, and lies about 150 yards west of the tramway-station. It contains a series of historical paintings illustrative of the epoch of the Conquest.

Horse-cars leave Puebla for Cholula several times daily. The pyramid may also be reached by carriage-road.

The City of Mexico.

Hotels, Restaurants, etc.—Hotels: *Iturbide, San Cárlos, Gillow, Comonfort, Guadiola, Humboldt, Nacional*, and others.

Restaurants: *Iturbide, Concordia, Maison Dorée, Café Anglais*, and *Café de Paris*.

Theatres.—Principal, *Gran Teatro Nacional, Arben*.

Post-Office (*Casa de Correos*), in the *Calle de la Moneda*.

Express-office in the Hotel *Iturbide*.

Telegraph-offices in the several railway-stations.

Baths: *De Vergara*, adjoining the *Teatro Nacional*.

Modes of Conveyance.—Carriages: first class, with *blue* flag, $1 an hour; second class, with *red* flag, 6 *reales* an hour; third class, with *white* flag, 4 *reales* an hour.

Horse-cars start from the *Plaza Mayor* for all parts of the city and suburbs. Fare, ½ *real*—i. e., a *medio*—in city limits, and 1 *real* in the suburbs.

Location, Climate, History.—The City of Mexico is the capital of the Republic, and lies in an oval-shaped valley about 45 by 30 miles in area. It is situated in latitude 19° 25′ 45″ N., and longitude 101° 25′ 30″ W. of Paris. Its elevation is 7,347 feet above the sea-level. Mexico is built on ground that was formerly an island in Lake Texcoco. It is one of the finest cities in the Western Hemisphere, and it has been called the Venice of the New World.

The valley of Mexico contains six lakes, all of which are salt except *Xochimilco*. Their names are—beginning on the north—Zumpango, Xalcotan, San Cristobal, Texcoco, Chalco, and Xochimilco.

The *climate* of the capital is at first trying to a stranger. The mean annual temperature is about 62° Fahr., and there is but little difference between summer and winter. There is, however, a great diurnal range of the thermometer. In the middle of the day, if the weather be fair, the mercury will rise to 75°, while immediately after sunset it will sink rapidly to about 50°; and before morning the temperature may be as low as 40° Fahr. Occasionally the thermometer reaches the freezing-point. The coldest part of the night is just before daybreak.

The air is exceedingly dry, and the new-comer will suffer from thirst and chapped lips until he has become acclimated. He is also liable to be affected with headache by the highly rarefied atmosphere of the table-land. There is a great difference between the temperature of the air in the sun and in the shade. Strangers are apt to become overheated while walking in the sun, and to cool off too suddenly on entering the hotel or some other edifice. Accordingly, extreme caution should be taken to avoid catching cold, as it is very difficult to recover from the effects of it. Hats should be worn as much as possible in all buildings. The rainy season lasts from June to October. The annual rainfall is 59 inches.

The ancient capital of Mexico was founded by the Aztecs in 1325. The country was called *Anahuac*, and the capital *Tenochtitlan*. The latter word signifies "a cactus upon a rock." This emblem, surmounted by an eagle holding a serpent in its talons, has been adopted as the escutcheon of Mexico. On the 8th of November, 1519, the Spaniards under Cortez entered Tenochtitlan. After a residence of less than eight months the intense hostility of the Aztecs caused the invaders to evacuate it, with great loss, on the night of July 1, 1520. This date has ever since been termed the *noche triste*, or the "melancholy night."

In the following year, with the aid of numerous allies, the conqueror attacked and subsequently besieged the ancient capital. The siege lasted 75 days, during

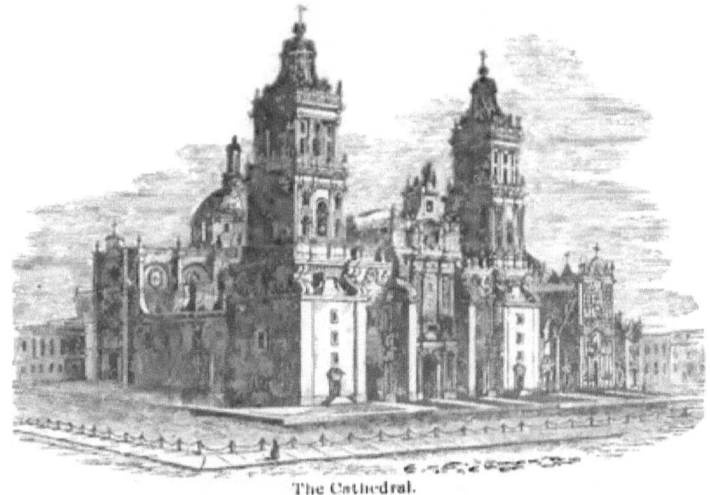

The Cathedral.

which time the sufferings of the inhabitants were so great that they are unsurpassed in the pages of history.

On the 15th of August, 1521, the Aztecs surrendered to Cortez. The city was immediately razed. A few monuments and idols which were incapable of destruction were buried. A new city was founded on the site of Tenochtitlan, and to-day scarcely a vestige remains of the ancient capital. At the time of the Conquest the population of the capital was about 300,000. In 1803, according to Humboldt, it was 135,000, and in 1885 the city may be said to have 225,000 inhabitants.

Streets and Drives.—Nearly every block in Mexico has a different name. The "Broadway" is the *Calle de San Francisco,* the continuation of which is called the *Plateros.* This street runs from the Park or *Alameda* to the *Plaza Mayor.* The principal hotels, stores, and shops, are on this thoroughfare. The fashionable drive is the *Paseo de la Reforma.*

Prominent Buildings.—1. The *Museum,* containing many **Aztec** idols and antiquities. 2. The *Palace,* in which the sights are, the *Sala de Embajadores* and *Maximilian's coach.* 3. The Academy of *San Cárlos,* in which are found paintings by the best native artists as well as those of several of the old masters. 4. The *Mining-School,* which has a collection of rocks and minerals. 5. The *Mint.* 6. The *National Library.* 7. The *Reform School.*

Churches.—The *Cathedral* (ascend the tower for a view—fee, 1 *real*). The churches of **Santo Domingo,** *La Santísima, La* **Profesa, Santa Teresa,** and *San Fernando,* are worth a visit.

Places of Resort.—The **Park,** or *Alameda.* The canal and market. The floating gardens. The **Tivoli Gardens.** Bull-fights take place at the suburb of *Huisachal* on Sunday afternoons.

Suburbs.—The castle of *Chapultepec,* which has been occupied in turn by the Emperors Iturbide and Maximilian.

The village of *Atzcapotzalco,* on the way to which is the famous *noche-triste* tree, where Cortez stopped and wept over his misfortunes on the night of the evacuation. *Tacubaya,* containing the Military School, *San Cosme,* and *Guadalupe,* which is noted for its cathedral and chapel. Excursions may be made to *Cuernavaca,* 47 miles by diligence; to *Toluca,* 45 miles by rail; to the pyramids of *San Juan Teotihuacan,* 27 miles by rail; and to the volcano of *Popocatepetl* and to *Cuautla.*

Central Mexico.

Querétaro is distant 152 miles by rail from the capital. At a point about 30 miles from the city, the railroad **enters the cañon** known as the famous *Tajo de Nochistongo,* through which a canal was dug to drain the valley of Mexico in the early part of the seventeenth century. This gigantic scheme was not successful, although it cost about $12,000,000. The leading hotels are the *Diligencias, Del Ferrocarril Central,* and *Del Aguila Roja.* The post-office and bath-house are in the *Calle de Locutorios.*

The **Places of Interest** are: 1. The *Hercules Cotton-Mill,* which gives employment to 1,400 operatives. It is by far the largest establishment in Mexico. Visitors are welcome. 2. The *Cerro de las Campanas,* or hill at which the Emperor Maximilian was shot, on June 19, 1867, lies about a mile southwest of the main *Plaza.* 3. The *Alameda,* which has a beautiful grove of ash-trees. 4. The churches of *San Francisco, San Antonio, San Augustin, Santo Domingo, Santa Rosa, El Carmen,* and *Santa Clara.* The last named contains exquisitely-gilded carvings of wood, and is well worth a visit. *Querétaro* is the capital of the State of the same name, and has about 28,000 inhabitants. According to Humboldt, its elevation is 6,363 feet above the sea-level.

Guanajuato is reached by the Mexican Central R. R. It is 252 miles from Mexico City. The town is built in a narrow valley encompassed by barren, rolling hills. The leading hotels are the *Suiza, Bayas,* and *Diligencias.* The city is the capital of the State of the same name. The population is about 60,000, and the elevation is 6,836 feet, according to Humboldt.

The Places of Interest are: 1. The *Mint.* 2. The Church of *La Parróquia.* 3. The *Prison,* which was formerly used as a castle, and was the last stronghold of the Spaniards in the State. 4. The *silver-mines.* 5. The *silver-mills,* or *haciendas de beneficios,* about fifty in number. The *Veta Madre,* or mother vein, is one of the most remarkable ore-deposits in the world. The mines on it have been worked for three hundred years. The well-known *patio,* or cold amalgamation process, is used in the mills. Steam has been introduced at one of them to run the machines employed for crushing the ores.

Guadalajara is about 130 miles, by diligence, from *Lagos*, on the Mexican Central R. R. The latter town is 294 miles from the capital. The leading hotels are the *Hidalgo, Nacional, Diligencias*, and *Nuevo Mundo*. Population, 78,600; and elevation, 5,052 feet above the sea-level. *Guadalajara*, the capital of the State of Jalisco, is the second city of the Republic.

The Places of Interest are: The *Cathedral*, on the *Plaza de Armas;* the *Government Palace;* the *City Hall;* the *Mint;* the *Bishop's Palace;* the *Custom-House*, and *Alameda*. The city is noted for the manufacture of silk, thread, cotton, and woolen goods.

Aguascalientes is 66 miles north of *Lagos*. It lies in a broad plain. There are warm springs here, adjoining the *Alameda*. The city can boast of a fine park. The best hotels are the *Diligencias* and *Nacional*. Population, 32,000. *Aguascalientes* has been for a very long time a favorite resort for the sick, its name being derived from its numerous hot springs. Zacatecas, the capital of the State of the same name, lies in a gorge at an elevation of about 8,000 feet above the level of the sea. The adjoining region is very barren. The best hotels are the *Zacatecano, Comercio*, and *Nacional*. The climate is cool and dry. The objects of interest are, the *Cathedral* and 14 churches, the *Palace*, the *Mint*, the *silver-mines*, and the hill called *La Bufa*, whose summit commands a fine view of the city. The mines of Zacatecas began to be worked in 1548. The principal vein is known as the *Veta Grande*, which is next in magnitude to the *Veta Madre* of Guanajuato. There are about 100 mines in the vicinity, several of which are owned by English and American capitalists. The silver-reducing mills are in the suburb of Guadalupe. Population, 32,000.

NORTHERN MEXICO.

The Republic may be entered on the north by rail, either at *Laredo* or at *El Paso*, both of these towns being situated on the Rio Grande. The Mexican National R. R. runs southward from *Laredo* to *El Salado*, a distance of 323 miles. It is being extended beyond this point toward *San Luis Potosi*. *Monterey* lies 170 miles from *Laredo*. The best hotels are the *Iturbide* and *Monterey*. The notable buildings are the Cathedral and Bishop's Palace. The mean annual temperature is 71° Fahr. A pleasant excursion may be taken to the *potrero*, 14 miles distant. Population, 15,300. Saltillo (Hotel *San Estaban*), the capital of the State of Coahuila, is 68 miles from Monterey. The famous battle-field of *Buena Vista* lies 8 miles distant.

Chihuahua.

The Mexican Central R. R., starting from *Paso del Norte*, on the western bank of the Rio Grande, runs to Chihuahua (distance, 220 miles). The intermediate country is well adapted to stock-raising. The city of Chihuahua is the capital of the State of the same name. It lies in latitude 28° 35' 10'' N. The leading hotel is the *American House*. The places of interest are, the Cathedral, several churches, and the Aqueduct. The Mexican Central R. R., connecting with all the principal trunk lines in the United States, now runs without break through to Mexico City, a distance of 1,224 miles.

The Volcanoes.

There are four semi-active volcanoes in Mexico, viz., Popocatepetl, Orizaba, Jorullo, and Colima. They lie on or near the 19th parallel of north latitude, and on the same great vent in the earth's crust. The first-named mountain is the only one that is generally visited by tourists. It is much easier of ascent than Orizaba. Jorullo, in the State of Michoacan, possesses charms for the geologist and lover of scenery, but it is somewhat inaccessible. Accordingly, we will confine ourselves to Popocatepetl.

This volcano may be ascended either from Puebla or Amecameca. The latter route is preferable. Starting from Mexico, the tourist can reach Amecameca by rail in about four hours. He should at once provide himself with horses, guides, provisions, alpenstock, etc. Don Francisco Noriega, who keeps a store on the north side of the *Plaza*, can furnish the traveler with the articles needed. Each guide will cost $5 for the ascent. Leaving the town, the night will be passed at the ranch of Tlamacas, about 12 miles distant. This spot lies just below timberline, on the ridge which connects the peak of Popocatepetl with Iztaccihuatl. An early start must be made on the following morning (by 4 o'clock, if possible), as six hours of constant climbing will be requisite to reach the top of the volcano. Goggles or a veil should be worn to protect the eyes from the glare of the sun reflected from the snow; and leggings should also be used to keep the ankles as dry as possible. The view from the summit is very extensive. Nearly one quarter of the surface of the Republic lies within the field of vision on a clear day.

The crater is about half a mile in diameter. Sulphur is taken out of it and carried down the mountain-side by *peons*. It is a source of profit to the owner, General Sanchez Ochoa. The traveler should not remain more than one hour on the summit. The descent will be very easy if the snow be not too hard, as the guide will arrange a piece of matting or *petate* for the tourist to "coast" down the slope of the peak. If no accident takes place, the traveler can reach Amecameca on the same evening, and return to the capital by the morning train, thus making the trip in two days.

N. B.—It may be added that the new-comer had better not attempt the ascent of Popocatepetl until he has been on the table-land for several weeks, so that his lungs have become accustomed to its rarefied atmosphere.

The Mines.

Owing to the fame and richness of the Mexican mines, the tourist should not leave the Republic without visiting at least one of them. The following trip will give the observer a very complete idea of the ore-deposits:

Starting from the City of Mexico, let the tourist go to *Morelia* by rail and examine the *Tlalpujahua, Chapatuato, Sinda*, and *Ozumatlan* districts; then return to *Acambaro* and travel to *Guanajuato* by rail; then proceed to *Aguascalientes* and visit the district of *Bolaños* in Jalisco. From the latter point, the journey may be continued to *Zacatecas*, either directly northward by trail, or *via Aguascalientes* by train. Leaving Zacatecas take the diligence to Fresnillo, Sombrerete, Guarisamey, and Durango. The Mexican Central Railway now furnishes easy access to the last-named town, from which the traveler may either proceed to Chihuahua or return to the national capital. There are fair hotel accommodations at most of the above-mentioned localities. We may add that the stranger will receive courteous treatment from the superintendents and miners generally. The best time to go underground is in the morning. If, however, one has but a few days to spend in the country, the most convenient mining town to visit is *Pachuca*, which is reached by tramway from *Irolo* on the line of the Mexican Railway (Hotel *San Carlos*). Pachuca possesses some of the oldest mines in the Republic. Millions of British capital have been invested here. Including the adjoining village of *Real del Monte*, the district contains about 300 mines. Excursions may be made on horseback from *Pachuca* to the towns of *Regla* and *El Chico*.

(For further information, *see* "Appletons' Guide-Book to Mexico," just published.)

OTHER RESORTS.

ATLANTIC CITY.

How to reach.—From Philadelphia, Atlantic City is reached *via* the West Jersey R. R. in 1½ hour (distance, 60 miles; fare, $1); also by the Camden & Atlantic R. R. or the Philadelphia & Atlantic City R. R. From New York *via* Pennsylvania R. R. to Camden, and thence *via* West Jersey R. R. or Camden & Atlantic R. R. (distance, 146 miles; time, 4½ hours; fare, $3).

Hotels and Boarding-Houses.—There are about 60 hotels and large boarding-houses, of which the most important are the *Brighton House* ($3 to $4 a day); the *Waverly* ($3 to $3.50 a day); the *United States* ($15 to $25 a week); *Congress Hall* ($12 to $20 a week); the *Berkeley*, the *Haddon*, and the *Seaside*. Good but less expensive hotels are the *Mansion*, *Schauffler's*, *Chalfonte House*, *Fothergill House*, **Ocean House**, *Senate*, *Ruscombe*, and the *Dennis*.

ATLANTIC CITY dates from 1818 as a settlement and 1854 as a city; it is situated on Absecon Beach, New Jersey, between Absecon Inlet and Great Egg Harbor Inlet. The resident population has increased within six years from 2,200 to nearly 10,000, while in the summer the visitors increase the number to 100,000. There are several good schools, with an attendance of 1,500 school-children, Roman Catholic, Episcopal, Presbyterian, Methodist, and Baptist Churches, and a large and attractive City-Hall. Hundreds of pretty and neat cottages, with their gardens of well-kept flowers, extend along the miles of broad avenues and walks; the dry, hard, and smooth streets, with ten miles of a beach-drive; the drive to the open country, excellent sailing and fishing from the Inlet, and gunning in the bays, a board-walk or promenade extending along the beach-front for two miles, the *Park Bath-House*, a winter ocean parlor inclosed in glass, afford much pleasure to the visitor.

Of late, Atlantic City has been frequented as a fall, winter, and spring resort by many who wish to make a temporary escape from the rigors of less favored places. Its climate is considered milder and more equable than that of most points on the North Atlantic coast, and its location is in other respects exceptionally healthful. February, March, April, and May are thought to be the months in which invalids experience greatest benefit from a residence there.

EASTMAN, GEORGIA.

How to reach.—Eastman is situated directly on the line of the Georgia division of the East Tennessee, Virginia & Georgia R. R., 56 miles southeast of Macon, 200 miles south of Aiken, S. C., and 150 miles north of Jacksonville. It is easily accessible, much of the direct travel to Florida from the west and northwest passing through this place. From the north and east it is accessible *via* Savannah to Macon, on the Georgia R. R., and thence by the East Tennessee, Virginia & Georgia.

EASTMAN is the county town of Dodge County, Ga., one of the central counties of the State, occupying one of the most attractive portions of the beautiful, rolling country known as the Uplands District, and famous for the loveliness of its scenery and the salubrity of its climate. It is situated in the western part of the great pine belt which intersects the State, and is 600 to 700 feet above tide-water—entirely away from the low, flat, and swampy lands of the coast counties, and yet sufficiently far south to secure freedom from the cold winds which blow down from the mountain-region. For some 15 or 20 miles in all directions from Eastman the land rolls off like a Western prairie. The woods have but little undergrowth, and present an aspect like that of an English park. The soil being of a stiff loam, firm enough to bear wheels, the rides and drives in every direction are very charming, being wholly free from the sand which is so great a drawback in other places of a similar character. The air of these pine uplands is thought to have a healing virtue in nearly all bronchial and pulmonary complaints, and is recommended by many physicians.

Encouraged by the advantages of the location, some Northern capitalists have built a large hotel at Eastman (the *Uplands Hotel*) with accommodations for 150 guests. The hotel is also managed by Northern men, and is provided with all the conveniences and appliances of hotels at the Northern resorts.

OLD POINT COMFORT.

Old Point Comfort has been for many years a popular watering-place, and since the construction of the new *Hygeia Hotel* ($3.50 a day, $15 to $20 a week), it offers greater attractions than ever before. It is situated within 100 yards of Fortress Monroe, Va., at the entrance of Hampton Roads, about 13 miles north of Norfolk; and may be reached from New York daily by the steamers of the Old Dominion Steamship Co., or by the New York, Philadelphia & Norfolk R. R., to Cape Charles, thence by steamer, and from Norfolk, Richmond, or Washington, by steamers. The hotel is located on the beach, at the head of the steamboat-landing. Fortress Monroe, the largest in America, with an armament of 370 guns, is always open to visitors, and contains many features of interest. The famed Artillery School has its establishment within the fortress; and the dress-parade, with the music of a fine band morning and evening, and the open-air concerts given by the band in the evenings, afford the visitor a pleasure which is enjoyed at no other watering-place save Newport. The climate is delightful, with an average of 45°, 44°, and 42°; and the Hampton Normal and Agricultural Institute, the National Military Home, the National Cemetery, and the venerable old town of Hampton (containing one of the oldest churches in America), are all within the easy limits of a ride or sail. The *Hampton Normal and Agricultural Institute* is well worth a visit. It is designed especially to train colored youth as teachers of their own race, by giving an English and industrial education, while affording students an opportunity to defray a portion of their expenses by labor. It is open to both sexes. The grounds comprise about 200 acres, of which 150 acres are under cultivation by the boys. There is also a successful printing-office operated by the students.

The climate of all this region is remarkably mild and healthful in late autumn and early spring, and the *Hygeia Hotel* is a favorite place of temporary sojourn for those *en route* to or from the more southern resorts. The *Hygeia* is open all the year round (see "Some Useful Hints").

LAS VEGAS HOT SPRINGS, NEW MEXICO.

How to reach.—The Hot Springs are reached from all points *via* the Atchison, Topeka & Santa Fé R. R. to Las Vegas, and thence by a short branch, 6 miles long, to the springs.

Hotels, etc.—The leading hotel is the *Las Vegas Hot Springs Hotel*, built by the railroad company to replace the Montezuma House, burned a short time ago. An older hotel, the *Hot Springs Hotel*, is one of the most comfortable in the West. The rates at these houses are from $2 to $4 a day, and from $12 to $25 per week.

LAS VEGAS HOT SPRINGS are situated 6 miles above the city of Las Vegas, in the foot-hills of the Spanish Range of the Rocky Mountains. The swift and beautiful river Gallinas flows from the mountains through a gorge, and, just where it enters the plateau, the hot springs, to the number of 40, bubble from the red granite ledge, varying in temperature from 110° to 140°. Long before the coming of the white men, the Indian traditions clustered about these thermal springs as a marvelous agency of healing, and among the Spanish population they have always been a much-prized resort. Until 1879 the only hotel accommodations were adobe buildings. But during that year the Atchison, Topeka & Santa Fé R. R. purchased the property and inaugurated a series of extensive improvements, which have resulted in fine hotels, a large park, and grounds laid out with fountains, graveled walks, bluegrass lawns, shade-trees, and flower-beds; an aqueduct system, palatial bath-houses, livery-stables, and fine carriage-roads 70 miles long, conducting through the Cañon of the Gallinas into the heart of the finest scenery in New Mexico. In connection with the *Montezuma House* is a large conservatory, and a museum containing an interesting collection of mineral, Indian, and early Spanish curiosities. The springs are only half a day's ride by rail from Santa Fé, one of the most quaint and interesting cities, as it is one of the oldest, in the United States. Aside from the quaintness of the city itself, it lies in the midst of the curious relics of a civilization old when the Spaniards came. The deepest interest attaches to this region on the score of historical and antiquarian considerations. In point of climate Las Vegas Hot Springs claim an advantage over all other thermal waters of like property. The location is on a southern slope, and at an elevation of 6,767 feet above the sea. This gives a pure, invigorating atmosphere, absolutely free from malaria, and a temperature so mild and even that invalids may spend a portion of the day in the open air every day in the year. The mean temperature in the shade from Christmas, 1882, to New-Year's day at noon, was 52°; during January, 41°; for February, 49°; for March, 56°; for April, 58° Fahr. The waters are taken both internally and externally, and a comparison of them with those of the celebrated Carlsbad, Bohemia, shows them to be nearly identical. The diseases for which they are specially recommended are chronic and acute rheumatism, gout, scrofula, stiff joints, cutaneous diseases, syphilitic complaints, enlargements of the glands, general debility, spinal disease, mental exhaustion, sciatica, lumbago, paralysis, neuralgia, and nervous disorders; catarrh, asthma, dyspepsia, liver disorders, Bright's disease, diabetes, blood-poisoning, and female diseases. It is also claimed that, where pulmonary difficulty is not too far advanced, the use of these waters, in connection with the dry, pure air, and perfectly even, mild climate, proves of great benefit. The hot baths are administered in a great variety of forms by skillful attendants, amid the most luxurious surroundings, and under the charge of competent medical authority. The waters principally used, both for bathing and drinking, are derived from three of the springs, although new ones are discovered from time to time. The analysis of these, made by Prof. F. V. Hayden, is as follows:

CONSTITUENTS.	Spring No. 1.	No. 2.	No. 3.
Sodium carbonate	1.72	1.17	5.00
Calcium carbonate. } Magnesium carbonate }	1.08	10.63	11.43
Sodium sulphate	14.12	15.43	16.21
Sodium chloride	27.26	24.37	27.34
Potassium	Trace.	Trace.	Trace.
Lithium	Strong trace.	Strong trace.	Strong trace.
Silicic acid	1.04	Trace	2.51
Iodine	Trace.	Trace.	Trace.
Bromine	Trace.	Trace.	Trace.
Temperature	136° Fahr	123° Fahr.	123° Fahr.

For those visitors to the Las Vegas Hot Springs who are not strictly invalided, the surrounding country offers the greatest attractions. Independent of the historic interest of the region, the neighboring scenery is of the grandest character, and good roads give easy access to it by carriage or horseback. Devotees of the rod and gun, too, will find here one of the best fields on the continent for the exercise of their skill. The brooks and streams are full of mountain-trout, and throughout the whole country deer, elk, antelope, mountain-grouse, ducks, wild-turkeys, etc., may be found in abundance. Those ambitious for nobler game may easily meet the bear and puma. No finer game-parks can be found than the mountains west and north of Las Vegas Hot Springs.

LAKEWOOD, NEW JERSEY.

Lakewood, a new winter resort, formerly known as Bricksburg, lies on the New Jersey Southern Division of the Philadelphia & Reading R. R., about 58 miles from New York. It has within the last three years achieved a marked popularity. The Lakewood air is supposed to have a peculiar efficacy in diseases of the throat and lungs. The soil, of pure light sand, creates a dryness of atmosphere, and perhaps serves as a reservoir of heat, causing the thermometer to range at any given date about ten degrees above the temperature of New York. Pine-woods begin at the outskirts of the village and surround it for miles on every side. Whatever breezes blow can not fail to bring with them balsamic and healing virtues. The hotel (the *Laurel House*, $3 to $4 per day) is specially adapted for invalids, having corridors and piazzas covered in with glass, and with provision for wood-fires in each bedroom. There are also boarding-houses in the village. There are two lakes in the woods, from which the place derives its name; and numerous drives and walks in the pines are the great resource of visitors.

NEWPORT NEWS, VIRGINIA.

This place has begun to attract great attention as a winter resort. It is situated on Hampton Roads, eight miles above Old Point Comfort and twelve miles from Norfolk. It is reached *via* Chesapeake & Ohio R. R., and its connections (Newport News is the deep-water terminus of the former road), or by Bay Line, or Old Dominion steamers from New York. The locality is full of historic interest, and the contiguous waters were the scene of some of the most important naval battles on record. The surrounding country is very attractive, and the waters of Hampton Roads teem with the finest fish, making excellent sport for the fisherman. The climate is very mild, being about that of Old Point Comfort, the thermometer seldom registering 20° Fahr., and the average winter temperature being 47° Fahr. The *Hotel Warwick* (300 guests, $3 to $4 per day; $17.50 to $21 per week) is situated on high ground overlooking the sea, with splendid marine views of from eight miles to twenty miles. It has every requirement and luxury of a completely equipped hotel, and is conducted on the most liberal principles. The artesian-well water used at the hotel is claimed to have healing properties not unlike the waters of the Virginia Springs. For those invalids who are able to take frequent outings, this resort seems to afford great attractions, as the fishing, boating, and shooting are all good, and there are many beautiful drives.

BAILEY SPRINGS, ALABAMA.

This resort is accessible *via* the Memphis & Charleston R. R. to Florence, Alabama, thence nine miles by stage. These springs have long been known for their healing qualities, and the waters are shipped to all parts of the country. They are seven in number: the Free Stone, the Soda, the Brick or Chalybeate, the Alum, the Rock or Mineral, the Iron, and the Sulphur. The waters are peculiarly beneficial in dropsy, scrofula, dyspepsia, diseases of the urinary organs, and women's diseases, and all of the springs differ from one another in taste and quality. The scenery is very picturesque and beautiful, the climate almost perfect in its balminess and uniformity. The increasing numbers which throng here every year prove the attractiveness of this winter sanitarium. The hotel buildings are situated on the summit of a semicircular range of hills which curve grandly round the mineral springs at their base. The houses are three hundred feet above the level of Shoal Creek, a little over a quarter of a mile away. They are comfortable, old-fashioned structures, with large rooms and an abundance of doors and windows and verandas. The extensive grounds are turfed with natural grasses, and densely shaded with forest trees of large growth and infinite variety, among which graveled walks wind in every direction. All the customary amusements are supplied. Music, dancing, boating, bathing, archery, ten-pins, cards, chess, excursions, barbecues, and other pleasant entertainments are called into frequent use for the pleasure of the visitors. The services of a competent resident physician are always available.

CAMDEN, SOUTH CAROLINA.

This place of winter resort can be reached from the North via the Charleston steamers to Charleston, and thence by South Carolina R. R.; though railway transit can be had on any of the trunk lines running to Charleston or Columbia, South Carolina. Lying in the middle country of the State—a section known as the "Sand-Hills," varying in width from five to twenty-five miles—Camden possesses an inter-tropical climate, the bracing mildness of the temperate zone, and none of the moist heat of the tropics, so enervating to invalids. The veritable home of the long-leaf pine, the atmosphere, saturated with the resinous exhalations of its immense forests, is of the purest and most invigorating character, and above all others beneficial to diseases of the throat and lungs—in proof of which, the mortuary records of Camden for the past thirteen years show but an average annual death-rate of twenty-five persons in a population of two thousand, with cases of genuine native consumption so extremely rare as to warrant the strong assertion of its being unknown in the neighborhood. The mean winter temperature is 46° Fahr., and in the months of December, January, and February there is little or no rainfall. It is claimed that the climate of Camden will cure all throat and lung difficulties in their incipiency, and in their more advanced stages will prolong life. The climate has also been found highly efficacious in convalescence, nervous debility, insomnia, brain-troubles, and women's weaknesses. The *Hobkirk Inn*, formerly the residence of a gentleman whose wealth permitted the full indulgence of his taste for arboriculture, is surrounded by rare and costly trees and shrubs, curiously trimmed and trained, affording charming pleasure-grounds of genuine botanical merit and beauty. It is claimed that to those desiring to winter South, either for pleasure or health, the Hobkirk Inn offers the comforts and independence of a good hotel, with the seclusion of a gentleman's private park and residence. The many points of historic interest in and about Camden, the numerous and varied drives and rides among the pines, and the many fox-hunts during the season, make the chief winter amusements of the town—riding, driving, and following the hounds.

COLUMBIA, SOUTH CAROLINA.

This beautiful city, the capital of South Carolina, is situated on the bluffs of the Congaree River, a few miles below the charming falls of that river. It is reached by rail via the Richmond & Danville R. R. to Charlotte, and thence by the Charlotte, Columbus & Augusta R. R.; or via steamer to Charleston, thence by South Carolina R. R. The soil of the region is dry and sandy, giving perfect drainage, and the air is aromatic with the breath of pine-forests. It is famous for beautifully shaded streets and flower-gardens. There are many handsome private residences and imposing public buildings; among the latter the State-House, which, when completed, will cost $4,000,000. The social attractions of the city are great, and the invalid or pleasure-sojourner during the winter months will find them a very pleasant feature. In the suburbs are beautiful parks and pleasure-grounds. The weather during January, February, and March is peculiarly fine, the air being very dry, the skies clear, and the thermometer ranging from 50° to 75° Fahr. The pleasures and amusements of Columbia will, probably in many cases, be a valuable accessory of the healthfulness of the city, and act as a moral tonic. For those invalids who find the air of Florida too enervating, as is often the case, the winter climate of Columbia is perfect. There are two good hotels (*Wright's Hotel* and *Grand Central*), at which the charges are reasonable. The country about the city is full of charming landscape views, and the walks and drives are highly attractive. The number of winter tourists who make Columbia a place of somewhat lengthened sojourn is increasing every year.

MOBILE, ALABAMA.

This city, one of the most beautiful in the South, and the original seat of French colonization in the Southwest, having been for many years the capital of the colony of Louisiana, is the largest town in Alabama, and the only seaport. It is situated on the west side of the Mobile River, just above its entrance into Mobile Bay. The site is a sandy plain, rising as it recedes from the river, and bounded at a few miles back by high and beautiful hills. The city is beautifully built; with broad and shady streets, and many handsome public buildings and private residences. A feature of Mobile is found in the noble oaks that line the streets, and the handsome private grounds and gardens which surround the dwellings. The Gulf Shell Road, which extends nine miles along the Gulf, is the favorite drive, and is one of the most charming in the country. The climate of Mobile in the winter months is very much the same as that of Jacksonville, Florida, except that it is not liable to the northers which at times make Jacksonville disagreeable. The atmosphere is somewhat humid, and the temperature in December, January, and February ranges from 60° to 75° Fahr. If the invalid finds the Mobile climate a little trying on account of its occasional dampness, the wise pleasure-seeker, who seeks to avoid the rigors of a northern climate, will be delighted with the balmy and even temperature, and the rich summer bloom of vegetation. The fishing and sailing on Mobile Bay can not be surpassed anywhere. Mobile may be reached from New York by any one of three or four great trunk routes (fare, $34.65), and from the West by Louisville, Nashville, and Great Southern lines. The hotels are the *Battle House*, *St. James*, and *La Clede House*, the rates being from $2 to $3 per day, and from $12 to $15 per week.

TABLE OF RAILWAY AND STEAMBOAT FARES

FROM NEW YORK TO THE LEADING CITIES AND PLACES OF INTEREST IN THE UNITED STATES AND CANADA.

☞ *The Railway named is that by which the traveler leaves New York.*

☞ The rates given are those which obtain at the time of going to press, but are liable to slight variations. They are both for unlimited and limited tickets. Unlimited tickets are good until used, and permit of stop-over at any place and for any time *en route*. The limited tickets are good for continuous passage only, and will not permit of stop-over. We do not give the price of excursion tickets (good for passage both ways), as these **are so** variable at different times and are issued to but few points.

NEW YORK TO	VIA	Unlimited.	Limited.
Aiken, S. C.	Baltimore, Washington, and Lynchburg	$26 60	$23 65
" "	Baltimore, Washington, and Richmond	28 85	23 65
Albany, N. Y.	Hudson River *or* West Shore R. R.	3 10	
" "	Steamboat	2 00	
Atlanta, Ga.	Harrisburg, Luray, and Roanoke	26 70	24 00
" "	Baltimore, Washington, and Richmond	32 10	24 00
" "	Washington, Lynchburg, and Danville	24 00	
Atlantic City, N. J.	Pennsylvania *or* New Jersey Southern R. R.	3 25	
Augusta, Ga.	Baltimore, Norfolk, and Weldon	27 90	23 00
" "	Washington and Richmond	26 90	23 00
" "	Washington, Lynchburg, and Danville	25 95	23 00
Baltimore, Md.	Pennsylvania R. R.	5 30	
Berkeley Springs, Va.	Pennsylvania *or* Baltimore & Ohio R. R.	10 05	
Boston, Mass.	New York & New Haven R. R.	5 53	5 00
" "	Fall River, *or* Stonington, *or* Providence, *or* **Norwich** steamers	4 00	
Buffalo, N. Y.	New York Central, Erie, **or** West Shore R. R.	9 25	
Burlington, Iowa	New York Central R. R.	29 40	26 15
" "	Erie **or** West Shore R. R.	29 40	24 65
" "	Baltimore & Ohio R. R.		
" "	Pennsylvania Central R. R.	32 65	26 15
Burlington, Vt.	New York Central & Hudson River R. R.	8 25	
Cape May, N. J.	New Jersey Southern *or* Pennsylvania R. R.	4 25	
Charleston, S. C.	Baltimore, Norfolk, and Weldon	25 60	23 00
" "	Washington and Richmond	27 50	23 00
" "	Washington, Lynchburg, and Danville	27 50	23 00
" "	Steamer (Pier 27 North River)	20 00	
Chattanooga, Tenn.	Harrisburg, Roanoke, and Bristol	26 25	23 75
Chicago, Ill.	New York Central R. R.	24 25	20 00
" "	Erie *or* West Shore R. R.	23 25	18 50
" "	Baltimore & Ohio R. R.		
" "	Pennsylvania Central R. R.	26 50	20 00
Cincinnati, Ohio	New York Central, Erie, *or* West Shore R. R.	21 25	16 50
" "	Pennsylvania Central R. R.	21 50	18 00
Cleveland, Ohio	New York Central, Erie, *or* West **Shore R. R.**	14 25	13 00
" "	Pennsylvania Central R. R.	16 50	13 00
Colorado Springs, Col.	New York Central R. R.	58 00	48 50
" " "	Erie *or* West Shore R. R.	58 00	47 00
" " "	Pennsylvania Central R. R.	61 25	48 50
" " "	Baltimore & Ohio R. R.	61 25	
Columbus, Ohio	New York Central, Erie, *or* Pennsylvania R. R.	18 40	16 25
Cooperstown, N. Y.	New York Central & Hudson River R. R.	6 15	
Delaware Water-Gap, Pa.	Morris & Essex (D., L. & W.) R. R.	2 55	
Denver, Col.	New York Central R. R.	56 00	50 75
" "	Erie *or* West Shore R. R.	56 00	49 25
" "	Pennsylvania Central R. R.	59 25	50 75
" "	Baltimore & Ohio R. R.	59 25	49 75
Detroit, Mich.	New **York** Central, Erie, *or* Pennsylvania R. R.	16 25	15 00
Fernandina, Fla.	Baltimore, Norfolk, and Weldon	37 40	31 60
" "	Washington and Richmond	37 10	31 00
" "	Washington, Lynchburg, and Danville	37 10	31 00
" "	Steamer (Pier 20 East River)	21 50	
Frankfort, Ky.	New York Central, Erie, Pennsylvania, *or* Baltimore & Ohio R. R.	24 85	21 25
Galveston, Texas	N. Y. Cent., Erie, Penn., *or* Balt. & Ohio R. R. (Western Route)	56 60	44 30
" "	Washington **and** Lynchburg (Southern Route)	57 45	44 30
" "	Steamer (Pier 20 East River)	40 00	
Halifax, Can.	New York & New **Haven** R. R.	20 53	18 00
Hartford, Conn.	New York & New Haven R. R.	2 65	
Hot Springs, Ark.	Pennsylvania Central, **Erie**, Balt. & Ohio, *or* N. Y. Central R. R.	43 90	36 30

Table of Railway and Steamboat Fares. (Continued.)

NEW YORK TO	VIA	Unlimited.	Limited.
Houston, Texas	N. Y. Cent., Erie, Penn., or Balt. & Ohio R. R. (Western Route)	$54 85	$42 80
" "	Washington and Lynchburg (Southern Route)	55 95	42 80
Indianapolis, Ind	New York Central, Erie, Pennsylvania, or Baltimore & Ohio R. R.	22 50	19 00
Jacksonville, Fla.	Baltimore, Norfolk, and Weldon	37 20	30 20
" "	Washington and Richmond	36 90	30 20
" "	Washington, Lynchburg, and Danville	36 90	31 00
" "	Steamer (Pier 20 East River)	28 00	
Kansas City, Mo.	New York Central R. R.	35 75	29 50
" "	Erie or West Shore R. R.	35 75	29 50
" "	Pennsylvania Central R. R.	39 00	29 50
" "	Baltimore & Ohio R. R.		
Kingston, Can.	New York Central & Hudson River R. R.	9 20	
Leadville, Col.	New York Central R. R.	68 50	63 25
" "	Erie or West Shore R. R.	68 50	61 75
" "	Pennsylvania Central R. R.	71 75	63 25
" "	Baltimore & Ohio R. R.	71 25	61 75
Little Rock, Ark	New York Central, Pennsylvania, Erie, or Baltimore & Ohio R. R.	40 85	33 00
Long Branch, N. J.	Central R. R. of New Jersey	1 35	1 00
" "	New Jersey Southern (Pier 14, North River)	1 00	
Louisville, Ky	New York Central, Erie, or West Shore R. R.	24 75	20 00
" "	Pennsylvania Central R. R.	25 00	21 50
" "	Baltimore & Ohio R. R.		
Lynchburg, Va.	Pennsylvania or Baltimore & Ohio R. R.	12 00	
Madison, Wis.	New York Central R. R.	24 15	23 90
" "	Erie or West Shore R. R.	24 15	22 40
" "	Pennsylvania Central R. R.	30 40	24 60
" "	Baltimore & Ohio R. R.	30 40	22 40
Mauch Chunk, Pa.	Morris & Essex or New Jersey Central R. R.	3 60	
Memphis, Tenn.	Cincinnati and Louisville (Western Route)	35 90	27 70
" "	Washington and Lynchburg (Southern Route)	35 55	27 70
Mexico, Mex	N. Y. Cent., Erie, West Shore, Balt. & Ohio, and Penn. Cent. R. R.	120 95	118 05
Milwaukee, Wis.	New York Central R. R.	26 00	22 75
" "	Erie or West Shore R. R.	26 00	21 25
" "	Pennsylvania Central R. R.	29 25	22 75
" "	Baltimore & Ohio R. R.	29 05	21 05
Minneapolis, Minn.	New York Central R. R.	34 25	31 50
" "	Erie or West Shore R. R.	37 25	30 00
" "	Pennsylvania Central R. R.	38 00	31 50
" "	Baltimore & Ohio R. R.	38 00	30 00
Mobile, Ala.	Cincinnati and Louisville (Western Route)	45 00	30 25
" "	Baltimore or Washington (Southern Route)	34 65	30 25
Montgomery, Ala	(Same routes as to Mobile)	39 60	26 75
Montreal, Can.	New York Central or New York & New Haven R. R.	11 50	10 00
Nashville, Tenn.	Cincinnati and Louisville (Western Route)	30 45	26 00
" "	Washington and Lynchburg (Southern Route)	30 80	26 00
New Haven, Conn.	New York & New Haven R. R.	1 75	
New Orleans, La	Cincinnati and Louisville (Western Route)	49 50	32 00
" "	Harrisburg, Roanoke, and Chattanooga	36 90	32 00
" "	Washington, Lynchburg, and Atlanta	38 90	32 00
" "	Steamer (2 lines)	35 00	
Newport, R. I.	New York & New Haven R. R.	5 00	
" "	Fall River steamers	3 00	
Niagara Falls	New York Central, or West Shore, or Erie R. R.	9 25	
Norfolk, Va.	Pennsylvania Central R. R.	8 50	
" "	Steamer	7 25	
Northampton, Mass.	New York & New Haven R. R.	4 25	
Oil City, Pa.	Erie R. R.	12 60	
Omaha, Neb.	New York Central R. R.	36 25	33 00
" "	Erie or West Shore R. R.	36 25	31 50
" "	Pennsylvania Central R. R.	39 50	33 00
" "	Baltimore & Ohio R. R.	39 50	31 50
Ottawa, Can.	New York Central & Hudson River R. R.	11 20	
Philadelphia, Pa.	Pennsylvania or New Jersey Central R. R.	2 50	
Pittsburg, Pa.	Pennsylvania or New Jersey Central R. R.	12 50	10 50
Pittsfield, Mass.	New York & New Haven R. R.	3 50	
Plattsburg, N. Y.	New York Central & Hudson River R. R.	9 05	
Portland, Me.	New York & New Haven R. R.	9 00	
" "	Steamer to Boston, thence by railroad	7 50	7 00
Portsmouth, N. H.	(Same routes as to Portland)	6 20	
Providence, R. I.	New York & New Haven R. R.	5 00	4 50
" "	Steamer (Pier 29, North River)	3 25	
Quebec, Can	New York & New Haven R. R.	13 00	
Raleigh, N. C.	Pennsylvania Central R. R.	18 50	15 20
Richmond, Va	Pennsylvania or Baltimore & Ohio R. R.	11 25	10 85

Table of **Railway and Steamboat Fares.**—(*Continued.*)

NEW YORK TO	VIA	Unlimited	Limited
Richmond, Va.	Steamers (foot of Beach Street, North River)	$8 50	
Rutland, Vt.	New York Central & Hudson River R. R.	6 15	
Sacramento, Cal.	New York Central R. R.	94 90	$80 50
" "	Erie or West Shore R. R.	94 90	79 00
" "	Pennsylvania Central R. R.	97 75	80 50
" "	Baltimore & Ohio R. R.	97 75	79 00
St. Augustine, Fla.	Baltimore, Norfolk, and Weldon	38 70	32 50
" "	Washington and Richmond	38 90	32 50
" "	Washington, Lynchburg, and Danville	39 40	32 50
" "	Steamers to Savannah	26 50	
St. John, N. B.	New York & New Haven R. R.	16 00	13 50
St. Joseph, Mo	New York Central R. R.	35 75	31 75
" "	Erie or West Shore R. R.	35 75	30 25
" "	Pennsylvania Central R. R.	39 00	30 25
" "	Baltimore & Ohio R. R.	39 00	30 25
St. Louis, Mo	New York Central R. R.	30 50	24 25
" "	Erie or West Shore R. R.	30 50	22 25
" "	Pennsylvania Central R. R.	31 50	24 25
" "	Baltimore & Ohio R. R.	31 50	22 25
St. Paul, Minn	New York Central R. R.	34 75	31 50
" "	Erie or West Shore R. R.	34 75	30 00
" "	Pennsylvania Central R. R.	40 50	29 50
" "	Baltimore & Ohio R. R.	58 00	30 00
Salt Lake City, Utah	New York Central R. R.	87 35	80 50
" "	Erie or West Shore R. R.	87 35	79 00
" "	Pennsylvania Central R. R.	90 60	80 50
" "	Baltimore & Ohio R. R.	90 60	79 00
San Francisco, Cal.	New York Central R. R.	94 90	79 00
" "	Erie or West Shore R. R.	94 90	79 00
" "	Pennsylvania Central R. R.	97 75	80 50
" "	Baltimore & Ohio R. R.	97 75	79 00
Saratoga Springs, N. Y.	New York Central & Hudson River, or **West Shore** R. R.	4 20	
Savannah, Ga.	Baltimore, Norfolk, and Weldon	31 85	24 00
" "	Washington and Richmond	30 20	24 00
" "	Washington, Lynchburg, and Danville	29 90	24 00
" "	Steamer (Pier 35 North River)	20 00	
Sharon Springs, N. Y.	New York Central & Hudson River R. R.	4 90	
Springfield, Ill.	New York Central, R. R.	28 00	23 75
" "	Erie or West Shore R. R.	28 00	22 25
" "	Pennsylvania Central R. R.	29 60	23 75
" "	Baltimore & Ohio R. R.		
Springfield, Mass.	New York & New Haven R. R.	3 80	
Staunton, Va.	Pennsylvania or Baltimore & Ohio R. R.	11 50	
Toledo, Ohio	New York Central, Erie, or Pennsylvania R. R.	17 50	16 25
Toronto, Can.	New York Central, Erie, or Pennsylvania R. R.	11 85	
Trenton Falls, N. Y.	New York Central & Hudson River R. R.	5 54	
Washington, D. C.	Pennsylvania or Baltimore & Ohio R. R.	6 50	
Watkins Glen, N. Y.	Erie or New York Central R. R.	7 10	
White Mountains, N. H.	New York & New Haven R. R.	9 75	
" "	Any steamer route to Boston, thence by railroad	8 00	
White Sul. Springs, Va.	Pennsylvania or Baltimore & Ohio R. R.	14 30	
Wilkesbarre, Pa.	Morris & Essex or New Jersey Central R. R.	5 00	
Wilmington, N. C.	Pennsylvania or Baltimore & Ohio R. R.	18 20	18 00
Winnipeg, Manitoba	New York Central R. R.	52 80	49 55
" "	Erie or West Shore R. R.	52 80	48 05
" "	Pennsylvania Central R. R.	54 65	48 05
" "	Baltimore & Ohio R. R.	54 65	48 05
Yosemite Valley, Cal	New York Central, Erie, Pennsylvania, or Baltimore & Ohio R. R.	139 90	

INDEX.

Aguadilla, Porto Rico, 116.
Aguascalientes, Mex., 141.
Aiken, S. C., 49.
Alachua Sink, Fla., 15.
Alameda, Cal., 84.
Algiers, La., 103.
Almaden Quicksilver Mines, Cal., 89.
Alta Luz, Mex., 137.
Amicalolah Falls, Ga., 41.
Apizaco, Mex., 137.
Appalachicola, Fla., 26.
Arecibo, Porto Rico, 116.
Arkansas Cañon, Col., 77.
Asheville, N. C., 59.
Atlantic City, N. J., 143.
Atoyac, Mex., 137.
Atzcapotzalco, Mex., 140.
Augusta, Ga., 36.
Bahama Islands, 109.
Bailey Springs, Ala., 146.
Bald Eagle Lake, Minn., 68.
Baldwin, Fla., 15.
Balsam Mountains, N. C., 64.
Barbadoes, West Indies, 117.
Batabano, Cuba, 109.
Baton Rouge, La., 96.
Bayamon, Porto Rico, 116.
Bermuda Islands, 121.
Boiling Springs, Col., 77.
Bota, Mex., 137.
Breckenridge, Col., 79.
Brevard, N. C., 64.
Bridal Veil Falls, Minn., 69.
Bridgetown, Barbadoes, 118.
Cæsar's Head, S. C., 54.
Cairo, Ky., 93.
Calhoun Lake, Minn., 69.
Calistoga, Cal., 91.
Camaron, Mex., 137.
Camden, S. C., 147.
Cañon City, Col., 77.
Cape Haytien, Hayti, 115.
Carrollton, La., 103.
Cashier's Valley, N. C., 60.
Cataracts of Tallulah, Ga., 40.
Catoosa Springs, Ga., 39.
Cedar Keys, Fla., 14.
Cedar Lake, Minn., 69.
Chalybeate Springs, Ga., 39.
Charleston, S. C., 42.
Charlotte Amalie, St. Thomas, 116.
Charlotte Harbor, Fla., 27.
Cheyenne Cañon, Col., 76.
Chicago Lakes, Col., 77.
Chick's Springs, S. C., 53.
Chihuahua, Mex., 141.
Chimney Rock, Minn., 69.
Chimney-top, N. C., 61.
Cholula, Mex., 138.
Christiansted, West Indies, 117.
Clarksville, Ga., 39.
Clayton, Ga., 39.
Clear-Water Harbor, Fla., 26.
Clingman's Dome, N. C., 58.
Colorado Springs, Col., 75.
Columbia, S. C., 147.
Columbus, Ky., 93.

Como Lake, Minn., 68.
Conestee Falls, N. C., 64.
Congress Mineral Springs, Cal., 90.
Cordoba, Mex., 137.
Cuba, West Indies, 104.
Cuernavaca, Mex., 140.
Curaçoa, West Indies, 118.
Dahlonega, Ga., 39.
Daytona, Fla., 22.
De Funiak Springs, Fla., 24.
Denver, Col., 75.
Dominica, West Indies, 120.
Drayton Island, Fla., 20.
Dry Tortugas, Fla., 28.
Durango, Mex., 142.
Eastman, Ga., 143.
Eastatoia Falls, Ga., 41.
El Paso, Tex., 141.
Enterprise, Fla., 20.
Escurial, Mex., 137.
Esperanza, Mex., 137.
Ewa, Sandwich Islands, 130.
Fairplay, Col., 79.
Falls:
  Amicalolah, Ga., 41.
  Bridal Veil, Minn., 69.
  Conestee, N. C., 64.
  Eastatoia, Ga., 41.
  Hiawassee, Ga., 41.
  Minnehaha, Minn., 69.
  Slicking, S. C., 55.
  St Anthony, Minn., 69.
  Tallulah, Ga., 40.
  Toccoa, Ga., 39.
  Towaligo, Ga., 39
Faribault, Minn., 70.
Federal Point, Fla., 18.
Fernandina, Fla., 14.
Flat Rock, S. C., 60.
Fort Capron, Fla., 21.
Fort Pillow, Ky., 94.
Fortin, Mex., 137.
Frederickstadt, West Indies, 117.
French Broad River, N. C., 62.
Frontenac, Minn., 70.
Gainesville, Fla., 15.
Garden of the Gods, Col., 76.
George Lake, Fla., 20.
Georgetown Col., 77.
Geyser Springs, Cal., 91.
G en Cannon Falls, N. C., 64.
Glen Eyrie, Col., 76.
Glenn Springs, S C., 53.
Gonaives, Hayti, 115
Gordon's Springs, Ga., 39.
Grandfather Mountain, N. C., 59.
Grand Gulf, Miss. 95.
Grand Lake, Col., 79.
Gray's Peak, Col., 78.
Great Yuma Desert, Cal., 87.
Green Cove Springs, Fla., 16.
Green Spring, Fla., 20.
Greenville, S. C., 54.
Grenada, West Indies, 120.
Gretna, La., 103.
Guadalajara, Mex., 141.
Gudalupe, Mex., 137, 140.
Guadeloupe, West Indies, 120.

Guanabacoa, Cuba, 107.
Guanajuato, Mex., 140.
Guayama, Porto Rico, 116.
Gulf Coast, Fla., 26.
Hamburg, S. C., 37.
Hamilton, Bermudas, 122.
Hanalei, Sandwich Islands, 134.
Harbin's Springs, Cal., 91.
Harbor Island, 110.
Harney Lake, Fla., 21.
Harriet Lake, Minn., 69.
Havana, Cuba, 105.
Hawkinsville, Fla., 18.
Hawk's Bill, N. C., 60.
Hayti, West Indies, 112.
Hiawassee Falls, Ga., 41.
Hibernia, Fla., 18.
Hickory-Nut Gap, N. C., 60.
Hilo, Sandwich Islands, 131.
Hogarth's Landing, Fla., 18.
Honolulu, Sandwich Islands, 128.
Hot Springs, Ark., 71.
Hot Sulphur Springs, Cal., 85.
Hot Sulphur Springs, Col., 78.
Idaho Springs, Col., 77.
Indian River, Fla., 21.
Indian Springs, Ga., 39.
Inolo, Mex., 142.
Iron Banks, Ky., 94.
Island No. 10, 94.
Isle of Pines, 109
Jackson Lake, Fla., 22.
Jacksonville, Fla., 6.
Jacmel, Hayti, 115.
Jalapa, Mex., 137.
Jamaica, West Indies, 110.
James Island, S. C., 48.
Jérémie, Hayti, 115.
Jocasse Valley, S. C., 55.
Jorobado, Isle of Pines, 109.
Kaalea, Sandwich Islands, 130.
Kahana, Sandwich Islands, 130.
Kahuku, Sandwich Islands, 130.
Kauai, Sandwich Islands, 132.
Keulakeakua Bay, Sandwich Islands, 132.
Keowee River, S. C., 55.
Key West, Fla., 27.
Kilauea, Sandwich Islands, 131.
Kingston, Isle St. Vincent, 117.
Kingston, Jamaica, 112
Koloa, Sandwich Islands, 130.
Lafayette Lake, Fla., 22.
Lagos, Mex., 141.
Lahaina, Sandwich Islands, 130.
Lakewood, N. J., 146.
Lakes:
  Bald Eagle, Minn., 68.
  Bradford, Fla., 25.
  Calhoun, Minn., 69.
  Cedar, Minn., 69.
  Cherry, Fla., 23.
  Chicago, Col., 77.
  Como, Minn., 68.
  George, Fla., 20.
  Grand, Col., 79.
  Harney, Fla, 21.
  Harriet, Minn., 69.

INDEX. 153

Jackson, Fla., 22.
Lafayette, Fla., 22.
Little Lake George, Fla., 20.
Minnetonka, Minn., 69.
Monroe, Fla., 19.
Pepin, Minn., 69.
Pontchartrain, La., 103.
Salt Lake, Fla., 20.
San Luis, Col., 79.
Santa Fe, Fla., 15.
White Bear, Minn., 68.
La Palma, Mex., 137.
Laredo, Mex., 141.
Las Animas, Col., 77.
Las Vegas Hot Springs, New Mexico, 144.
Leesburg, Fla., 27.
Limestone Springs, S. C., 53.
Linville Gorge, N. C., 60.
Little Lake George, Fla., 20.
Little Manatee, Fla., 27.
Looking-Glass Falls, N. C., 64.
Los Angeles, Cal., 86.
Madison Springs, Ga., 39.
Madison, Fla., 23.
Magnolia, Fla., 16.
Maltrata, Mex., 137.
Manatee, Fla., 27.
Mandarin, Fla., 18.
Manitou Springs, Col., 75.
Marianao, Cuba, 107.
Martinique, West Indies, 120.
Matanzas, Cuba, 105.
Matanzas, Fla., 13.
Maui, Sandwich Islands, 130.
Mauna-Haleakela, Sandwich Islands, 131.
Mauna-Kea, Sandwich Islands, 131.
Mauna-Loa, Sandwich Islands, 132.
Mavaguez, Porto Rico, 116.
Mellonville, Fla., 18.
Memphis, Tenn., 94.
Merida, Yuc., 136.
Mexico, 134.
Mexico City, 133.
Middleburg, Fla., 18.
Middle Park, Col., 78.
Milot, Hayti, 115.
MINERAL SPRINGS:
  Boiling, Col., 77.
  Catoosa, Ga., 39.
  Chalybeate, Ga., 39.
  Chick's, S. C., 53.
  Congress, Cal., 90.
  Geyser, Cal., 91.
  Glen Alpine, N. C., 60.
  Glenn, S. C., 53.
  Gordon's, Ga., 39.
  Green, Fla., 20.
  Green Cove, Fla., 16.
  Harbin's, Cal., 91.
  Hot, Ark., 71.
  Hot, Las Vegas, N. M., 144.
  Hot Sulphur, Cal., 85.
  Hot Sulphur, Col., 78.
  Idaho, Col., 77.
  Indian, Ga., 39.
  Limestone, S. C., 53.
  Madison, Ga., 39.
  Manitou, Col., 75.
  Million, N. C., 59.
  Moncrief's, Fla., 7.
  Napa Soda, Cal., 91.
  New Holland, Ga., 39.
  Paso Robles, Cal., 87.
  Porter, Ga., 39.
  Powder, Ga., 39.
  Red Sulphur, Ga., 39.
  Rowland's, Ga., 39.
  Silver, Fla., 25.
  Sulphur, Fla., 13.

Tarpon, Fla., 27.
Thundering, Ga., 39.
Wakulla, Fla., 23.
Warm, Ga., 38.
Warm, N. C., 62.
White Sulphur, Cal., 91.
Williamston, S. C., 54.
Wilson's, N. C., 60.
Minneapolis, Minn., 68.
Minnehaha Falls, Minn., 68.
Minnetonka Lake, Minn., 69.
Miragoane, Hayti, 115.
Mississippi River, 92.
Mobile, Ala., 14.
Moncrief's Spring, Fla., 7.
Monroe Lake, Fla., 19.
Montecito, Cal., 85.
Monterey, Cal., 90.
Monterey, Mex., 141.
Monticello, Fla., 23.
Monument Park, Col., 76.
Morganton, N. C., 60.
Mosquito Inlet, Fla., 29.
Mount Island, N. C., 63.
Mount Currahee, Ga., 41.
Mount Lincoln, Col., 79.
Mount Mitchell, N. C., 58, 63.
Mount Pleasant, S. C., 48.
Mount Pisgah, N. C., 59.
Mount Tamalpais, Cal., 90.
Mount Yonah, Ga., 40.
Nacoochee Valley, Ga., 40.
Napa City, Cal., 90.
Napa Soda Springs, Cal., 91.
Napoleon, Ark., 95.
Nassau, Bahama Islands, 110.
Natchez, Miss., 95.
Natural Bridge, Fla., 24.
Na-Wiliwili, Sandwich Islands, 134.
New Britain, Fla., 22.
New Madrid, Mo., 94.
New Orleans, La., 97.
Newport News, Va., 146.
New Smyrna, Fla., 21.
North Park, Col., 78.
Nueva Gerona, Isle of Pines, 109.
Nuevitas, Cuba, 109.
Oakland, Cal., 84.
Ocala, Fla., 15.
Ocklawaha River, Fla., 25.
Old Point Comfort, Va., 144.
Orange Mills, Fla., 18.
Orizaba, Mex., 137.
Pablo Beach, Fla., 14.
Paso del Macho, Mex., 137.
Paso Robles Springs, Cal., 87.
Pensacola, Fla., 23.
Pepin Lake, Minn., 69.
Pescadero, Cal., 90.
Petrified Forest, Cal., 91.
Picolata, Fla., 18.
Pike's Peak, Col., 76.
Pilatka, Fla., 18.
Pines, Isle of, 109.
Pisgah Mountain, N. C., 59.
Ponce, Porto Rico, 116.
Pontchartrain Lake, La., 103.
Popocatepetl, Mex., 141.
Port-au-Prince, Hayti, 115.
Port de la Paix, Hayti, 115.
Port Orange, Fla., 22.
Porto Rico, West Indies, 115.
Powder Springs, Ga., 39.
Puebla, Mex., 137.
Pueblo, Col., 77.
Puentes Grandes, Cuba, 107.
Puerto Pinta, Santo Domingo, 114.
Puerto Principe, Cuba, 109.
Punta Rassa, Fla., 27.
Queen's Cañon, Col., 76.

Querétaro, Mex., 140.
Quincy, Fla., 23.
Red Sulphur Springs, Ga., 39.
Red Wing, Minn., 69.
Riverside, Cal., 87.
Roan Mountain, N. C., 59.
Rowland's Springs, Ga., 39.
Saba, West Indies, 119.
Sacramento, Cal., 87.
Saint Marc, Hayti, 115.
Salt Lake, Fla., 20.
Saltillo, Mex., 141.
Saluda Gap, S. C., 60.
Samana Bay, West Indies, 114.
San Bernardino, Cal., 86.
Sand Point, Fla., 22.
Sandwich Islands, 127.
San Diego, Cal., 85.
Sanford, Fla., 20.
San Andres, Mex., 137.
San Francisco, Cal., 83.
San German, Porto Rico, 116.
San Gorgonio Pass, Cal., 87.
San Jacinto Mines, Cal., 87.
San José, Cal., 89.
San Juan de Porto Rico, 116.
San Juan Teotihuacan, Mex., 137.
San Luis Lake, Col., 79.
San Luis Park, Col., 79.
San Luis Potosi, Mex., 141.
San Mateo, Fla., 18.
San Rafael, Cal., 90.
Santa Barbara, Cal., 84.
Santa Barbara, West Indies, 114.
Santa Clara, Cal., 89.
Santa Clara Valley, Cal., 89.
Santa Cruz, Cal., 90.
Santa Cruz, West Indies, 117.
Santa Fé, Isle of Pines, 109.
Santa Fé Lake, Fla., 15.
Santiago de Cuba, 109.
Santo Domingo City, 114.
Savannah, Ga., 32.
Savana la Mar, West Indies, 114.
Silver Cascade, Minn., 69.
Silver Spring, Fla., 25.
Slicking Falls, S. C., 55.
Soledad, Mex., 137.
Soltepec, Mex., 137.
South Park, Col., 79.
Spanish Town, Jamaica, 112.
Spartanburg, S. C., 53.
St. Anthony, Minn., 69.
St. Augustine, Fla., 8.
St. Croix, West Indies, 117.
St. Eustatius, Isle of, West Indies, 119.
St. George, Bermudas, 122.
St. John's River, Fla., 16.
St. Kitts, West Indies, 120.
St. Louis, Mo., 93.
St. Lucia, West Indies, 120.
St. Mark's River, Fla., 24.
St. Paul, Minn., 67.
St. Thomas, West Indies, 116.
St. Vincent, West Indies, 117.
Stockton, Cal., 88.
Stool Mountain, S. C., 54.
Sullivan's Island, S. C., 49.
Sulphur Spring, Fla., 13.
Summerville, Ga., 37.
Summerville, S. C., 49.
Swannanoa Gap, N. C., 60.
Table Rock, N. C., 60.
Table Mountain, S. C., 54.
Tacubaya, Mex., 140.
Tajo de Nochistongo, Mex., 140.
Tallahassee, Fla., 22.
Tampa, Fla., 26.
Tejeria, Mex., 137.
Thomasville, Ga., 38.

Thunderbolt, Ga., 36.
Thundering Springs, Ga., 39.
Titusville, Fla., 22.
Toccoa Falls, Ga., 39.
Tocoi, Fla., 18.
Toluca, Mex., 140.
Towaliga Falls, Ga., 39.
Trempeleau Island, Minn., 69.
Trinidad, Col., 77.
Turk's Island, 110.
Ute Falls, Col., 75.
Ute Pass, Col., 75.

Vallejo, Cal., 90.
Vera Cruz, Mex., 136.
Vicksburg, Miss., 95.
Visalia, Cal., 88.
Volusia, Fla., 18.
Waalua, Sandwich Islands, 130.
Waimea, Sandwich Islands, 132.
Wakulla Spring, Fla., 23.
Waldo, Fla., 15.
Warm Springs, Ga., 28.
Warm Springs, N. C., 62.
Weiaka, Fla., 19.

White Bear Lake, Minn., 68.
White Bluff, Ga., 36.
Whiteside Mountain, N. C., 61.
White Sulphur Springs, Cal., 91.
White Water Cataracts, S. C., 55.
Willemsted, Curaçoa, 118.
Williamston Springs, S. C., 54.
Wilson's Springs, N. C., 60.
Winona, Minn., 69.
Yonah Mountain, Ga., 40.
Zacatecas, Mex., 141.

OTHER RESORTS... 143
TABLE OF RAILWAY AND STEAMBOAT FARES.. 149

SOME USEFUL HINTS.

There are certain things with which every traveler must supply himself before starting on his journey, and certain facts, a knowledge of which will be useful to him while on his way. For this reason, a little time devoted to an examination of our advertising pages will doubtless be profitably spent.

None but first-class Hotels are invited to advertise in the HAND-BOOK, and the fact that they appear is a guarantee of their character.

The following hints to travelers may be of interest: It is better to telegraph in advance for rooms at hotels. A single room means a room for one person; a double room means a room for two persons; a double-bedded room means a room with two beds. Always mention the day of the week and train or boat by which you will arrive.

Lakewood, N. J.—Lakewood is at once beautiful and healthful—a combination of attractions which have given the village and its surroundings a foremost place among the most famous winter resorts. The village proper, containing nearly one thousand people, is tidy, and well-kept, with neatly trimmed hedges guarding broad streets and avenues, all of which, passing the Presbyterian, Episcopal, and Baptist Churches, lead to the pleasant walks and drives beyond. Many of the walks have been permitted to retain their natural rusticity, while others have received the touch of the pruning-hook to form convenient intersections and add variety to the scene. The roadways are more largely a later growth than dependent upon old landmarks, and the handiwork of a landscape-artist has made them a series of constantly changing thoroughfares, among the richest verdure of evergreen and autumnal foliage and the greatest variety of wild flora in the country: here a cathedral arch of overhanging pines; there a square, and thence a winding course amid oak and chestnut groves, and about them all a girdle, skirting the lakes and entering the town at any desirable point. Some idea of the possible artistic beauty of the drives, compassed within seventeen thousand acres of forest, carefully designed and elaborately constructed, may be conceived, and the Lakewood Land and Improvement Company have employed the best skill to subdue their large tract with such success that it is both picturesque and inviting. So well protected are many of the drives, that one may ride for hours in a high wind without being made aware of its existence, save by the soughing of the stately pines. The healthfulness of the climate has grown into an axiom, and eminent physicians bear constant testimony to its healing virtues in pulmonary, asthmatic, and bronchial troubles.

The Laurel House, now as widely known as the most famous hostelries at home and abroad, stands at the southeastern entrance to the village. The appointments of the house are in every sense the best, and are so arranged that comfort is constant, and luxury responds to the touch of the electric bells. Its large and cheerful rooms, all warmed by open wood-fires and lighted by gas, are home-like in the tidiness and convenience of home. Broad halls running at intervals into extensive glass-inclosed piazzas, well-fitted and tastefully designed parlors, and commodious entertainment-rooms, all kept at an even temperature night and day; water, flowing in clear and sparkling purity from an artesian well, which has received the highest scientific indorsement of being unexcelled; unseen but perfect drainage, and every sanitary care observed—all these features combine to make the Laurel House what it has been justly pronounced, one of the most comfortable and attractive winter resorts in the country.

Hotel Warwick, Newport News.—There are many who find it necessary or agreeable to seek relief from the rigors of a Northern winter by moving southward, especially to Florida. It has also become the custom of late to stop on the way to and from extreme Southern points at what may properly be called half-way houses, in the early fall and spring, and at the same time avoiding the blustering and disagreeable weather incident to Northern localities during these periods.

The most satisfactory "middle ground," yet discovered, both as to climate, agreeable surroundings, and hotel accommodations, is undoubtedly within the capes of Virginia, and in the vicinity of Hampton Roads, as attested by the great success, as a resort, of Old Point Comfort.

In this vicinity, so favored by nature, is located the new summer and winter sanitarium, known as HOTEL WARWICK, having accommodations for three hundred persons. Open all the year.

The climate at this point is salubrious, rarely reaching the extremes of heat and cold, and is exceedingly favorable to those suffering with catarrhal and bronchial affections, hay-fever, and kindred maladies, relief from which is speedily experienced upon entering the genial atmosphere of Newport News, and drinking the pure water to be found there. Notable instances are on record where guests of the WARWICK have found relief from the above-named ills and are bearing testimony of the same to their friends.

HOTEL WARWICK is built of brick, having been constructed in a thorough and substantial manner; it is situated on an elevation at Newport News, eight miles above Old Point Comfort, commanding a marine view of great beauty and extent. The views to be had from the hotel windows are also particularly fine, combining marine and park effects in one picture, to which additional life is given by the presence of handsome buildings in the foreground.

Particular attention is called to the fact that HOTEL WARWICK is well adapted for the comfort of those who *seek quietude*, the provisions for the amusement of guests being supplied in buildings *entirely separate from the hotel proper*.

The drainage and sewerage of the house are perfect, and the water-supply is excellent.

The surroundings of HOTEL WARWICK are pleasant. In front of the house is a park shaded by full-grown trees through which the carriage-way from the steamboat-landing and railway-station passes. On the left, as you enter this park, is a beautiful summer-house, nestling in the shrubbery. Directly in front of this is a pleasure dock three hundred feet in length, running out into the water, on the end of which is a large pavilion.

An excellent sandy beach extends along the shore for miles above this dock, back of which is a luxuriant growth of evergreen foliage on the face of a high bank, forming bathing-grounds which are safe and beautiful.

HOTEL WARWICK is conveniently located, and accessible by favorite routes of travel from all parts of the country.

THE CHARLESTON HOTEL is the leading house in Charleston, S. C., and is fully described in the body of the work. It has just been newly furnished and embellished throughout, one of Otis Brothers' best hydraulic elevators put in, and everything that could add to the comfort, convenience, and pleasure of its guests has been provided for.

THE NEW ATLANTIC HOTEL, Norfolk, Va.—This house is recommended to the traveler as one in all respects complete in everything that can add to the comfort and enjoyment of its guests. Its accommodations are ample, its table provided with the best and in abundance, and is furnished with all modern improvements for convenience and safety.

THE GRAND HOTEL TELEGRAFO, J. BATET, Proprietor, Havana, Cuba.—Tourists visiting Cuba will find the comforts and conveniences of a first-class hotel at this house.

WILLARD'S HOTEL, Washington, D. C.—We call the particular attention of our readers to this house in their visits to the metropolis of the nation. Washington is well worth visiting by every citizen of the Republic. Its magnificent public buildings, private homes, beautiful avenues, monuments, and numerous points and objects of historic interest, make it a city more worthy of a visit than any other city in the world. Willard's is most admirably located and handsomely furnished. Its table leaves nothing to be desired; for, deservedly high as its reputation has been, Mr. Staples is determined that it shall be excelled.

THE COLONNADE HOTEL, Philadelphia, Pa.—No pleasanter or more home-like house can be found. Its genial proprietors; its excellent table, furnishing every luxury; the perfection of its cookery, and many other attractions, make it a most attractive home to the visitor to Philadelphia.

GRAND UNION HOTEL.—Persons *en route* by rail to the city of New York will do well to keep their baggage-checks in their pockets, and on arrival at the Grand Central Depot walk across the street to the Grand Union Hotel, register, hand their baggage-checks to the clerk, who will dispatch a porter and have their baggage in their room in a few minutes, and return it to the depot when desired, free of charge. The transfer of baggage to and from Hotel without expense is an important saving. Conducted on the European plan. Its 600 rooms, $1 per day and upward. Elevators and all modern improvements. Horse-cars and elevated railway pass the door to all points.

OLD POINT COMFORT.—Old Point Comfort has been for many years a popular watering-place, and since the construction of the new *Hygeia Hotel*, comfortably accommodating 1,000 guests, it offers greater attractions than ever before. It is situated within 100 yards of Fortress Monroe, Va., at the entrance of Hampton Roads, about 13 miles north of Norfolk, and about 180 miles south of Baltimore and Washington. It may be reached from New York daily by the New York, Philadelphia and Norfolk R. R., *via* Cape Charles (new short route); the Pa. R. R. to Baltimore, thence by the Old Bay Line, or every other day by the steamers of the Old Dominion Steamship Co., *via* Norfolk or Newport News. From Norfolk or Washington, by steamers direct, and from Richmond by C. & O. Ry. or steamers. The hotel is located on the beach, at the head of the steamboat-landing. Fortress Monroe, the largest in America, with an armament of 370 guns, is always open to visitors, and contains many features of interest. The famed Artillery School has its establishment within the fortress; and the dress-parade, with the music of a fine band morning and evening, and the open-airconcerts given by the band in the evenings, afford the visitor a pleasure which is enjoyed at no other watering-place save Newport. The climate is delightful, with an average of 45°, 44°, and 42°; and the Hampton Normal and Agricultural Institute, the National Military Home, the National Cemetery, and the venerable old town of Hampton (containing one of the oldest churches in America), all are within the easy limits of a ride or sail. The *Hampton Normal and Agricultural Institute* is well worth a visit. It is designed especially to train colored youth as teachers of their own race, by giving an English and industrial education, while affording students an opportunity to defray a portion of their expenses by labor. It is open to both sexes. The grounds comprise about 200 acres, of which 150 acres are under cultivation by the boys. There is also a successful printing-office operated by the students.

The climate of all this region is remarkably mild and healthful in late autumn and early spring, and the *Hygeia Hotel* is a favorite place of temporary sojourn for those *en route* to or from the more southern resorts. The *Hygeia* is open all the year round.

DECKER BROTHERS' PIANOS.—One of the busy establishments of New York City is the Manufactory of the celebrated Piano-forte makers, Messrs. Decker Brothers, whose instruments have attained a world-wide reputation. Here, under the personal supervision of the founders of the house, the vast detail of all that appertains to the manufacture of a perfect instrument goes on. Being practical artisans themselves, and familiar with the capabilities of every man employed in the business in New York, they find no difficulty in securing the services of the highest skill for each department. The instruments manufactured by this firm fully realize the standard of what a well-made piano, for tone and durability, should be. The firm is one of the most prominent of representative piano-forte makers in the world, having won this proud position by the intrinsic merits of the instruments of its make. Their warerooms, at 33 Union Square, is also a pleasant place to visit. Here will be found many superb specimens of artistic skill in this direction, both as to musical excellence and exquisite exterior ornamentation and finish. Strangers, even if not intending to purchase, but who wish to examine, will be welcomed, and afforded every opportunity for testing the tone and for the inspection of the finish of their pianos. The location of the building is convenient, being on the most prominent thoroughfare in the city.

THE QUEBEC STEAMSHIP COMPANY.—The QUEBEC STEAMSHIP COMPANY, of Quebec, Canada, run a direct line of steamers from New York to Bermuda, under a mail contract with the Bermuda Government. The steamers of this line are all British-built iron steamers, of about two thousand (2,000) tons, and run with an unexampled regularity. They have cabin accommodation of the most approved style for one hundred first-class passengers, and with numerous water-tight compartments and every improvement for safety at sea and for the comfort of passengers. The tables are furnished with the best of everything procurable in the New York markets. The QUEBEC STEAMSHIP COMPANY also run mail steamers to the West India Islands. Persons desiring may, by connecting lines, make an excursion, visiting these ports as well as Nassau and Florida.

THE NEW YORK LIFE INSURANCE COMPANY is an institution which it is safe either to commend or to insure with. It is one of the old, purely mutuals, and has grown with the growth of life insurance in this country, in which it has been a conspicuous figure. In popularizing the system, and in adjusting the equities of policy-holders, it has, perhaps, done more than any other company. Its management has been distinguished by great energy and prudence, and by a high sense of the responsibilities of so great and sacred a trust. The last report of the Insurance Superintendent commends it as "deserving of the greatest praise." It is now one of the largest as well as one of the most rapidly growing companies in the world. Its system of policies includes all the approved forms, including ordinary Life, Endowment, Tontine, and Annuity Policies, and its experience and patronage are so large as to afford safe averages and desirable results. It has recently applied the non-forfeiture principle, introduced in 1860, to its Tontine Policies, rendering them at once a desirable investment and a safe form of assurance. In short, THE NEW YORK LIFE offers a variety of advantages, and a combination of strong points, which only age, success, a large business, approved methods, and skillful management can afford.

THOMAS COOK & SON, TOURIST AND EXCURSION AGENTS.—This firm arrange circular tourist tickets for all chief lines of travel in America, including all the noted pleasure resorts in the Eastern and Western States and in Canada. It is sometimes of great convenience to travelers to arrange their trip in advance and to know what the expense will be, how long a time should be devoted to the various places of interest *en route*, and to the whole trip. Messrs. COOK & SON will give all necessary information on these points, and in many cases a saving is effected by taking advantage of tickets issued by them specially for pleasure travel during the season. The address of the New York office is 261 Broadway, and branch offices are to be found at other important centers.

ALL people who go South, whether for pleasure or for health, wish to be strong enough to enjoy their trip, and to return home strengthened and invigorated. The mere fact of going away creates a great tax on the nervous system, and every thoughtful person knows that nervous irritation carries off more strength than a large amount of bodily labor. If we spend in mental labor or nervous excitement the brain-nutriment, we must return an equivalent, or we suffer depression. Our foods contain but little special brain-food; and so food and rest restore brain and nerve strength but slowly. We need a special brain and nerve food, and the best physicians of the present day find it in CROSBY'S VITALIZED PHOSPHITES. It has been used by them for the last fifteen years for the purpose of restoring weakened vital energies, nervousness, lassitude, and overtaxed powers. It has been used, for the purpose of restoring the bodily and mental vigor, by Bismarck, Gladstone, Emily Faithfull, and the Emperor Dom Pedro, and thousands of the brain workers of the world. Dr. CHURCHILL says, "It stamps out consumption." It is universally acknowledged to be a specific for night sweats, and this one fact alone proves its great value to strengthen the nervous system. School-teachers acknowledge that it directly aids a child to learn, and aids in the bodily and mental development of children. The President of the New England Medical Society says that it "promotes good digestion." All who are traveling for their health should take *Vitalized Phosphites* with them, and not mistake it for the inert acid laboratory compounds or other useless phosphates. This is a vital not a laboratory compound. The advertisement on the last page of this book tells where it is to be found.

THE MAGNOLIA HOTEL, St. John's River, Florida.—This new and elegant hotel is situated twenty-eight miles south of Jacksonville—conceded to be one of the finest and healthiest places on the river. The house is large and airy, contains all modern improvements, and every requisite for the comfort of its guests. This Hotel, having the advantage of a commanding site and superb river-view, is unusually striking and attractive. The improvements on the lawn and wharves in front make this the handsomest landing on the entire river. This grand hotel is always full of guests, and is lighted at night by the electric lights, making a magnificent view from vessels passing up the river.

ST. AUGUSTINE, FLORIDA, is by far the most ancient city in North America. It is situated on a peninsula formed by the St. Sebastian and Matanzas Rivers. It is a most delightful winter resort, and filled with remarkably interesting historical and picturesque buildings and scenery. A very full and good description of the city will be found in the body of this work, pages 8 to 13, and to it we refer the reader.

In this wonderfully attractive winter resort is found THE HOTEL SAN MARCO, under the management of Messrs. AINSLIE & MACGILVRAY, of the "Magnolia Hotel," St. John's River, and also of the "Maplewood Hotel," White Mountains. The house is, in everything, first-class in all its appointments; entirely new, and handsomely furnished. An advertisement, with full particulars, will be found in back part of this work.

ACADEMY AND COLLEGE, DE LAND, FLORIDA.—A first-class Academy for both sexes. Five courses: College Preparatory, Higher English, Normal, Business, Industrial Drawing. First-class Art and Music Departments. Fine new dormitory buildings, enabling us to furnish board

Stetson Hall.

De Land Academy.

and tuition at reasonable rates. The purpose of this Institution is to give, in the delightful climate of Florida, as thorough and liberal an education as can be secured in the best New England schools. De Land College will also receive students of both sexes, prepared to enter the freshman class.

Dormitory, Stetson Hall.—The citizens of De Land and vicinity, together with generous friends of education in the North, have erected a spacious and elegant dormitory building, thus supplying a very urgent need of the institution. Among these noble helpers are the names of C. T. Sampson, of North Adams, Mass., of the C. T. Sampson Manufacturing Company, and John B. Stetson, of Philadelphia, Pa., the great manufacturer of hats. Mr. John B. Stetson has already paid and pledged an amount equal to about one-third of the entire cost of the building; therefore the trustees have decided to call the Dormitory Building Stetson Hall. The first floor of this building is supplied with reception and music rooms, office, dining-room, etc. The dormitory rooms are large, well furnished, and pleasant, and the entire building is heated by steam. The president and family, as well as other teachers, will reside in the building, and parents may thus feel assured of a careful oversight of and interest in their children. The young ladies will be under the direct control of the preceptress, Mrs. Helen B. Webster.

Location.—The city of De Land is in Volusia County, on the east coast of the Peninsula, about one hundred miles south of Jacksonville. It is accessible by both river and rail, located on high, rolling pine-land, not near any water, standing or running, and is remarkable for its general healthfulness. The Mutual Life Insurance Company, of New York, grants its policy-holders a *perpetual* permit to live in De Land the year round. The famous Ironduquoit Dairy established here furnishes the city with absolutely pure milk from Jersey cows, and the large ice-factory adds another luxury. The climate is almost a specific for throat and lung troubles, catarrh, rheumatism, etc. The population numbers about 1,500 white people and is far superior to most Northern towns of the same size in its moral and intellectual tone. There are in the city six white churches, all possessing houses of worship, a well-organized public school, and a Kindergarten. Three weekly papers are published in De Land, also. The general healthfulness and beauty of the city, its accessibility, together with the high character of its inhabitants, and the stimulating, intellectual, moral, and religious influences, make this an ideal location for an institution of learning. Students who are unable, from delicate health to attend school during the winter in the North, find it possible to pursue their studies here regularly, and yet constantly improve in health.

General Statement.—De Land Academy owes its existence to the generosity and foresight, of Hon. H. A. De Land, of Fairport, N. Y. The purpose of its founder was to establish in Florida a Christian high-school, *for both sexes*, inferior to none in this country in character and rank.

It was assumed that there was a demand for such an institution on the part of two large and rapidly increasing classes of students: *First*, the young men and women of the State of Florida—a State whose population is increasing perhaps faster than that of any other State in the Union; and, *secondly*, the large number of young men and women who, from delicate health on their own part or that of their friends, are compelled to spend the winter in this more congenial and kindly climate.

This assumption has been fully verified, and these classes of students have both been largely represented among our pupils. The institution is now fully organized, possessing fine buildings, admirably furnished, and supplied with apparatus and illustrative material of all kinds, equal and in many cases superior to that possessed by the best institutions of a similar grade in the North; with courses of study well adapted to meet the varying needs of those who may desire a liberal education, and a faculty in charge composed exclusively of teachers of liberal culture, wide experience, and marked success. The Board of Trustees, therefore, confidently invite students to avail themselves of these advantages.

"*A Florida College.*—It is no longer necessary for those who find it desirable to pass the winter in a warm climate to hesitate about going because of the poor educational facilities heretofore existing in many of the Southern States. Parents can now take their children to De Land, Florida, with the comforting assurance that no break need occur in their course of studies, for there is established at this delightful and flourishing village an academy and college that is first class in every particular, affording every opportunity offered in the best schools here in the North, securing a thorough and liberal education. Board and tuition are supplied at reasonable rates, and students sent there will receive the same kindly care as at home."—*Christian Intelligencer, September 1, 1886.*

Send for catalogue to J. F. FORBES, President, De Land, Florida; or, H. A. DE LAND, Fairport, N. Y.

We call attention to the card of THE NORFOLK COLLEGE FOR YOUNG LADIES. It will be found in connection with the advertisement of THE NEW ATLANTIC HOTEL.

www.ingramcontent.com/pod-product-compliance
Lightning Source LLC
Chambersburg PA
CBHW030242170426
43202CB00009B/598